Universe, I Trust You

- A MONTH IN SRI LANKA -

ROBERTA MUSSATO

BOOKS BOOST BUSINESS
Books Boost Business UK booksboostbusiness.com.

EDITION
First edition in Italian
©2020 Roberta Mussato
First Edition in English
©2022 Roberta Mussato
www.booksboostbusiness.com
Book: Universe I Trust You–Roberta Mussato
ISBN-13 978-1-913501-63-1

robertamussato@gmail.com
Updated version 15 May 2022

COVER
Andre Radke
www.etcetera23.com
Back cover photo by Rodney Pedroza

*To all the women who feel stuck
and to all those who are awakening.
May all of you find the strength to blossom.*

*To the family in which I chose to be born:
to my parents, Maria and Silvano,
to my brothers, Mauro and Alessio,
and to Elena, Adele and Lorenzo,
who chose to join us.*

'It is only in our darkest hours that we may discover the true strength of the brilliant light within ourselves that can never, ever, be dimmed.'

Doe Zantamata

'Happiness is when what you think, what you say, and what you do are in harmony.'

Mahatma Gandhi

ACKNOWLEDGEMENTS

Having learnt that gratitude is one of the best energies to cultivate, I'd like to start by thanking all those who have helped me, one way or another, to bring this book and its English translation to life.

My first, immense *grazie* goes to my translation assistant, proofreader and editor Sarah Little. Thanks to my Italian book, which you were interested in buying to brush up your Italian, our paths crossed again, as if by magic, almost ten years after our last encounter. While chatting briefly I discovered that you now run your own Italian-to-English translation business – just when I was considering hiring an editor to help me with my own translation. It was totally the Universe that sent you my way, Sarah, and deciding to bring you onboard was the easiest of choices. Thank you for your professionalism, for your attention to detail, for often stepping in and re-writing things way better than I could have done. Above all, thank you for reining in my Italian irreverence when needed and (hopefully!) keeping me from offending anyone by pointing out culturally sensitive issues.

My second thanks goes to my amazing travel buddy Andre Radke, who gifted me the beautiful cover of this book and helped me (obliged me?) to practise letting go of attachments and expectations. Thanks for all the great memories. Till we meet again thank you so, so much.

I want to thank Lucio, who gave me permission to talk about our co-creation, despite the pain this could have caused him. You have no idea how much this mattered to me.

I want to thank my fantastic, crazy friends: Alessandra de Michele, Sara Covarelli, Elena Mantovani, Chiara Tixi, Maria Giovanna Biscu,

Marisa Savoia and Marzia Zani for proofreading some of my batches and in general for your ongoing support. A special mention goes to Claudio Bendazzoli who has become my official interviewer since the launch of the Italian book.

Another thank you, though he'll probably appreciate a beer (or three) more, goes to Brian Kreel, who has helped me with the translation and some proofreading, and supported me along the way with his trademark caustic and dry sense of humour when I felt I was losing my voice in this English translation.

Talking of dry humour, I also have to thank Kevin Armstrong for his contribution to the proofreading (albeit a tiny one, let's be honest, Kevin). More importantly, for renewing my appreciation of the English sense of humour at a time when I felt it was strangling my Italian one.

Thanks also to Oliver Mayes, a published author whom the Universe sent straight into my home through Airbnb, and who repeatedly reassured me that I was doing something good with this book. Thanks for all the linguistic support, and I wish you all the best in your career.

I also want to thank my relationship coach Anna Garcia and her tribe. Thank you, Anna, for teaching me so many of the concepts I touch on in this book, and thank you to those tribettes who took the time to give me their opinion on some of the most culturally delicate passages of the book.

I really want to thank all those who encouraged me and listened to me during this interesting and challenging journey.

Funnily enough, in a way I also want to thank the people who played a part in making me feel so bad, to whom I had unconsciously given permission to do so. All that sorrow brought me to a point where I started looking inside myself and saying, 'Enough'. Without all that pain, this three-month trip, and therefore this book too, would not have happened.

One *grazie* for so many things goes to Franco Ranieri, even if he dislikes being thanked. Thanks for the journey we've taken together, and for sharing your beautiful, golden heart with me.

ACKNOWLEDGEMENTS

I thank my family, who have always left me completely free to choose my path and have always been there for me. *Papà, mamma, Alessio* and *Mauro*, thanks for all the laughter and for the lessons you continually teach me. Thank you, Adele and Lorenzo, for having brought so much sweetness and love into my life, and thank you, Elena, for bringing them into this world.

Last but not least, you know what? I'm going to thank myself, too. I acknowledge you, Roby, for never losing your sense of humour and trust in life, even when things were not looking particularly bright. Thanks for the courage you have shown in picking yourself up and starting again every single time, and thanks for the resilience and discipline you showed in bringing this book to light.

I end this long but certainly not exhaustive list with a silent 'Thank you' to the Universe, with my eyes closed and a big, warm smile. Thanks for the beauty in this world and for giving me the ability to see it everywhere and no matter what.

FOREWORD

It is so true that our darkest moments are also those in which we discover our brightest light.

My book was born out of the desire to reiterate this truth, given that I have experienced it for myself, and because I firmly believe in the power of vulnerability.

I dedicate it to all the women who somehow recognise themselves in my story or can relate to what I share here. I believe that the years between 35 and 40 are particularly difficult for women, or at least they have been for me. Talking about my story and my various wounds is an act of sisterhood which I hope can make those women who are suffering feel less lonely. Maybe I will succeed in making you feel better and, by comparing your situation with mine, you will reach the conclusion that, no, in fact you are not doing so badly.

I have never understood the point of hiding one's sorrow and pain and presenting the world with a fake version of yourself. Let me rephrase that: I do understand the reason behind it, which is generally connected to fear in its various forms, but I have never understood what purpose it serves. It is by sharing our life story that we can be a beacon of light for others. It is precisely by being vulnerable that we realise our essence as human beings, and it is thanks to vulnerability that we can save ourselves and help each other. For years I have been telling myself that choices have to be made out of love, not out of fear and, as Brené Brown says, there can be no courage without vulnerability.

However, I am perfectly aware that not everybody agrees with or understands this love of mine for truth and sharing, and that is why I have changed some names in the book to respect people's privacy.

I feel compelled to explain that this book brings out the writer's side of me, and for comic effect, I often give my typically Italian irreverence free rein. After this journey, I embarked on years of courses, which saw me become a life coach and NLP Practitioner, and I just wanted to reassure you that in my coaching practice I am definitely more compassionate and less judgemental. What you are going to read is my story, told by the person I was in 2018, which is so many versions of me ago.

This book first came out in Italy on December 28th, 2020, right in the middle of COVID, when travelling was so difficult and complicated. I wanted it to help readers dream of those beautiful, distant lands that thankfully we can now visit again, and I also meant it as my way of spreading some lightness and positivity in such a terrible year for the whole world.

With the war in Ukraine and the COVID aftermath, it seems that times have only slightly improved, so once more I hope that this book can gift readers with a few pleasant hours and even more pleasant thoughts. My hope is to inspire people, demonstrating that we are only ever one decision away from feeling better, and that every change starts within us. But even if I simply manage to raise the odd smile or, even better, make you laugh in such a difficult time for the whole world, I will be more than satisfied.

Enjoy.

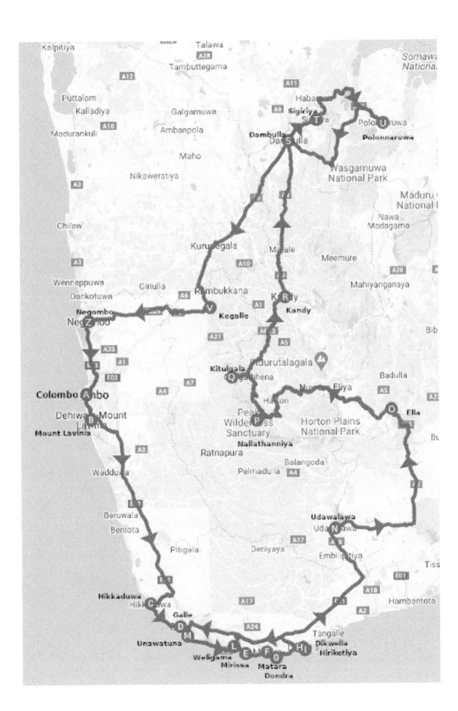

DAY 1
'Does this leaflet refer to my flight?'
-Heathrow, London, Monday 12th February 2018-

My weight at departure: 74.2kg
Weight of my backpack: 13.8kg
Number of modes of transport I took to get to the airport: 1 bus and 2 tubes
Last person I said goodbye to: Lucio
Layers of clothing: 4
Song playing nonstop in my mind: The shamanic chant *'Eu chamo a forca'*
Joy level at the idea of going away: Stratospheric
Aeroplanes I have to take: 2
Conviction upon leaving: This is the best beginning ever!

Finally. Here I am at the airport, ready to depart. I'm a mixture of adrenaline, enthusiasm, sweet anxiety, joy, excitement–and hunger, too, just for a change.

But there's no rush. I have some time to kill and, as I've been doing for decades now, I spend it writing in my beloved journal. Every single gram in my backpack is important, and I will have to carry it with me for the next three months, so it may seem odd that I have packed my journal in my military green backpack, a faithful companion from journeys past. In fact, I've been keeping a journal since I was nine years old, and I am absolutely adamant that those pages will be filled with magnificent places, interesting people, tragicomic anecdotes and abundant reflection. Stretching ahead of me at this precise moment is one month in Sri Lanka, to begin with, then another in India, before I finish my journey with one month in Nepal. My soul is smiling simply writing these words.

As well as my habit of keeping a journal, which I began as a child, and my love of writing and the deep reflection it enables, another trait people associate with me is my passion for travelling–the more adventurous the better. I adore the kind of experience that not only takes you away from the greyness and everyday grind of London, in my case, but tears you out of your comfort zone, forcing you to discover new sides of your personality. The kind of travel that draws new resources, previously unknown to you, to the surface, filling your eyes with beauty, your heart with gratitude and your memories with interesting stories to tell your friends at dinner parties.

In London I am constantly busy, running here and there with hardly a moment to catch my breath. For this reason, when I travel one of the things I yearn for and cherish the most is having the time to sit down and watch people, smiling at their follies, great and small. Above all, I love to take my time and talk with the locals, listening to their stories so that I can understand a tiny bit of their culture, of the people's mentality, and immerse myself even further into my new reality.

I could write whole pages about what travelling means for me, and maybe I actually will shortly. Today, on Monday 12th February 2018, travelling for me is both a way out of the heavy situation stifling my London life in recent months, and a way back to seeing the beauty in life. Travelling is a means of recharging my batteries, rediscovering myself. There are too many things I don't like in my current life, things that are not going the way I expected, and I need some time away from it all to breathe and understand where I went wrong.

Yes, because at the end of the day I know that the responsibility for our happiness falls always and only on us. Or our unhappiness, for that matter. Even simply accepting certain situations, repeating the same behavioural patterns thinking that at some point they will yield a different result, or putting other people's needs and well-being before our own: these are all choices that we make, the responsibility for which lies wholly with us.

It took me a while to realise this. And, boy, did it hurt. It was so much nicer and easier to play the victim and have people feel sorry for me as I recounted my incredible string of dating disasters or lamented my friends' not being there for me or lack of sensitivity. Today I am aware of the role I've played in my unhappiness, the role I played in seeking things out and making them happen, in accepting certain situations and in the way I reacted to others.

Anyway, here I am at the airport, waiting for my lunch to be served, ultra-excited and smiling broadly because I am really having the best of all beginnings. Listen to what just happened.

After only four hours of sleep, which weren't exactly peaceful either, this morning, having taken the mandatory selfie with my backpack, all set to leave, I boarded my last tube until May and sat on the Piccadilly Line all the way to Heathrow.

I go to the desk to check in for the Jet Airways flight to Mumbai, my stopover, where I would then pick up the connecting flight to Colombo. The woman at check-in doesn't say a word, but there's a leaflet on her desk, and I start reading it while she is processing my boarding pass. It says, 'There is a chance of overbooking on this flight. We are looking for volunteers who are willing to leave at a later stage in exchange for 500 pounds compensation'.

Is this for real? I mean, can my trip really be starting under such a lucky star?

'Excuse me, does this leaflet refer to my flight?' I ask her.

'Yes, indeed. We don't know yet if all the passengers will show up, so we don't have a clear idea of whether the flight really is overbooked or not. However, we are taking note of people who volunteer to leave a bit later, just in case', she explains.

'Okay, and how much later are we talking? I mean, are we talking days?'

'No, you would be assigned a seat on a Qatar Airlines flight leaving five hours later, in the afternoon, and you would reach Colombo tomorrow morning at 9am.'

So, to sum up: they are potentially offering me 500 pounds cash in hand, just to wait for five hours, board a Qatar Airlines flight–ten times better than the unknown quantity that is Jet Airways–which would land in Colombo at a decent time instead of 4am, as per my itinerary.

'But this is just brilliant! I totally volunteer!'

'Fantastic, I'll put your name down. You are the third person to step forward, a couple has already volunteered.' (Typical.) 'However, given that we won't know until the very end if we need anyone to stay behind, we'll follow the normal procedure for now. So I'll prepare your boarding pass anyway, and then once you arrive at the gate please wait until last to find out what to do. When all the other passengers are on board and seated, my colleagues will let you know how many people, if any, have to stay here.'

I'm loving it. My trip has barely begun and already the unknown is stepping in, and 'let's see how it goes' is the name of the game, which is exactly what I want.

At the last minute, when all the other passengers had boarded the plane, we were informed that only one person had to stay here. Since five of us had volunteered, and the other four were two couples, for once, being an old maid proved an advantage. Three massive cheers for spinsterhood! (Oh my God, did I really just say that?)

Yep, because besides being a writing and travel enthusiast, another fun (oh, what fun indeed…) fact about me is that I've been single for three and a half centuries. But who knows, maybe this trip will change that. Although the change I really need–and the one I owe myself–is to give up constantly obsessing about it and stop entertaining thoughts like these.

Anyway, this is awesome! In one go I have saved myself from worrying about the financial impact of a month's travelling, ensured my room will be ready when I get to the hotel in Colombo, even earned a ten-pound lunch voucher and got to make an early start on my favourite pastime when abroad: people watching. I simply adore observing people's marvellous eccentricities and making up stories about their lives. The best beginning ever, indeed!

And so here I am, sitting in a Lebanese restaurant at Heathrow airport, with three hours to kill. At last, I can relax. Yesterday was so stressful. Basically, I ran around like a crazy woman from morning till night feeling the anxiety mounting, because for every single thing I did, I thought of three more I had to sort out. At some point, in the evening, while contemplating the huge pile of stuff on my bed, trying to decide what to bring with me and what to leave at home, completely out of the blue I started crying. Big fat tears were rolling down my cheeks and I even indulged in some sobbing.

I'm over the moon at the idea of leaving. I've been waiting eagerly for this very moment for months, yet yesterday a sort of dejection took hold. There is joy, curiosity and hope that this trip will fill my soul to the brim, that it will be a turning point for me. But there's also something else. Calling it 'fear' would be wrong, especially given that in the last few years I've made a point of fighting my fears. Perhaps it's not knowing where my life is headed next, or the possibility that something bad will happen to me or the people I'm leaving behind… Part of me wonders if three months away is too long. The fact that I really cannot picture myself in the coming months, that I have no clue what will happen, creates an emptiness that feels a bit frightening.

'Mind-blowing', indeed. That's the correct word for such a state. A thought that makes your mind explode, because you are trying so hard to picture something but your mind keeps drawing a blank.

Or maybe it was just the adrenaline leaving my system, burning off in those few sobs which caught me by surprise and definitely left me more peaceful afterwards. Who knows? Maybe this is just the apprehension that comes with maturity. Years ago the immense joy I used to feel at the idea of taking a plane and going away on a trip left no space for anything else. It was all-consuming. Today, on the other hand, I am aware of how many things can go wrong.

From air tragedies (give those crown jewels a superstitious pat![1])
to fracturing my ankle while trekking (touch wood), from having
my passport stolen (Our Father, who art in heaven…), to having my
debit card blocked (Barclays, don't you dare…), from food poisoning
leading to a diarrhoetic seaquake (May the force of Imodium be with
me) to possible tsunamis (Hail Mary, full of grace…), from having
an allergic reaction to insect bites (touch and knock on all kinds of
wood), to losing my mobile somewhere and with it all my contacts
and photos (For Apple's sake! That would be a tragedy).

After that short but shattering attack of sobbing I found myself
calling upon the spirits, for the first time since that evening at the
spiritualist church. I prayed to *Zia* Lidia, *Zio* Rino, but also *Nonno*,
my grandfather, and *Nonna*, my grandmother, to stay close to me
and protect me.

The spiritualist church… Yes, that was an important evening for
my now imminent trip. Actually, thinking about it, it was the very
same week that I bought the plane tickets.

Three hours to go before boarding my new flight. I have my
beloved journal in front of me, many of its pages already densely
packed with words and thoughts, others waiting patiently to be
filled with fantastic and tragicomic anecdotes in due time. Even if
I already know how these stories end, I always enjoy reading them
again, months after I wrote them, observing myself from a detached
position. Reading extracts of my journal here and there, I can clearly

---

[1]   Readers might like to know that to come up with this solution I exchanged
      quite a few emails with my proof-reader/editor Sarah, discussing what
      English-speaking men do with their testicles. In Italy, men might touch or
      shake their genitalia as a way of keeping bad luck at bay, but I was told that
      in the UK there's no such colourful practice. 'Cross your fingers and toes'
      didn't remotely have the same conceptual strength, so we opted for 'crown
      jewels', which you can't however shake in quite the same way… I hope that
      this solution sounds good to you, and you are welcome for this insight into
      Italian superstitious practices.

see the jigsaw that has been coming together, piece after piece, revealing the final image of me, Roby, wearing heavy, black trekking trousers with several side pockets, trekking shoes for walking along Nepalese mountain paths and who knows where else, a red fleece sweater to keep me warm on my journeys by night bus, sitting at a restaurant table at Heathrow, my journal in my hands.

THE MONTHS BEFORE
-General overview of my emotional wreckage-

London, Thursday 24th August 2017

It's been two years since I first had the strong feeling that potential alternative careers lay within me. The problem is I can't decide which ones.

If God had given me fewer gifts, that might narrow things down a bit, but no, He made me smart and capable, so here I am racking my brains, faced with so many different choices, like detective, speech therapist, psychologist, profiler, counsellor... I've even considered going to Asia to set up an orphanage or a school. I distinctly feel that I want to do something more useful, that I want to do a job where I can help people. Yes, my job as a subtitler for the hard of hearing is quite important for those who cannot hear. Okay, without me interpreting for them, those Italian couples coming to London for medical or fertility treatments might feel even more lost and confused. The same for the families of children with eye problems who come to Moorfield's Eye Hospital here in London with all sorts of medical issues. And yet, what real difference do I make in the grand scheme of things? I feel I have so much love to give, but to whom, and how?

I don't know. Much as I like my jobs as an interpreter, a subtitler and a voice over artist, I feel I want a change. Maybe it's simply 'the London effect'. In Italy, you almost feel obliged to hang on for dear life to that one job you got out of God's grace. Whereas, here in London, it's never too late to completely change your career. I know people in their fifties who are getting a new degree, studying in the evenings and weekends.

At the end of the day you need to listen to your dissatisfaction. God forbid, I'm not remotely close to the levels of 'mental vomit', as I call it, that I was experiencing when I decided to leave my hometown of Treviso in the northeast of Italy back in 2006. Not at all, thank God. That, incidentally, was a mixture of dissatisfaction with the job I was doing and with the Italian bubble that seemed way too small for me. It was as if I was supposed to be grateful for the amazing opportunity I'd been given to earn 900 euros a month in an exports department dealing with shipments, sales and item returns, which I wasn't at all interested in. And when I went out and met someone new I felt like I already knew their life story up to that point: what cartoons they'd watched when they were little, what they had studied at school, what traditions they had for Christmas, which university they'd studied at. Little by little, I was splitting myself in two. I was doing things in my everyday Treviso life whilst imagining doing others in London, a city I had fallen in love with the moment I saw it, when I came to see my elder brother Alessio, who was living here at that time. When I was driving down the narrow country roads to go to work I would picture myself rushing down the escalator and just about making it onto the tube, where I would then sit down to read a book, casting glances around me once in a while to admire the diversity of the faces and clothes. When I was in a café with my friends I would visualise myself going into a pub, packed with men in suits who had just flocked out of their offices in the City.

In the end, when my request for a pay rise was turned down for the third time, and also to safeguard my mental health, given that these alternate realities were becoming increasingly insistent, I decided to move here. London has welcomed me in its multiple crazy and colourful arms, almost like a psychedelic Kalì goddess, and the pace of my life has picked up. Thinking back on those years, I feel like I've lived I don't even know how many lives.

No, I'm not doing remotely as badly as back then. I still like my jobs. The thing is, I don't feel this is my 'calling'. And by the way, what a big, heavy word that is: calling. Blessed are those who understand theirs and are able to follow it.

I don't know. I feel very confused. I don't understand myself. The truth is, I'm also very tired, physically and even more psychologically. This isn't exactly a happy period for me. Okay, who am I trying to be all diplomatic for? It's pure shit. There are many things contributing to my feeling stuck, oppressed, unhappy, sad, gloomy inside...

London, Sunday 24th September 2017

I think I've come to a major as well as sad turning point with Lucio, my best friend. I'm emotionally drained. I have a thousand voices in my head arguing with each other, but I don't want to listen to any of them anymore. Enough. I knew that sooner or later I would have to tell you about him. It's incredible how I have avoided writing to you for months about what was going on with him. Lucio was filling my thoughts. He was basically the central theme of each one of my counselling sessions. So when I sat down to update you on my life I almost wanted to claim a... Lucio-free oasis. I certainly can't say I claimed a peaceful oasis, because I haven't felt peaceful at all these last months. I kind of forced myself to write about all the other things, because I will remember this difficult chapter of my life forever, even without talking about it on the pages of my journal.

Eighteen months ago I discovered that Lucio has an addiction. Lucio is a friend I met at primary school and whom I have always been close to. It was one of those friendships that really shapes your sense of identity, because Lucio and I were an inseparable duo. We were always playing together at break times, and were often doing our homework together, too, either at his place or mine. When at high school we used to spend our Sunday afternoons going around together on our bikes, or fishing at the lake, talking about everything. When we went on the parish camping trip, we invented a whole series of characters that made everybody laugh. I pretended I was a journalist, and he in turn would play Batman, or a sex maniac in a raincoat jumping out from behind the tents, who was depressed because there were never any damsels to impress with his unbridled masculinity. I would interview him, asking him the weirdest questions. There was almost an unspoken competition between us over who could invent the most stupid things. Roby and Lucio, always together, making each other laugh, mutually feeding the creativity and imagination that seemed to be our prerogative. The most incredible thing is that we were so different. I was a studious overachiever, whereas he would often skip school. At 16 I was already dreaming of leaving my village and peppering my sentences with English words, while he revelled in local dialectal expressions and provincial traditions. When we went to secondary school, we still spent so much time together, even though we were at different schools. He would spend whole afternoons at my place telling me about his great, immense unrequited love for the sister of a friend of mine. With his romantic spirit, exacerbated by adolescence, he would find himself putting up banners in the fields bearing declarations of love and writing heart rending songs accompanied by those few chords he'd managed to teach himself on the guitar. Thinking back on everything his unrequited love drove him to do, I don't know if I'm more inclined to laugh or feel tenderness towards him.

In response to those long summer afternoons I'd spend listening to Lucio, my mum used to say, 'In my opinion, è innamorato di te'. He's in love with you. 'And you are in love with him, obviously. But you don't have the courage to admit it to each other.'

Time never proved her right. Lucio moved from one girlfriend to the next in Treviso, while in Forlì I was studying super hard and dancing even harder at the university parties. Every time I came home to the village, however, Lucio was always there to take me out on a Saturday evening for a Spritz, or four, while we updated each other on our respective lives.

My move to London could have meant the decline, if not the end, of our friendship, but three years after I left, he moved here, too. 'I'm looking for a better job', he used to say. And I would take the piss, 'No, you are looking for more variety in terms of women, and because you've already shagged the whole Veneto region'.

And so: Roby and Lucio in London, discovering the city together, walking in the parks, drinking in pubs, having barbecues with friends, picnics, dinners and so many nights out dancing together. Until one day, having met me in a pub at the end of his working shift, leaning on the bar, Lucio says to the barman, 'Okay, a glass of Prosecco for her, and...'

A long pause. At first I thought he was simply undecided, maybe eyeing the different bottles to get some inspiration. I looked at him, and he seemed absent and distant. His eyes were lost in a completely different dimension. The silence went on far beyond a normal pause. I'm talking about thirty seconds of pure silence. Alarmed, I looked at the barman who, in turn, was looking at me, worried. I didn't understand what was going on. 'Lucio, *stai bene?* Are you ok?' I asked, touching him on his shoulder. 'Yeah, sure', he said, having awoken from his strange blackout, adding, 'A Peroni for me'.

The rest of the evening went on normally, but the silence had gone on for too long and left me feeling slightly uneasy.

That was the first in a long series of worrying blackouts that were happening all of a sudden, out of the blue. It might be just the two of us, or we might be with friends. Once in a while it seemed like he was really switching off. His smiling, green eyes would lose their focus, as if gazing far into the distance, words would only come out with a lot of effort and were slurred, and it would take him forever to form the easiest of questions. Sometimes it seemed as if he was having hallucinations, not understanding what the biscuit in his hand was, or that strange device we had given to him to take a picture of us with. He would recover after a few minutes, trying to make up for his mental absence, trying to show he was in his right mind, as if nothing had happened. And probably, for him, nothing had happened.

He would be back with us, yes, but without the faintest memory of what had been said two minutes earlier, making everybody feel uncomfortable and embarrassed for him. They would look at me, worried, almost asking, 'Roby, what's up with him? You have to do something. Lucio is not well'. They would take me aside at parties to tell me this, or they would phone me the day after, concerned by what they had seen. I've introduced Lucio to my friends, so for all of them, as well as for his family, I am the point of reference if anything is wrong with him. 'You have to do something, Roby', I was being told from multiple sides. In that spur to action, I was already being condemned; it foreshadowed the end of a friendship that for me was a permanent fixture, a fundamental landmark in my life.

Only God knows how much I've done. Clearly too much. I've brought up the problem with Lucio countless times, trying to make him see that something was wrong and that he should go to a specialist. He absolutely didn't want me to involve his family, given that, living in Italy, they couldn't do anything apart from worry anyway. Following the advice of my brother, a nurse, I had insisted Lucio see a neurologist. A brain tumour, early dementia, even Alzheimer's, although unlikely because of his age, all seemed like valid if terrible explanations for those strange episodes he was suffering out of the blue.

And while I was becoming increasingly worried, and even more frustrated, because it seemed like I cared about this whole thing more than he did, and I was more determined than he was to find out the truth, the shit truly hit the fan. Splattering over the walls and slapping me hard in the face, I might add. A phone call that changed everything. A phone call during which they told me that, no, Lucio doesn't have any neurological disorders. The problem is a different one, and it's a monster that's all around us.

I felt as if the world had collapsed. Because of how serious the problem was, on the one hand, but even more because of everything underlying it: the lies, all the things left unsaid, his not opening up to me, his suffering in silence, my naivety at never considering that option, my feeling betrayed. I was asking him to go and see all these doctors, while he knew damned well that it was a completely different problem. I couldn't believe I'd never noticed anything. The sad awareness that I have reached an age where people do have problems, and big ones too. All of a sudden, I transition from saying my life looks like a movie, to actually being in one. Unfortunately, it's a movie that I didn't choose to star in, a drama where I cannot even decide what role to play.

For more than a year I've handled things his way, respecting his feelings when, from the very beginning, I would have dealt with the problem in a completely different way. While Lucio wanted to keep things secret and play them down, I saw in this behaviour an amplification of the problem, obliging all of us to wear more masks, layer upon layer of pretence, trapping us in a vicious circle that has, in the end, eaten our friendship away.

More than once I put my hurt ego aside, that little voice calling me a stupid idiot, at first, because I hadn't noticed anything was wrong. Then it called me a pathetic Pollyanna, who hadn't been able to consider other possible explanations. It finally called me a naïve fucking fool, who would confidently respond to her friends' concerns, 'No, come on, I'm the one gulping down bottles of Prosecco! Lucio is always very moderate in his alcohol consumption. If he had a problem with substances, it would be with cigarettes'.

Later on that same voice whispered to me that this isn't about me, and we should think about him, about how much he must have suffered to get to that stage, unable to ask for help and open up. And I really couldn't understand what we had been talking about for hours and hours, if I had never known anything about this pain he was carrying, so well concealed. What had our friendship been based on? I thought I knew everything about him. I mean, he would sometimes share details with me about his sexual prowess, and he had never once hinted at the void that was eating him alive? And what does this say about me as a friend? What responsibility have I had in all this? How come I never remotely suspected anything?

At first I felt compassion for him, and I was moved by a desire to help him. Little by little, though, these feelings have been replaced by frustration and a strong anger at seeing him relapsing when the path out of that mess seemed so clear to me. His determination to hurt himself, his denying the obvious. His weakness.

14

And my anger mounted. Silently, at first, feeling guilty because I couldn't really help him, which made me feel like a shitty friend, who had never thought there could be other explanations, and who was not happy about the motherly role she now had to play. Yes, because while before we were on the same level, since this bombshell struck, I feel like I'm the one who has to check on him, who has to reproach him, guide him, encourage him, even tell him off. When we meet up, it's different now. We tend to stay at home more and watch movies, rather than going out for dinner or to a pub. When we organise barbecues and picnics, I'm always keeping an eye on him, trying to pick up on any changes that would give away his drinking secretly in the bathroom. I don't have fun with him like I used to. That's the truth of it. And in saying this I feel like a horrible person because that's really not the point. It is so not the point. Yet, when you yourself have a hundred other things and problems to think about, and you need to have fun and let your hair down, you want your social outings to provide you with exactly this: relaxation, fun, laughter, joy. If they stop giving you all this and actually add to your insecurities, frustration, anger, disappointment, sadness... Well, they are becoming a burden.

The straw that broke the muddy, dirty, exhausted camel's back came last night, while I was talking in the garden with Lucio, who was smoking one of his many cigarettes, taking a break from the noisy house party we were at with some friends. Once again I was trying to encourage him to face the problem. 'Lucio, why don't you take a break from work? It's been stressing you out a lot lately, and we both know how you react when you are stressed. You should reduce the number of things that cause you to drink. I mean, tell me, how much stress does your job cause in the big picture of your current life?'

'Fifty percent', he answered. And, after a short pause, exhaling the smoke in a little cloud, he added, 'And you, with your constant worrying and checking on me, cause the other fifty percent'.

Boom.

15

Wow.

What a blow.

I do believe I missed a few heartbeats, hearing him talk that way. Not only for months on end have I gone against my judgement, respecting his feelings when I could clearly see that things were not improving at all. Not only did I find myself having to deal with a humongous problem, basically on my own, which had nothing to do with me. Not only did my heart and soul fill with sadness, anger, nostalgia for what we used to be, fear for his and our future, uncertainty, doubts, a sense of guilt and helplessness. No, there's more. All this had yielded the opposite result, actually adding to his stress.

Something really broke inside me at that point. And, at the same time, I put down this extra heavy luggage I'd been carrying for months.

Enough. ENOUGH. *Basta.*

I feel almost sick at saying this, and I have no idea how I will manage to distance myself from him, but there's really nothing I can do to help him if he doesn't want to be helped. Not only was it all in vain, but it had even made things worse for him.

Enough. *Basta*, for real. I can't take it anymore. In light of all of this, I take back my energy and care and I direct them towards myself, whom I have so violated and neglected throughout this whole story. I have no idea how, but I need to go back to thinking of myself.

London, Wednesday 27th September 2017

My eyes are red from crying. I don't know if I feel more sad or... outraged, and furious. Actually, I feel all three. I feel sad for myself and furious with life, which is so unfair in how it distributes its gifts, giving them to so many people who don't even want them or who don't understand how precious they are because it all came so easily to them, and I feel outraged at how there can be adults walking around with only kilos and kilos of shit in their heads.

Earlier on I was on Match.com, checking out the profile of this

16

cute guy, a doctor, and it's weird how, just by reading someone's profession, a whole set of stereotypes and assumptions pop up in your mind: 'A doctor. Therefore he must be sensitive, with a human touch, altruistic, educated'.

I started reading the few lines that accompanied his beautiful pictures, and Mr Sensitivity was careful to specify, on the third line: 'Women over 37, please refrain from contacting me as you are very likely infertile, and I want children'.

....

Boom.

....

There you go. The power of words. And of gratuitous cruelty.

In a split second I felt a seaquake of anger and pain mounting up and then suddenly exploding in sobs. Like that, out of the blue.

For the last two years I have been living with the pain of a diagnosis of low fertility, at an advanced biological age, and of a failed attempt, made alone and abroad, to freeze my eggs. I've been trying to come to terms with this for months, thinking about how I can address this problem, what alternatives I am left with... And I have to encounter as big a piece of shit as this who dares come out with something so horrendous?

I screamed my contempt for him. I called upon karma to take care of him, I reported him to the dating app, managing to get his profile shut down, but I've been left with this open, aching wound: my muted anguish at the passing of time combined with the men I see around me. Especially because the intensity of my reaction made me understand that I haven't remotely dealt with or accepted what the doctors told me. And, to be honest, I have no idea where to start.

London, Sunday 15th October 2017

Today is a rainy Sunday, both inside and out. My mood is at its lowest.

For too many months, I've been focused solely on what I haven't achieved. I focus my thoughts on the children I don't have and don't know if I ever will, on the partner I never found over the years, despite starting my search afresh with renewed energy and optimism each time. I focus on having lost my life-long friend, my shoulder to lean on since forever, and what scares me even more is that I'm talking about our friendship in the past tense, while in fact we are still both here.

I look for answers in self-help books, which all invite you to listen to yourself and align with your soul.

If there is one sentence I have probably heard around a thousand times by now, but which still leaves me a bit confused, it's the famous LET IT GO. How would we say it in Italian? Let things fall away? Release your grip on everything?

If we follow their reasoning, it would appear all our pain comes from attachment. We get attached to something and then, if we lose it, everything goes to hell. We should instead work on having no attachments. I read it and hear it everywhere. Even when I forget to attach my files in an email.

Okay, let's assume for a moment that this is true. So, specifically, what would I be attached to? To my family? Not really. They live in Treviso and Padua. We talk regularly on the phone, and I try to go home every two to three months, but I live my life here quite happily.

Could I maybe be attached to my career? I wouldn't say so. I'm definitely not a workaholic, killing myself with long hours. I devote a lot of time to my personal life and my hobbies, and I've never been afraid to go away and travel for a bit in the past, even if it jeopardised my client base, which it took me years and continued efforts to build. Am I perhaps attached to material things? Definitely not. Technology, designer clothes, cars, luxury holidays: I couldn't care less. Could I possibly be attached to my sweet little home, where everything speaks volumes about me, the purchase of which left me skint, with barely my socks and a G-string to stand up in? Well, yes and no. I care about it, of course, but I have no problem renting out my room to strangers on Airbnb while I am travelling. I don't hesitate to leave half my stuff on display for the newcomers to see,

18

even if I always make sure to empty the bedside drawer and hide its… less than saintly contents, let's say.

So, what am I attached to? If everybody has some attachments that cause them pain, what are mine? Friends? I wouldn't say so. Because of the work I do, I spend way more time alone than the average person. A partner? But how so, given that I've been single for as many years as there are letters in the word 'spinster'?

In this precise moment, I've had an epiphany, a sudden realisation.

Maybe I'm attached to the *idea* of a partner.

The idea of how my life should have been.

This certainty that I would fall in love, get married and have three children.

This is what was supposed to happen in my life. I've had that vision since I was a child. As a matter of fact, following the initial reasoning, all the pain I've felt in the last few years comes from the fact that this ideal life I'd sculpted in my mind has never become a reality.

That's my attachment. Some preset ideas about the man I will meet, how things between us will develop and my having to become a mother, given that I've always seen myself in this role.

Expectations. Here's another concept that goes hand in hand with the famous let it go and with attachments. I'm surely not the only one tussling with this trio, and I'm really trying to understand their true meaning.

Expectations, those bastards. Yet, how can you not have any? Every time I meet a new guy, I repeat to myself, 'Roby, take it slowly. Try not to have too many expectations'. Yes, I tell myself these things rationally in my head, but my heart just ignores them. How can you not be disappointed when you don't receive according to how much you have given?

I don't know. These concepts seem so abstruse and difficult to put into practice. And I do wonder if, at the end of the day, I'm really interested in living a life this… cold, almost, detached from other

19

people and things, where you don't get emotionally involved, where you keep a protective distance from everything and everybody.

In the midst of this multitude of things I don't understand, at least there's one thing I've learnt. Your body doesn't lie.

Or the soul if you will.

I mean that all this confusion and mental mud, which seem to trap me hopelessly inside the mangled body of a car, happen on a rational, intellectual level. That's where I am not able to understand what I want, what I have to do. My body, however, sends me clear signals.

There are people who get ulcers, others who get a mega-incredible psoriasis and still others who get alopecia, bouts of dandruff or an explosive outbreak of spots.

Me, I get tearful.

Just like that, all of a sudden. Bam! A flood of tears.

London, Tuesday 28th October 2017

Yesterday I was on the phone with my mum for our usual weekly chat when I found out, to my shock and desolation, that at the venerable age of 72, and having been married to my father for 43 years, my mum's sex life is more active than mine. I addressed a silent thought to God, 'How can You allow such atrocities to happen?'

If I think about my love life and dating activities over the last two years, I feel like buying a ticket to Lourdes. A one-way ticket.

The last guy I really lost my mind over was a certain Gareth, who I met on a plane last year coming back from a fab weekend in Palma de Mallorca. Love clicked immediately, as it almost always does for me. We share two amazing weeks during which I find myself, for the first time in my life, posting something on Facebook that hints at the fact my pupils are turning heart shaped; two weeks during which I learn that Gareth has an utterly shocking family history: he knifed his brother, his sister was raped by their father, and other such niceties. And yet my inner Florence Nightingale is screaming at the top of her lungs that she'll make up for all the love he never got,

20

that his life will be beautiful through her and more slush of this kind. For the first time in years everything seemed so real and intense. The sunsets are more brightly coloured, the squirrels are even cooler, waking up at dawn is not a problem. I am in love and so happy to be in love again.

However, one evening, only twelve days after we got together and completely out of the blue, things change dramatically. During a normal conversation between Gareth and me, his eyes suddenly fire up, he makes a face I'd never seen before and barks, 'Shut that trap, you fucking bitch'.

....

Like that, out of the blue. Excuse me?????!

A completely unjustified outburst, which shocked me even more because of how incongruent the tone of voice and the words were with the Gareth I knew. I would like to say it left me baffled, because I find that an elegant word, but disturbed, confused, shaken give a better indication of how shocked I was.

'Where did that come from?' I asked him, after being left totally frozen at first.

'From Gary. So far you have met Gareth, but there's also Gary inside me. I created him in order to survive in that family where emotional abuse was the order of the day. Without Gary, who knows, I might have already committed suicide. Or I would have killed someone. For sure, I wouldn't have remained normal.'

....

Oh, I see. Well, sure, you remained perfectly normal.

I was missing a double personality disorder in my repertoire of doomed romances. Thank goodness I managed to bind and gag old Florence long enough to beat a hasty retreat. However, this whole story has not only left me shocked and shaken, but also quite confused about my judgement skills. How on earth did I not notice anything weird during those two super intense weeks?

With Lucio, too, I had not noticed anything. And I've known Lucio my whole life.

And yet I consider myself a receptive and attentive person. But am I really so? Or has my emotional compass already gone haywire? Can I really trust my intuition next time I think, 'You like this guy. Go for him'?

I don't know. I don't even trust myself anymore. I doubt the soundness of my thinking. And when you doubt yourself so much, every step becomes incredibly difficult. And when every step becomes incredibly difficult, you end up not taking any, and you stay still. Stuck, indeed.

In September, I met Antonio during a shamanic journey in Italy. In between ayahuasca-induced bouts of vomiting, this handsome Venetian, who had caught my eye straight off, asked for my phone number. We shared numerous cuddles that morning, spurred on by the loving spirit of that plant circulating big time in our systems. We then went out a few times to get to know each other better. There followed a whole month of daily text messages and regular phone calls, and Antonio promised to come and see me in London. The date approaches. He hasn't bought the ticket yet, but he keeps reassuring me that he's coming until a week before the fateful date.

It's only when I insist on knowing whether he's coming or not that he explains, '*Guarda* Roby, look, I would really love to come and see you, but maybe I shouldn't, since I've just started going out with a girl here in Venice... There's an incredible energy between us, even if things are a bit complicated because she has a boyfriend...'

Ah, ecco. Oh, I see.

No, I really think you shouldn't come, then. So, not only, despite all your sweet words and compliments, did you manage to get interested in another woman, not only is your word worth about as much as an unfinished handjob, but you even prefer a cheater to me. Fantastic. And, of course, I don't wish you both all the best.

But here I am, giving love another go, once more and despite everything. Christmas is approaching, and I don't really fancy walking all by myself again along Oxford Street, bursting with Christmas lights and decorations, wondering how it is possible that

22

a woman like me is still as alone as a dried-up cow pat in a Swiss field at dawn. Last week I started chatting with a cute guy living outside London, and we spent whole days writing each other long messages exchanging our deepest thoughts on life. I immediately noticed that he had some rigid, narrow perspectives which would not marry well with my open-minded world view. However, I told myself that it would still be nice to meet him in person. I then decided this would be pointless when, having asked him, 'If you had a magic rubber, what would you cancel from this world in order to make it a better place?' he answered, 'Dogs, fireworks and most babies'.

Fantastic.

Let's put Mr Herod aside and see what male specimen turns up next, for Quest for a Soulmate's sake!

London, Thursday 2nd November 2017

A few weeks ago I started a 30-hour course, 'Introduction to counselling', to see if this might lead to my next career move. We watched a movie about Carl Rogers, founder of the person-centred therapeutic approach. It included some of his filmed sessions with patients, some of the awards he received, revealed how much work he had done to develop this new approach and how much he had believed in it from the very beginning, and silent tears were falling down my cheeks. I was moved by his clear vision. And I was so envious of it. How successful can a person be when they know exactly what they want? How much good can a single person do when that thing they want is useful to the world? And how much courage and resilience is needed to devote oneself entirely to a cause?

Those tears were the same I cried last week when on the internet I stumbled across Maggie Doyne, a 31-year-old who is currently the adoptive mother of 53 Nepali orphans.

53 Nepali orphans.

Fifty-three.

53.

The more I read of her story, the more the floodgates opened up inside me. My eyes filled with tears, and I found myself sobbing in my bedroom. Like a mad woman, basically. I get goosebumps when I read stories like hers.

When she was 19 years old, Maggie went to Asia on her gap year. While in Nepal, she locked eyes with this seven-year-old Nepali girl who was carrying a sack filled with heavy stones up the mountain. Meeting that girl's eyes left Maggie devastated. A question immediately popped up from her heart, so simple and direct, and yet so terrible: why does this girl have to do such a heavy job at her young age, every day, for like just two dollars a day, while I am here enjoying life travelling the world simply because I was lucky enough to be born in a Western country?

From then on, she basically had no choice. First, she got the girl out of that job and paid for her education. Then, Maggie told herself that, since she had helped one girl, she might as well help another one. Later on, the opportunity arose to buy a piece of land for 5,000 dollars. Maggie called her parents in New Jersey asking them to send over all her savings from years of working as a baby-sitter. After that, the buying of the land, building a school on it with the help of local men and taking in orphans was just one thing leading to the next.

I was listening to one of her interviews. She was fresh faced, and her eyes shimmered with love. 'I told myself I couldn't save all the eight million children who live in the streets, having lost their parents, but I could at least save one'.

So direct and simple.

I always get so struck by people like her, who don't build any barriers between their life and what they'd like to do. They go all in, without worrying about how far they'll get. Sometimes, when we think about where we want to go, our destination or goal can seem so blurred and confused that we don't even know where to start. Or it might be clear in our mind, but it seems so huge that we feel it's impossible to reach, and we don't even start moving and working in that direction. Whereas Maggie shows us that what really matters is taking the first step, without worrying about how things might evolve. Go for it. Dive in. Believe in it. And trust yourself, trust your capabilities, and trust the Universe. Trust the incredible possibilities and plot twists It has in store for us every day, including pulling the rug from under us when we plan too much.

Trust your capabilities and trust the Universe.

Yeah, right.

These words stir something inside me. I've always perceived myself as a colourful spinning top, constantly in motion, yet for the last two years I've felt faded. Maybe that's not visible from the outside. I'm still more active than half of the people I know, but I know that something inside me has changed.

Here in London I feel oppressed. In my attempt to save Lucio, doing it my way, I've emotionally drained myself. Worrying about other people's problems, my loneliness and being unable to understand what I wanted to do with my life all weighed me down like never before. I had pictured freezing my eggs, then I started researching adoption for single women, now I've changed my mind again and decided I might as well go straight ahead with IVF treatment. So many ideas, notions, thoughts crowd my mind, and none speaks to me more clearly than the rest. In all these scenarios, where is the man I've always thought would be by my side throughout this phase of my life? Not only is he not here, but the men who do darken my door are one-hit wonders, flashes in the pan, fleeting meteors that disappear without explanation. Each retreating figure reiterates that you can't expect commitment and silently reminds you that, when it comes down to it, you are basically not good enough. You're not good enough to make them fall in love and stay. At the end of the day, at the end of the long list of reasons you can reel off for why you've been single for years, there must be something in you that makes you unlovable.

London, Monday 6th November 2017

Eleven 'no's. Eleven. I could see the silver lining in this and focus on the fact that I have at least eleven people I regard as friends, while so

25

many other people I know say they have at most two or three friends. But, indeed, what kind of friends are they if one after another, for their various reasons, they all said 'no'? Or is this just me wanting to play the victim and take things personally again? What I know is that for years, no, ever since I was a child, I've always dedicated so much time and energy to keeping in contact with people and organising meetups. I'm always the one who's available and enthusiastic, always saying 'yes', and if I don't organise anything myself, you can be sure that nobody else does. I've always invested a lot in my friendships, because it's in my nature and maybe also because I tend to have more spare time than people working in normal office jobs, tied to working hours.

Yet, even when you think you have a good number of friends to rely on, be it for going out or just someone to talk through your worries with... Just when you think that all that time and care and attention you invested into other people's lives will pay off when you need it most... Right when you are entertaining all these illusions, life slaps you down hard, almost Giacomo Leopardi style, to remind you that at the end of the day we are born alone, and we'll die alone (what a happy prospect!).

Yesterday was the 5th of November, Guy Fawkes Night, a very British celebration. Basically they commemorate a failed attempt by this Guy Fawkes to blow up Parliament back in 1605. For the last three nights, London has been lit up with fireworks, and I simply adore fireworks. It may sound childish, but I wouldn't want to miss them for anything in the world. That explosion of colour, that unpredictable succession of bangs and lights, so beautiful and full and intense and noisy and unexpected and surprising, in constant motion... To me, they are both a representation and celebration of life.

Last week I asked eleven 'friends' if they were up for coming with me to see the fireworks, and eleven times I received a 'no', each one clear and justified, to varying degrees. When some of them told me they didn't like fireworks, I asked myself how many times I'd gone with them to do something I didn't particularly enjoy. When some of them told me it was cold and they were tired and they didn't feel like it, I asked myself how many times I'd travelled an hour by train to go and see them at their place, to spend time with these people who had little desire to go out but a huge desire to see me. One friend even went so far as to say I am co-dependent and never able to do anything on my own.

Me. Me? I'm never able to do anything on my own. Me.

First of all, I wondered how some people can be so casually mean; second, how it is possible that certain friends don't seem to understand the first thing about me; and third, if there is any truth in her words.

And now that I'm putting these thoughts down on paper, I'm getting so angry because the first thing that should come to mind, the very first one, is: fourth, how can I even consider someone who says something so untrue a friend? And fifth, why do I? I mean, it doesn't seem to matter that you've been working from home alone for eight years, which means that you've had no choice but to get used to your own company, and you even like it. Little does it matter that you've been single for years and, despite the suffering that has entailed, never have you compromised to ease the loneliness, unlike so many women around you do.

No, you, like the idiot that you are, even stop and ask yourself whether this friend of yours may be right, if it's true that you put your happiness into other people's hands. You, of all people, who see yourself as 'the independent one'. But Roby, there's something really wrong in your way of thinking. Maybe it's time to reassess your friendships, weeding some of them out. Maybe it's time to look deeply into what these friendships give you, what need of yours they satisfy. But I'd also like to understand why, in the heat of the moment, I don't feel outraged at her words but instead automatically assume there might be some truth in them. A propensity to soul-search may be a good thing and a rare quality, but isn't doing it all the time a sign of low self-esteem? And am I not supposed to be that 'strong and independent woman' so many people describe me as?

In the end, used as I am to doing things on my own, a lesson my mum taught me growing up, I went to see the fireworks anyway. And, following the same old script, I cried. Because of their incredible beauty, yes, but also because this time the loved-up couples around me made me feel ten times lonelier than in the past. Actually, eleven times lonelier (to be a little more precise).

London, Sunday 12th November 2017
I'm so mega fed up with my moods. Paranoia, fear, negative and limiting thoughts which deprive me of self-esteem and self-confidence. Full-blown chaos reigns in my head, and inside myself the perception that I am not living the life I want, for various reasons, is plaguing me.

I know this to be true. Otherwise Maggie Doyne's story wouldn't move me so profoundly; it wouldn't evoke such a strong and immediate reaction.

I need people like her in my life. Someone who inspires me, someone who is not afraid to give it a proper try, someone who lives fully what they feel. Someone who can show me that life is indeed marvellous, and that so many amazing things happen when we finally follow our hearts.

So, you know what?

I'm buying a ticket to Nepal, and I'm going to meet her. Also because doing this makes me someone who follows her heart and is not afraid to give it a try. I'm done with waiting around to meet someone so inspirational. Roby, why don't you become the source of inspiration you need?

All those voices inside and out, whether they're mine or not, can go and fuck off for a little while. Actually, I'll go and fuck off. Voices, you can all stay here.

Yes. I really need to get away from my normal life with all its associated emotional burdens. And since I'm not in a good place, one month would not be enough. I would need a week just to unwind, and a week before I actually fly back, I know I would already be thinking about London, which would basically leave only two weeks for any actual, real mental detachment from everything. I don't have to explain anything to anybody, thanks to the combination of being a freelancer and having been single for three and a half centuries, so... why not stay away for two months? Actually, now that I think about it, my last trip to Vietnam, Thailand and Malaysia lasted eight weeks. Let's do a longer trip now. Let's do a three-month one.

From Nepal, it almost seems logical to go to India, even if I've already been there several times. This time I could concentrate on the south of India, given that I haven't actually been there yet. Yes, let's spend a good month there. And then, from there...? Bangladesh? Oh gosh, it may very well be lovely, but I've never heard anyone praising its beauty. Actually, now that I think about it, I don't know anyone who's been there, which could be a great reason to go there myself. Or should I rather continue south towards Sri Lanka? My friend Marghe has been recommending it since we were at University, calling it something of an earthly paradise.

Maybe I'll sleep on it. But by tomorrow I want to have bought the tickets.

Yes, a long trip is exactly what I need to 'unblock' this situation.

London, Monday 13th November 2017

The trinity is confirmed: Sri Lanka, India and Nepal, in that order. I've just bought the tickets, and now it's for real. I already feel full of joy just at the prospect, and a little shiver of vitality shimmers up my spine, reaching my lips and tugging them upwards into a smile. Asia, here I come.

I come mentally destroyed, but here I come nonetheless.

Sri Lanka, land of serendipity, I'm on my way to discover you. Who knows? Maybe I'll be lucky enough to find something wonderful by pure chance, or stumble across something I wasn't even looking for, totally unexpected, while in fact looking for something else entirely.

I'm returning to the seductive embrace of the colourful, adorned arms of brutal Mother India, a lady as mind-achingly beautiful as she is deliriously out of her mind.

And I'm going to meet a girl who has no idea how much she has inspired me.

Three months on the road, just me and my backpack. And I want to come back feeling light inside. I feel like I want to plan almost nothing. I already have the plane tickets, now I'll take care of the visas and that's it. Whatever is going to happen in each country, I leave to Destiny. I don't want to force anything. If I like a place, I'll stay there as long as I want to. If I feel tired, and all I want to do is sprawl under the sun like a beached whale, I'll do that. If some of the backpackers I meet give me interesting tips, I will follow them and go to those places. And should a good vibe develop with another traveller, then maybe I will hang out with him for a while. Or her. But most likely him.

In other words, as busy as I am in London, where my life resembles a never-ending *Tetris* game, each piece dovetailing perfectly with the next, every manoeuvre timed to the millisecond to fully exploit my time and the resources of this beautiful city, that's how free I want to be when travelling, not bound to any plans or commitments. I don't want to have any expectations; I don't want to develop any preset ideas of what should happen. Let's see if I can really manage not to have any attachments, and if life flows better this way. Let's see if it's true that precisely when we stop trying to force things, and let life unfold, we receive the biggest surprises. Let's run this experiment for three months. Absolutely nothing organised or booked, apart from the flights and the hotel for my first night in Colombo.

Universe, I trust You.

London, Thursday 16th November 2017

Today I've been asked if I consider myself religious. No, not particularly. Not anymore. However, over the last two years I have definitely begun a spiritual journey, which I like to refer to as my 'walk in Hippyland'. Every single thing I've discovered has opened up a new door, creating a very long chain of so many interlocked rings. Some years ago, I had a tenant from New Zealand, Caroline, who was the epitome of the 'lost woman' in my eyes. She was 40 years old, single and vegetarian; she had a spiritual guru and saw a business coach and a psychologist. She would surely have been a *gattara*, a cat lady, if Emanuele and I had allowed her to keep any small felines, Emanuele being my friend and co-owner of the house. Caroline would swing in an almost charming way between not being able to take a single decision without consulting at least one of the above three people and taking decisions on her own that were definitely impractical, if not downright ridiculous. Watching her constantly going from one extreme to the other, I found myself telling Emanuele, 'If I get to 40 and I'm still that screwed up, please just put me down'.

Caroline would get by on the odd massage here and there, or by selling cakes to local cafés, and in the meantime, she would fill her life with esoteric readings, astrological consultations, meditation, numerous rituals, including one where she invited angels to spend five days with us (welcome to my world).

'You can shoot me in the head… or poison me. It's up to you, but please don't let me become anything like her', I would urge Emanuele, looking at Caroline's life, which seemed cut adrift, so… inconclusive.

Being from the Veneto region in Italy, accustomed to working, saving, productivity and practicality from day one, I couldn't help but have a negative view of this life in which nothing ever became substantial and where so much time was devoted to nothing real, as far as I could see.

Such is the irony of life that we often become what we once despised. A bit like when we realise that we have become like our mothers, despite having criticised them for years. Today I know that people work like mirrors for us, and we often dislike in them the things we don't accept in ourselves. At that time I couldn't know this, of course, and I want to underline that I never got to the stage

31

of inviting angels into my home (also because *everybody knows* that angels are always with us, so Caroline's ritual was basically useless). I simply thought that there was a chasmic divergence in our values and views on life.

Instead, five years later, here I am on my spiritual quest, my so called 'walk in Hippyland', where every practice sheds some light on dark corners of my being.

For me, everything began with biodynamic craniosacral therapy. For the first time in my life, I really felt energy flowing strongly inside me. Before my first session I had always perceived my body as something decaying and aging, from wrinkles around the eyes, to grey hairs, to tooth cavities, to age spots on my hands. However, lying on that treatment couch while the therapist held her hands close to my ankles without ever touching them, I was obliged to instantly change my view. I could feel proper waves flowing inside me, my eardrums and eyeballs were hurting, as if something was boiling and pushing forcefully to come out. My eyes were open, but for a few seconds everything went black, I could only see inky darkness, and despite being on that solid couch, I felt as if I was floating in the sea. I have never had such an intense physical reaction. 'Wow, I can feel you are responding very strongly. It's not often that I feel such energy waves in a patient coming here for the first time. Unfortunately, you have many blockages inside that won't allow the energy to flow. I suggest you try Qi Kung. Have you ever heard of it?' the therapist asked me.

No, I had never heard of it, but in that moment I suddenly felt like Lazarus, who had been shown that another dimension was indeed a thing, and couldn't go on ignoring it.

Thanks to the Universe's synchronicities, or simply because we notice the things that fill our thoughts, two days later, while walking in Brixton, I stumbled across a poster: 'Qi Kung and Tai Chi classes, every Tuesday and Thursday'.

And so here I am in a gym, surrounded by people standing with their eyes closed, bringing my hands closer and then moving them away from each other, feeling my blood throbbing strongly in each finger then a growing tingling sensation culminating in a small electric shock. Slow and repetitive movements, through which, for the first time, I could really see what was happening *inside*. I don't know how else to describe it. My eardrums and eyes would often hurt, my blood seemed to flow faster, more strongly, pressing everywhere, insistently, as though trying to force its way out. I had never realised how vitally charged we are, what incredible energy is held inside each of us. I was becoming more and more aware that there are worlds I never knew existed, and that venturing forth to discover them could be the most fascinating journey ever.

'If you like Qi Kung so much, and it gives you this sensation of well-being, you should try meditation. In a sense, Qi Kung is a standing up meditation. Try Mindfulness. I'm sure you'll love it', my teacher told me.

And so there I go, sitting in a circle with eight other people practising Mindfulness, closely examining a flower for two minutes, as if we had never seen it before, and then admiring it for two more minutes, as if we would never see it again. Mindfulness is a meditation focused on being totally immersed in the moment. With our eyes closed, we would sit, alert, waiting to receive sounds, discovering that there are always more sounds around you than you are initially aware of and welcoming even the loudest and most unpleasant ones as part of the symphony playing in that precise moment. Thanks to this practice, I discovered that my mind could translate some sounds into an explosion of colours; a fascinating synaesthetic experience. An aeroplane flying above me would be... Boom! An explosion of red. A passing lorry would be... Boom! A cloud of electric blue sprayed across my brain. Through Mindfulness, I came to realise how much richer and more intense life can be when we devote our full attention to it, living each moment as the precious and unique unit that it is.

'Have you heard of Eckhart Tolle? He's written a book, *The Power of Now*, which has sold millions of copies and deals with this very topic, staying in the moment. It underlines how the past and future are simply our own mental constructs and how, in fact, there is no other time except the one we are experiencing now', my meditation teacher told me one morning, when all the other students were leaving the class. 'If we manage to be fully present, to accept the moment we are living because it is the only one we have, and it's neither ugly nor beautiful, but simply transient, then we'll be able to experience the only possible joy, the joy of Being. You should read it.'

And so, there I go sitting on my colourful and comfortable sofa in my bright living room, with *The Power of Now* in my hands, progressing slowly as these concepts were so new and complex to me.

That's how it went, basically. Every step I took led me to the next, and, looking back, I love seeing how they are all linked together. My 'walk in Hippyland' went on to include sound baths, and for each sound of the gong I would see visions of animals, all of them white, which led me to start reading about totem animals and spirit guides. I then embarked upon a shamanic journey by trying ayahuasca which, once the initial puking session was over, left me full of love for everything and everybody for almost a month, even if it took away my ability to remember my dreams.

'Why do you do all these things?' I've been asked repeatedly by many people. 'It seems as if you are desperately seeking an answer, but what's the question?'

Uh... I don't know yet. But what I know, for the time being, is that this journey fascinates me, and it has opened up new worlds where I can feel good, and which are always available to me. Sometimes I tell myself that I am accumulating knowledge and experiences so that one day, if prompted to ask myself a question, as the Italian journalist Marzullo would always say, I will finally be able to give myself an answer, too.

For the time being, however, I feel like I'm in a vortex. 'Growth can be so messy. At times it may just look like chaos and confusion. In many aspects of your life, you don't recognise yourself anymore, and you lose so many certainties you used to have', my meditation teacher explained to me. Truer words were never spoken.

There is such a gap between what I rationally understand and what I feel. It's as if I'm putting up some inner resistance to the new concepts I'm reading about that nevertheless fascinate me. Deep down, I am not able to believe in them. Something is holding me back. In a way, I feel like a heron (okay, a 70kg heron) who would love to take flight, who knows that there are better places, but who has its foot trapped in something, without knowing exactly where and how.

A heron, now. My favourite animal of all time has always been the elephant, ever since I saw my first one at a circus when I was seven years old. I was sitting in the front row at an afternoon show for which they had given us tickets at school. I was sitting next to my mum when this huge animal slowly walked in. The... What do you call the guy who runs the elephant show? It doesn't matter. That guy was forcing the elephant to walk with its two front feet on a huge colourful ball. If I think about it now, that was so '80s. I was sitting so close to the circus ring that I could clearly see the huge tears that seemed to have crystallised in the corners of the elephant's eyes. And out of solidarity I also started crying, and a lot, too.

'Don't they see that he is too big to walk on that ball? He doesn't want to do it! They are bad boys. They're hurting his legs like that!', I started telling my mum, my face streaming with tears. She tried to explain that no, all animals have that liquid in their eyes. She went on saying that it was a bit like what we have in our eyes in the morning when we wake up. But I was inconsolable, and the only way to stop me crying was to take me out of that circus tent, into the open air, where I finally calmed down and forgot about the brutality I'd witnessed.

Over the years I have reasoned that this love I spontaneously felt for elephants might derive from the fact that I somehow identify with some of their traits. My brothers would of course say that the first thing we have in common is our physique, given that taking the piss out of my soft, doughy body seems to be their favourite way of expressing their affection. However, there is maybe some truth in this.

I've always felt like an elephant: having a tall father and having grown faster and earlier than my schoolmates, I was always the tallest and the biggest. Especially when I was little, I had a way with words, and I used them as a shield, giving the impression that I was strong, afraid of nothing and able to take hard blows, yet inside I've always been hypersensitive. I've always felt sorrow so strongly, both mine and other people's, and this empathy has often caused me pain. I don't have an elephant's rough, 5cm-thick skin. On the contrary. The thoughtless words and indifference of superficial people have left mini scars on my heart, with which I have learned to coexist. Elephants, then. And yet, for the last two years I've been filling my house with butterflies. I don't know myself where this new passion has come from. Elephants and butterflies. Like the song by that mega-cheerful Italian singer, Michele Zarrillo. Just like that, out of the blue, I started buying flowery, butterfly-strewn dresses and jeans. Wherever I went, I would buy butterflies in different materials and sizes to hang here and there in my house.

'Mmh, that's interesting', remarked a yoga teacher who had come to see my room with a view to renting it while I was away on one of my trips. 'The elephant represents your nature; the butterfly stands for the period you are going through. You want to be light. Enough with heaviness.'

Ehm. Easier said than done. I'm trying to be lighter. I'm trying. I'd love that. As I was saying, indeed, I'd love to fly towards the real me, towards a life that I feel is more aligned with what has been restlessly moving inside me, but Life continues to clip my wings. Or, getting back to the heron, it keeps my foot mysteriously stuck.

Anyway, I've decided that this Saturday I'm going to a spiritualist church. A friend of mine went there several times and told me about the interesting experiences she had there. That was enough to arouse my considerable, insatiable curiosity, which is both my blessing and my curse. This week has been particularly shitty, and I've told myself that going to see if the spirits have a message for me could make me feel better, provided they exist. Or it could make me feel worse. Or they could have absolutely nothing to say to me. Nevertheless, let's make another foray into Hippyland.

London, Saturday 18th November 2017
Wow. What a weird evening. I've just come back from the spiritualist church in Clapham Common, and I will remember this evening forever. I mean, today I received confirmation that there are other worlds, and that some people have the gift of seeing them.

Well, where to start? First of all, this spiritualist church is not exactly a church. It was more a hall with an altar, with around twenty chairs positioned in front of the altar to accommodate the public. I arrived there feeling a bit hesitant, a bit sceptical, not exactly awkward but definitely not perfectly at ease either. There was a table on the left with a full teapot and some biscuits, and two women and three men were standing in front of it chatting happily. I greeted them, and they were all very welcoming and smiley, apart from an obese gentleman with quite greasy hair who went on closely examining his teacup.

'Welcome. Is this your first time?' a blonde lady with glasses asked me. I understood her to be the one organising these evenings.

'Yes, it's my first time, and I don't really know what to expect', I answered.

'Oh, Peter will explain how it works. Every medium works in different ways. There are those who draw the faces they see, and then ask around if anybody can recognise that person, but Peter doesn't work in this way. But don't worry, just sit down with your heart open.'

Okay, then. I sit down with my heart open, somewhat reassured by the woman's words, even if she does seem to have walked straight out of an '80s TV series, judging by her outfit. In fact, when I started looking properly around, I realised I wasn't feeling better at all. I mean, okay, on the one hand, yes, because the other five people who were there all seemed to have either weight or personal hygiene problems, as well as some difficulties socialising most likely. Comparing myself to them, I could see I was not doing that badly. On the other hand, however, the idea that I was apparently the most together person in the room comforted me for, like, ten seconds, leaving plenty of time for the realisation to dawn that I was here with them nonetheless, so I was in fact doing way worse than everyone spending their Saturday evening dancing the night away, drinking like fish, shagging like rabbits or even just watching *The X Factor* and eating pizza with their partners.

After a five-minute wait, that I spend in silence, switching between examining the condition of my cuticles and the poor furnishing in that room, in comes a man around 65 years old; a handsome man who somehow reminds me of a rock-and-roll Paul Newman. He is tall, thin, with light blue eyes surrounded by a spider web of wrinkles, and a warm smile. His hair is white and short, and he's got a load of tattoos on his arms and a cross earring that seems out of place on a man his age. He's wearing jeans, a chequered shirt, a leather waistcoat and black boots. He greets the people he already knows, then asks me if I'm new, given that he has never seen me before.

'It's nice to meet you. Thanks for coming today. Let me explain how it works. One after the other, I will come to each of you and start telling you what I see and feel in relation to you; what the spirits are willing to share with me. Should I ask you any questions, please answer loudly because I might be mentally far away and not able to hear you properly.'

Okay, then. Let's hear what the spirits have to tell me in their wisdom. I mean, if they do exist. Actually, I haven't really asked myself this question, which might seem like a minor gap in my preparation for this event. Let's say that I like hearing the stories of those who believe in spirits and claim to have seen them, and that on a spiritual level I would really love it if they existed for real. I mean, spirits in the sense of our departed dear ones who protect us and guide us, not cursed souls who haunt terrible houses or possess our bodies. There you go. I've learnt that in life it's always better to be specific, especially when talking about your desires.

Yet, I've never had the remotest flicker of an encounter with ghosts and spirits... I would love to believe in them, yes, so I was really hoping for proof of their existence. I was sitting there, telling myself, 'Spirits, come and knock on my door. Help me somehow'.

The medium started with the gentleman to my right, an old black man who was clearly no stranger to a second (and maybe even third) helping at dinner.

'I can see your mother, sitting next to you. She is always by your side, and she protects you. She wants you to keep reading the Bible every evening.'

The old man was smiling, looking at his hands on his lap. The clairvoyant rocker had an almost blank look on his face. I couldn't understand exactly what he was looking at, but I could see he was very focused. 'Your mother insists that you tell Jason to get his liver checked', continued the medium, adding a whole series of specific details and explanations to which the gentleman was responding enthusiastically. The medium seemed to get it right, then. A good beginning.

And then he moved to me. I was curious and slightly excited. I had half a smile on my face, almost inviting him to prove his skills to me. I wasn't prepared at all for the exasperation he showed when, speaking loudly and stomping a foot on the ground, he burst out, 'I want to go away! I NEED to go away! You've been saying that for a while, and finally you've made up your mind'.

Inside me, everything stood still.

Boom!

Here's how to get 1000% of my attention in one second.

'I want to go away. I NEED to go away!' are the exact, precise words I told my friend Paola four days ago, sitting in front of a huge ice cream that raises my blood sugar just thinking about it.

'Paola, I'm not okay. I'm aware of this. I really need to make some space inside. I need to go away for a while, get a change of air… Too many things have piled up here, and I feel in such a mess. I have no idea where to turn, what to think. I am not able to make decisions, I feel stuck, and I don't even know exactly how or why. I only know that I feel like a broken record, and I'm so tired of myself. So I made up my mind, and I bought an aeroplane ticket. Well, tickets, plural', I told her.

'Super cool! And well done! Where are you going?' Paola had asked me, pretty as always with her brown curls, nose piercing, black eyeliner and ever-present red lipstick, as she put the spoon down, filled with semi-molten ice cream.

'Well, I started with the idea of going to Nepal, but then I told myself that in fact I want to have a proper long trip, so in the end I'm going away for three months. One in Sri Lanka, one in South India and the last one in Nepal.'

'I hate you', Paola answered, with her trademark smile.

Wow. It feels so weird to have a stranger telling me the same precise words that I uttered only a few days before with that same intensity and exasperation.

'You are blocked in a circle you are not able to break out from. You always go back to square one. You go around in circles. You need to break those patterns that you keep repeating', the medium explained to me.

Ehm. *Grazie mille.* Thanks a million. Stuff of little importance. 'You are out of balance. You are not in harmony with yourself. You need to slow down because you risk losing sight of what really matters', continued the spirit world's Paul Newman.

Uh, I know.

I generally perceive myself as positive and cheerful, optimistic and lively, but for months now I've been feeling as if I were constantly running on a low battery. I function, yes, but slowly and the power doesn't seem to last as long. I've become so focused on negative thinking and what is missing from my life, that I have lost sight of

40

the good and the beautiful. I know that it's there, and I know there's plenty of it, but I'm not able to focus on it. The negative thoughts occupy so much space in my mind and soul that, even if I hear a weak voice reminding me that life always has some surprises in store for us, my most bitter part bites back with 'Oh, yeah? Okay, then, where are they?'

'You have a dear friend who's been suffering for a long time, and you have been helping him a lot. The spirits are grateful for what you do', continued the rocker-medium. He was surely speaking about Lucio. So the spirits know, and they thank me for what I have done. At least someone does.

'I see a man with an almost Hitler-style moustache sitting next to you, and a lady who looks a lot like you, apart from her bouffant hairdo', added the other side's Paul Newman.

How to describe a man in only four words. He's talking about *Zio* Rino, Uncle Rino, a character I was lucky enough to meet and get to know a bit when I was his guest in Canada for a month at the age of 16. He was always smoking, always ready to laugh, with his thin nervous legs and, yes, his jet-black moustache. Lung cancer took away his vitality first, and then everything else in 1997.

The woman who looks a lot like me has to be *Zia* Lidia, Auntie Lidia, who in fact I hardly knew, since she died when I was little, but who nevertheless has appeared to me in dreams and visions three times already. And now the clairvoyant sees her sitting next to me…

'They are both guarding you closely. They are protecting you. They are sitting one on each side of you. Your trip will go well. Don't be afraid', the rocker-medium reassured me.

How come *Zia* Lidia is so close to me when she only ever knew me as a young child?

I don't know much about her life, apart from the fact that she passed away young, more or less at my age. The second time I saw her in a vision, an experience which left me quite bamboozled, I asked my mum to tell me a bit more about this sister of hers whom I remembered vaguely. From what my mum told me, with a serious expression and slightly teary eyes, I got the image of a woman who had been very unlucky in love, and who had suffered a great deal for it.

Maybe that's what keeps us close, my *zia* and me. For goodness' sake, I've never been stood up at the altar, cheated on or beaten up by a man. Thank God, no. But, no matter where I look around me, I only find confused and undecided men, eternal Peter Pans who don't want to commit and feel no particular urge to be honest, clear or well-mannered either.

So, yes, please, *Zia*, stay with me, because you can clearly see how badly I'm doing with men. Don't you worry, I still believe in love, and I still feel like putting myself out there. I still look for it and try, unlike some of my friends, who are now shielding behind such bitterness and self-sabotaging inertia that it's painful to contemplate, and which is still so alien to my way of being, despite all the disappointments I've faced.

The medium also told me two or three things which had nothing to do with me, to be honest, but the ones I've just written down were more than enough for me.

The most beautiful thing I brought home with me from this weird evening is knowing that my *zio* and *zia* are standing by me, that they are keeping an eye on me, that I'm never alone, but always protected. I was so excited that half an hour ago I called my mum to tell her about it. 'Can you believe it, *Mamma*? The medium saw *Zio* Rino and *Zia* Lidia next to me!' To which my mum replied, 'You don't need to tell me that. I already know they are always with us. Even your *nonna*, my mum, I feel her with me sometimes. If you prayed every evening, you would feel it, too'.

So just another pointed remark from mum on 'the power of faith' complete with a nice dampener on what had been a sensational discovery for me.

Anyway, now I know that the spirits are aware of my upcoming trip, that they will protect me and that everything will be fine.

(Maybe.)

DAY 1
'Does this leaflet refer to my flight?'
-Heathrow, London, Monday 12th February 2018-

Mamma mia, what a depression! I've written pages that put me in the mood for self-harm. It's always a bit weird rereading what I've written in moments when I was ready to gulp down a whole bottle of bleach (by the way, can you die like that?). Writing is a process that takes me deeper and deeper, and sometimes I indulge in self-pity and the victim's mentality that I actually want to move away from. But, of course, it's much better to spew all my sorrow into a journal, rather than breaking the balls of a friend who's probably heard it all before anyway, and no doubt has plenty of her own problems.

Anyway, if it were possible, reading this excursus on my own brand of misery over these recent dark months has got me even more excited at the idea of leaving! One hour to go before boarding!

Last Saturday I spoke with Piper, a friend of mine who just came back ten days ago from three months' travelling around Latin America, and who is enthusiastic about the whole experience. Like me, travelling brings her back to life. When things get crappy and stifling, travelling gives us both the chance to recharge our batteries, to put everything in perspective and detach ourselves from people, situations and above all our own oppressive thoughts.

Piper and I are so similar, and for this reason we have shared many experiences. We even explored Thailand and Laos together. She is sensitive, too, and with my same tendency to fry her brain with ceaseless thinking and pondering.

On Saturday, however, she sounded like a New Age guru, 'You will find your path because it's yours and only yours. Creativity will flow at the right moment. Don't worry about organising lessons should you ever want to be or find yourself volunteering with children. Trust yourself. Everything will happen at the right time. Human intelligence is microscopic in comparison to the Universe. Above all, be careful what you wish for, because you might get it.'

To an extent, she almost made me apprehensive and gave me some performance anxiety: what if my trip doesn't turn out to be as beautiful as hers? What if my journey doesn't bring me the peace, balance and happiness that shone from her every word?

And, while I'm writing this, I realise I've just fallen in the comparison trap. I rationally know that comparing yourself to others is pointless and, at the end of the day, impossible to do. As Piper says, I will find my path, and I really hope to find myself. Mojana, the tarot reader I contacted some time ago for a tarot reading, told me that only when I've become unstuck will I find harmony with myself, and only when I find myself will I also find Love.

Man, I know I am definitely walking in Hippyland, with these kinds of thoughts. Who would have thought I would end up like this? Had I seen this version of myself five years ago, I'd have been the first to say, 'No way, that'll never be me'.

By the way, what am I hoping to get from this trip, apart from some respite from all my negative thinking? I would especially like to come back with clear ideas and more inner space. I want to give myself some answers. Do I want to change career? Do I have to let Lucio go? If my life so far has not gone as I was expecting it to, what does this mean, and what can I do about it? Can some of my friends really call themselves 'friends'?

I want to learn to *let it go*, to leave behind everything that doesn't serve me and which, even worse, hurts me. I want to have a spiritual and emotional spring clean to clear out my negative thoughts, fears, self-doubts. I want to shrug off some of the sorrow I am carrying, without even knowing where it comes from. I want to get to the stage of UNDERSTANDING with my HEART, not intellectually, not

44

with my mind, that I just have to trust myself, my instinct and, in general, the Universe.

Like now, for example: the Universe loves me. It has just put 500 pounds in my hands, out of the blue. As per my personal karmic law, I will have to share this luck by giving some of it back once in Asia through generous tipping, doing some charity work or helping out the far too numerous poor people that you see everywhere.

Among the many things that Mojana told me, one struck me in particular: 'Always put God first. Ask for His help, find Him, surrender to Him'.

My parents would be happy to know that I feel God's presence much more strongly now than when I used to go to Mass just because I was supposed to. This whole spiritual journey these last few years, my famous walk in Hippyland, which they might see as moving away from God, has in fact drawn me much closer to Him.

I have distanced myself from the Church, made up of people and riddled with scandals, but I haven't moved away from God. And during these years, in so many of the things I do, I really see confirmation of this incredible and superior force which guides us all. Whether we then want to call it Energy, God, Universe, Higher Self, Source or whatever, *fate vobis*. So, besides invoking the protection of all my dear departed ones, I've also decided to wear one of those wooden bracelets with all the Saints and Madonnas. I remember that in the past a similar bracelet had been a huge hit among the Indians I met on my travels, who seemed to love anything kitsch and ultra-decorated.

Anyway, yes, I want to get to feel WITH MY HEART, INSIDE, AND NOT WITH MY HEAD, that we are all one, all united, and therefore never alone. We are all made of the same star dust. These are all concepts that I've read and reread. They have also come up in several conversations with people who are further along on their spiritual journey. I can repeat them, explain them in words, but I know that all this happens in my head. I don't feel them yet with the unshakeable faith of those who believe in them from the depths of their soul. I feel like I'm on the right path, I sense that every step I take makes me feel good, but at the same time I am aware that I'm still plodding along.

'You need to regain your balance', again, Mojana's words. Indeed, one of my many problems is that I give too much power to other people.

By the way, just to be disappointed until the very last minute or, rather, just TO ALLOW PEOPLE TO DISAPPOINT ME until the last minute, on Saturday night it looked as if Mr Potato Masher was coming by to say goodbye. This guy, who lives quite close to my place, earned this nickname because I met him via the app Shpock, through which I indeed sold him my potato masher (making the amazing profit of three pounds!)

'*In nomen, omen*', the wise Latins used to say. 'The destiny is in the name', and I have to say, he did go on to prove himself worthy of his vaguely erotic nickname.[2]

Now, for months nobody understood what this man wanted, from life in general and from me in particular. During the week, this model of perfectly understandable human behaviour would send me flirtatious messages to organise our Saturday-night date, when his children would be with his ex. However, when Saturday arrived, his formerly asymptomatic mixed-messagitis would suddenly flare up, and he would switch off his mobile, not answer my calls, come up with some last-minute emergency or fall asleep a few hours before our date. The day after, he might explain what had happened and being the basic moron that I am, one way or another I accepted his excuses. As some kind of deranged cross between Pollyanna and

---

[2]   The nickname *Schiacciapatate*, "Mr Potato Masher", sounds vaguely erotic in Italian because *patata* (and its endearing diminutive *patatina*), meaning "potato" and "crisp" or "French fry" respectively, is a common way of referring to the vagina. Do you get the joke now?

I trust you are now knowledgeable enough to appreciate it and, again, you are welcome for this further insight into Italian sexual vernacular.

Candy Candy, I told myself that yes, it's perfectly possible that his auntie has fallen sick and needs him right when he's supposed to come and see me, and yes, it's possible that he is so tired from his working week that he falls asleep on the sofa. He stood me up several times at the last minute, and I probably wouldn't have accepted it from someone else for that long, but this Mr Potato Masher lives only 400 metres from my place, and in a city like London, where it takes you an average of 45 minutes to go anywhere, this is no minor detail. Let's add to that a magnificent pearly smile and Lindor skin[3],

---

[3] I totally feel the need to write the longest footnote in history here. My fab editor strongly recommended I change my original, 'Let's add that magnificent white smile against that chocolate skin' because 'it has echoes of colonial legacy, with exoticisation/eroticisation of the non-white "other"'. Okay, let's speak about this. Trust me, I definitely think before I ink, and it took me two days of deep thinking, inner struggle, reading and talking about it to decide what to do with this sentence. I even conducted a survey among other Italian translators and interpreters based both in Italy and in the UK, and some native English speakers, both white and non-white, based in the UK. The results revealed strong, unilateral support ('Don't think twice about it!' 'Where exactly is the problem?') from the Italian, Italy-based people, a cautious warning from the UK-based Italian translators and a general 'Avoid it – it makes me feel uncomfortable, even though I cannot really explain why' rejection from the UK-based native white speakers. Interestingly, a few non-white people told me they were okay with it, and they too referred to their skin colour as chocolate. So, some very different positions. Deciding what to do has meant striking a careful balance between owning my voice and being sensitive about what is perceived in my target audience as a delicate topic.

Let's start with a reminder that this whole book is based on my diary entries, and the way I look at things is obviously affected by filters associated with being white, Italian and a Westerner, who always tries to speak from a place of peace and love (as well as a very irreverent, direct and outspoken sense of humour that especially loves to play with stereotypes. But that's another story.)

The survey showed that I clearly couldn't grasp the big problem with this sentence, so I delved into online forums to understand it better. A whole world opened up, and below are my thoughts on the several points raised.

It was argued that comparing skin tone to things like cocoa and chocolate amounts to fetishising, as there's an association with sexual desire. Well, hello? That's totally the case here! Mr Potato Masher was definitely someone I was attracted to. Do I feel the same unconditional attraction to all non-white people? No. Is this therefore a fetishising of dark skin? No. It's just a reiteration that I found Mr Potato Masher hhhhot.

Next point raised: comparing skin tone to food is dehumanising. Let's talk about this. I come from a culture where one of the most common things you tell little children is, *'Ti mangerei! Sei tutto da mangiare!'* 'I could eat you up!' I tell my niece and nephew all the time that I could eat their little feet, or that they'd better run away, otherwise I might eat them up, they're that cute. The whole world knows how much we Italians love eating, so it's only natural that for us the idea of wanting to eat someone reflects how much we like them (and no, we are not cannibals). Lovers often tell each other, *'Ti mangerei di baci'*, 'I could eat you with kisses'. So, what the forums say is dehumanising, in my culture is not only perfectly normal and acceptable, but totally endearing. Also, following this reasoning, shouldn't we remove the terms 'sugar' and 'honey' from English usage as terms of endearment? And another thing: throughout my life I have been called 'Miss Mozzarella', 'Vanilla cornetto' or even 'Peach', so many times. Have I ever been offended by this? They are all so delicious! Honestly, it never even crossed my mind. I am sure there are more serious issues to consider in this life.

Next: describing dark skin as 'chocolate' is 'about aggression and appropriation and has links to colonialism'. I'm really sorry that these are the images brought up for some of you because none of those concepts have any space in my mind. I know I come from a place of love. I know what intentions I have. I am here expressing my lustful desire to see Mr Potato Masher's beautiful, bronzed body once again. My intention is to compare him to one of my favourite things, and that's chocolate. What else so smooth and soft, those deep, dark eyes, that warm voice, and the fact that I have three months ahead of me where I have no idea how it will go in terms of men. The result was that the idea of seeing each other on Saturday night for a quick(ie?) goodbye didn't seem that terrible.

Instead, for the umpteenth time, after exchanging messages from the day before, which had created the right mood, he texted at 8pm on Saturday, 'Something unexpected just popped up, I probably won't be able to make it'.

After that text, the Big Nothing. Not a message to apologise, not one to wish me good luck and a safe trip, not even one to tell me that my potato masher works perfectly and that he had prepared fabulous mashed potatoes for his children. Nothing whatsoever.

But that's good, Roby. 'People stay in your life until you've learnt what they had come to teach you.' Some more words from the wise

---

do I like that is brown? Chestnuts? Nope. Snails? Bleurgh, please. Squid Ink risotto? Tasty, but just thinking of using this in a description makes me laugh. Next: the forums recommend using standard descriptions such as black, brown and so on. If we feel adventurous (and are able to distinguish different shades) we could go for specific hues and tones, like russet, sepia etc. Well, my intention here is to underline that I liked him, and I felt I could only convey that by referring to something I love eating.

Next: talking about 'chocolate skin' is a cliché. Yes, totally. Have I come up with enough original stuff in this book to be allowed one cliché? I like to think so. Am I going to miss out on a literary award because of this foray into Clichéland? No, I was never going to win the International Booker Prize anyway. Do you want something more original? Okay, I've turned it into 'Lindor skin', as that's one of my favourite kinds of chocolate. But I am not going to change it because someone might be offended. I am speaking from a place of love and peace (and lust for Mr Potato Masher!). I know my intention, and so do you now.

On a final note, I'd like to point out that when people want to comment on my paleness, they say that I am 'pale as death' or 'white as a corpse'. Now you tell me what is best!

49

Mojana. And Mr Potato Masher teaches me that I am responsible for what I accept and allow into my life. And as long as I allow these men to stay in my life, men who don't call me back, who cancel our dates without organising new ones, who disappear into thin air, I deserve the further disappointments and wounds that come with them. It's my fault if I allow these polluting elements to stay in my life and hurt me.

Take on your responsibilities, Roby. Because the moment you do that for real, you will understand that if you have accepted all this, you also have all the power to put an end to it and change your path. Make sure you understand this, and let's see what kind of people you will allow into your life over the next few months.

And now, Roby, get your (toned) ass onto that Qatar Airlines plane and chain watch at least four movies!

Last London meal: falafel and mixed salad
Last text I sent before boarding the plane: to my two brothers in the WhatsApp group chat 'Serendipity forever', which I created especially for this trip
People I've counted in the last hour with a red trolley bag: 11
Size of my trekking boots: 7 (or 40, if you prefer the *proper* size)
Pants I've brought with me: 8
Pairs of socks I've brought with me: 5
Imodium packages I've brought with me: 2
My seat on the plane: 46C
Refund for not having left on my actual booked flight: £528, 600
State of my hair upon leaving: acceptable

STILL DAY 1
'We could all die in this very moment'
-On the plane, evening between Monday
12th and Tuesday 13th February 2018-

I love long flights so much! For some years now, my approach to flights has been much the same as my approach to massages. Just like I wouldn't even consider a 60-minute massage, because it would end just as I was starting to relax and properly enjoy it, I get no particular joy from flights under five hours. You barely manage to watch two movies on a four-hour flight. I rarely go to the cinema, and so once I get comfortable in my seat, and before the plane takes off, I immediately check the movie menu and always find at least six or seven movies I'd like to watch.

I've just had a conversation with a cute Canadian guy wearing a bandana that really confirms this trip is all about *letting it go*.

He'd already caught my eye, so when I saw him going towards the toilet I thought it was the right time to stretch my legs a bit, thus preventing an unwelcome embolism. So I too walk towards the toilet where, waiting for my turn, I start running and jumping a bit on the spot, standing on my tiptoes, doing some stretching. Moving a little, basically. This handsome guy, thin and lean like someone who practises yoga seriously, smiles at me and so we start talking.

'Are you going on holiday or are you going back home?' I ask.

'I'm going back home. My girlfriend and I (*Ah, ecco.* Of course.) came to London to say our last goodbye to a dear friend, only 32 years old, who was dying of cancer.

....

Okay. I sense a cheerful conversation ahead.

'Oh, I'm so sorry...'

'I'm really glad I came, you know?' he continues. 'One morning there were six of us there with her, and we did laughter yoga all together. She really did love life so much and wanted to laugh right up to the end', he explains. I manage to keep my composure, but I start feeling a sharp pain in my chest and a knot in my stomach. 'She was ready to die, and yet till the very end she was clinging to life as much as she could. We were telling her, 'Come on, let it go. Go in peace'. She managed in the end. She died with all of us holding her hands.'

Shiny-eyed, a tear is ready to roll down my cheek. He is talking so smilingly about it, while I feel so immensely sad. The typical conversation you can expect to have when queueing for the toilet on a plane. Okay, ever since I turned 30, I've had neither the energy for nor the interest in superficial conversation and chit-chat, but I'd say things have gone a bit too intense too quickly.

'It's been an interesting experience, though, you know? It's made me think a lot about death', he continues, while my inner voice is blurting out, 'No shit, Sherlock!'

'This whole thing has really opened my eyes, you know? Seeing the exact moment in which we die... I'd now like to study death a bit, as it would be so special to free ourselves from the fear of dying.'

Ehm, okay... Although I'm sure there are more cheerful subjects to study, no? Just me?

'Because, if you think about it, death is always with us. We could all die in this precise moment', Mr Death-Is-A-Marvellous-Thing adds.

'Yes, we could, but if it happens now, that means the plane is crashing, and so I'd be dying, too. If it really has to happen, it had better wait until I'm on my way back from this trip at least, not now on my way out', I warn him, elegantly touching my wooden bracelet with all the Saints and Madonnas. Touch and knock on wood!

I come back to my seat, squeeze in one more movie and then finally take a look at my brand-new Lonely Planet guide to Sri Lanka.

And, guess what? I've discovered something that is as marvellous as it is shocking, at least for someone like me who should have already known this: Sri Lanka has the highest concentration of elephants in the world! I mean, at home I have something like 70 elephant pictures and statues of various shapes and sizes, scattered everywhere, and I've basically chosen by chance to go travelling in a country where I'll be able to see plenty of them!

'By chance', my (toned) ass. This is an incredible wink from the Universe. Wow. And I haven't even landed yet! So here's the first thing I absolutely have to do: a safari.

For the rest, I have no idea at all of which cities to see or what itinerary to follow. But no panic: I will surely do something, and the right time will come to decide what. I will meet other travellers who will give me their advice, fortuitous events will take me to one place rather than another, I'll make certain decisions and probably change others at the last minute. The right, divine timing for everything will come. Which is not now, because I feel like reading some more of your pages, my dear Diary. The vibe of the pages I've written today is already a world away from the negativity and sadness emanating from those I read in the afternoon, before boarding the plane. And I somehow think that the general tone of my entries was getting lighter and brighter as my departure approached. Or am I wrong?

Meal served aboard: pasta with a fantasy (read: unidentified and mysterious) sauce, chicken breast with mixed salad and potatoes, bread and butter, mini chocolate profiterole

Passengers sitting next to me: a lady, whom I believe to be Japanese and who is beating any records for longest uninterrupted nap on a plane, and a businessman, who earlier on was immersed in his laptop and is now sleeping bent over himself with his mouth closed, thank God

Movies I've watched so far: 3

Glasses of wine I've drunk so far: 2

Times the Canadian guy mentioned death: 7

Times the flight attendants mentioned it: 0, luckily
Temperature in London when I left: 11 °C
Little jumps I've done on the spot in order to reactivate my blood circulation and avoid an embolism: 16

THE MONTHS BEFORE
-Another overview of my emotional wreckage-

Look, dear Diary, as always things in London are happening so fast. I don't even have the time to start telling you about them before they are already over.

Two weeks ago I met this guy, Nick, on Tinder, and I immediately started investing time, curiosity and energy in him because he had that slight madness that I recognise in myself and that I love in others. As per my usual script, within three dates I'm in at the deep end. As per the same usual script, it's clear from the beginning that he is a problematic guy, having been both an alcoholic and a drug addict in the past.

Ah, ecco. Of course.

Okay, for some reason, I'm currently attracting this type of person. Perfect. He tells me anyway that he's been able to transform his past into a strength, becoming a psychologist specialised in managing addictions. He adds that he is currently taking a break because maybe he is a bit tired of constantly being in an environment that is not exactly overflowing with joy (*e ti credo!* I can well believe it!).

Tonight, on our way home from dining out, his pure, sincere soul pushed him to tell me, 'Roby, I have something to confess'. I am already bracing myself psychologically because, lately, when I like someone, things always follow the same pattern (meaning they go down the shit hole). However, I must admit that this time they went out with a serious bang; we're talking proper fireworks.

55

'Ehm... I haven't really been honest with you (a classic). I mean, I haven't exactly taken a break from my job (oh, you haven't?)... Let's just say they fired me because I had an alcohol relapse (yes, let's say that), and one day I went to work drunk (oh, what nasty people, firing you for that!). The point is... Ehm... I mean, I found myself jobless, so to make some money a friend of mine convinced me to produce MDMA at home (of course, all unemployed people try their hand as a poor man's Walter White). Unfortunately, ehm... Yes, the police caught us on the second day (bloody policemen) and basically, ehm... What I want to tell you is that in July I'll have to go to prison for 18 months.'

....

Ah, ecco. Oh, I see.

'But maybe we could write each other loads of letters, and you could come and see me on the weekends?' Nick tried to suggest.

I literally burst out laughing. I'm talking serious belly laughs, here. I swear.

'No, Roby, sorry, I'm not joking', he tells me, stopping in the street and even taking my hand. I squeeze his hand, with a smile that means 'Okay-Life-Universe-God-Whoever-You-are-I've-understood-that-it's-not-my-moment-and-I-surrender-for-fuck's-sake'. 'No, don't worry, I believe you, and I'm laughing because my life resembles a movie. What you just told me is absolutely aligned with everything else that has been happening to me. I'm laughing about how amazing the Universe is, and I'd say that you and I can say goodbye to each other right here, right now.'

And so Nick, too, is off the list. I'm happy with how I've managed the whole thing, as I don't at all fancy being a little Florentine scribe. And yet, while I'm writing this, I wonder what it is in me that only attracts people who have reached rock bottom? And how many more times can I simply put it down to bad luck before finally turning the lens inwards towards myself? Where am I going wrong?

In a few days I'm flying home for Christmas, so I'd say that my tragicomic dating life for 2017 is now officially closed. It's been a year in which I have believed, I have invested, I have hoped, and in the end, I've been royally shafted. From various angles. A bit like I was in 2016, 2015, 2014, 2013... And I'll stop here, because I can feel my grey roots growing longer just thinking about it.

Treviso, Sunday 24th December 2017

As per tradition, I'm at home for Christmas. I usually spend my Christmas holidays resting and reading by the heaters, but this year my brother Mauro broke the amazing, huge news that he is getting married! A decision taken quite last minute, with many changes of mind as per the type of ceremony to go for, and above all when to have it.

'Mauro, I'm leaving on 12th February. You can't tell me now that I'm going to miss your wedding, come on!', and so they have decided that they will get married on 3rd February. I mean, some people start organising their weddings over a year in advance. My brother, who is always swimming against the stream like a (not smoked) salmon, has decided to organise everything in less than three months. 'But Mauro, maybe some people won't be able to come because they have already booked their holiday in the mountains', I pointed out.

'In that case, it's their problem and it's better for us, as we save on the restaurant bill', he answered, very logical and to the point. Indeed, because if Mauro and Elena had begun with the idea of a small ceremony for a few close friends, this week the guestlist has reached 110 people. So much for a ceremony with 'just our two families and that's it'!

When Mauro told me, basically two weeks ago, I immediately got down to business. I have to prepare the mandatory video with the love birds' story and think about all the games to play at the wedding, as per our northern Italian tradition. In fact, I'd say I got down to business a bit too early, because when I texted his friend Beppuzzo, 'Ciao, Beppuzzo, fancy helping me organise the games for Mauro and Elena's wedding?' he replied, 'Whaaaaaattt? Mauro and Elena are getting married? And your human shit of a brother didn't say a word?'

Oooooops. Without meaning to, I've given him the big news before my brother Mauro did, for Small Detail's sake. There's my wedding-planner career nipped in the bud.

Anyway, I've already met with Beppuzzo, Bia, Ceccato and Mauro's other lifelong friends, jotting down ideas and delegating tasks, over a bottle of Prosecco and a mountain of *soppressa*.[4]

Another piece of news from this Christmas holiday is that last Thursday evening Antonio from the shamanic journey invited me out for dinner. At first, I didn't want to go, wondering what the point was, given that he is messing around with another girl, the famous cheater. In the end, though, I went out with him. I don't even know whether it was my usual mantra, 'you never know how things might develop', that nudged me or not.

Anyway, we saw each other again, and it was with some relief that I found him less handsome than I remembered. Better this way. The dinner was nice, and halfway through it I floored him by asking him very straightforwardly, 'Why are we here?'

'Because I like you as a person a lot, Roby (imagine if you didn't like me how you would have behaved!). You are a bit weird. I don't know anybody else like you. I mean, I'd like it if we could stay in contact.'

Oh, che carino. How sweet.

But in the meantime he's shagging the other one.

The whole thing kind of rolled right off my back. If I had to be disappointed, I had already been disappointed back in November, when he told me that he was not coming to London. The fact he hasn't kept his promise and prefers to involve himself in a love (Love?) triangle speaks volumes about how little he resonates with who I am.

---

[4] *Soppressa* is a typical product of the Veneto region in northern Italy. If you've never tried it, you are missing out. (Disclaimer for vegans and vegetarians: you don't want to read any further.) It's an aged salami made from pork, lard, salt, pepper, spices and garlic. It's generally very soft and soooo good.

So yes, we can keep in touch. I no longer have a crush on you.

It's only when we howled together at the magnificent full moon casting its bright light over our goodbye, in the Piazzale del Grano car park in Treviso, that my little inner voice whispered, 'Damn you! What a shame. Who else can I howl at the moon with like this?'

Who knows? During my trip I might meet some hhhhhhot backpacker, able to enjoy simple things, aware of how little it takes to be happy in this world and of how lucky we are. Someone who would play football with the local guys, blow balloons to bring a little joy to the street children and maybe serenade me by a bonfire on the beach.

Cooooome on, Roby! What happened to 'no expectations'!

Stop it, stop it, stop it.

If I'm already setting out with these dreams, I am setting myself up to being disappointed, and you don't need to be the Buddha to see that.

The idea of going without sex for three months triggers a few different emotions. Anxiety, resignation, anger over this humongous injustice I have been a victim of for too long.

Well, let's see what happens. Unfortunately, while Asia fascinates me and keeps calling me back, I find her men definitely outside my parameters. Of course I am going to make massive generalisations here, but I have noticed quite a few recurring patterns in the Asian men I encountered, whether they were Vietnamese, Indian, Cambodian etc. Also, before expressing my Italian, and therefore very likely politically incorrect views on Asian men, I should specify that while travelling in Asia I tend to spend most of my time in rural areas. So, to begin with, quite a curious phenomenon that I noticed most in India is that there seem to be only two or three haircuts that the whole male population adopts universally. Of course, the street barbers don't have the option of coming to London for creative cut-and-colour courses at the Toni & Guy Academy where I work as an interpreter, but they could still show a little imaginative flair. More drastic for me, being a muscle lover, is that you would probably need a telescope to spot any sculpted biceps. I also wouldn't underestimate the fact that the locals don't always have a full set of teeth, for Gap-Toothed Grin's sake. Let's add to this list the observation that 95% of them are half my size, both in height and build. So definitely, in physical terms, Asian men don't fit my ideal of a tall, protective, strong man. What do we want to do about it? Call me superficial, but I don't look at them much.

On the contrary, they seem to look at me a lot. Sometimes even too much. 'How can you blame them?' my cheeky side says. Mauro, instead, thinks that in India both men and women look at me so much because cows are sacred for them. What a jerk. My other brother, Alessio, is of the opinion that they are surprised at seeing a Westerner dressed so badly.

My two brothers are always very kind, albeit in completely different ways.

Anyway, the point is that there are multiple possible explanations for this. I think it's more to do with my height, my short hair and my very fair complexion. In any case, I've been repeating it for years now: should a woman feel insecure about her femininity, she should simply take a flight to India and all her problems will magically disappear. Once there, she will immediately feel like a demi-goddess, as beautiful as she is unattainable.

This is one of the world's paradoxes, given that Indian women are among the most graceful and feminine I've even seen, so pretty in their brightly coloured saris and always adorned with so many jewels, often despite their poverty.

Besides not being physically attracted to them in the slightest, the few Asian men I did interact with in Cambodia, Thailand, Vietnam, Malaysia, India and Laos had this jaw-dropping mentality, light years away from how I, as a Westerner, conceive relationships. They either struck me as effeminate, or they were the sweetest, purest souls, in neither case measuring up well to my ideal of an experienced, wily, worldly-wise man who takes you passionately, there and then, up against a wall.

So, in short, things are not looking bright. In Thailand, you can expect some lively beach parties that might be conducive to romantic encounters. On the other hand, in Nepal, the chances of such events taking place at all seem somewhat slim.

JesusMaryandJoseph, things are nooooooooot looking bright at all.

London, Wednesday 3rd January 2018

Happy New Year! Five weeks to go before my departure, and today I am repeating to myself, 'Universe, I trust You'.

Around two weeks ago I wrote to Maggie Doyne to say that from 12th April I'll be in Nepal and that I would love to volunteer in some capacity at her orphanage/school for a few weeks. My dream started from here, with the idea of going to meet her, and today that dream was torn to shreds. A member of her team got back to me, saying that they do not accept volunteers who are staying less than a year, in order to protect the orphaned children from the trauma of further separation and abandonment. Absolutely understandable and fair.

May this serve me somehow as a lesson in humility. I bought the flight to Nepal assuming that they would accept me. It didn't remotely cross my mind that someone would turn down, for whatever reason, the offer of free help, made with the best of intentions. On the contrary, I must understand that this is not always the case.

Just because one person wants to give, it doesn't mean that the other person wants to or can receive.

That's how it went in this specific case, as it does in so many other life situations. In relationships, for example, which have often left me disappointed, not only do some guys not reciprocate what I have to give, but they might even receive it reluctantly. Just because one person wants to give, it doesn't mean that the other person wants to or can receive.

This is the thing.

Oh, well. The dream is dead; long live the dream. There's plenty of dreams in my mind. But you know what? I'm not going to dream anything else. Universe, I fully trust You. I promised myself that for this trip I didn't want to plan anything, right? So, rightly and consistently, You take away the only thing I had set my sights on.

No expectations and no attachments to how I'd like things to turn out.

London, Tuesday 6th February 2018

Last Saturday my beloved little brother Mauro got married. I call him 'little brother' even though he's taller than me and 36 years old. Over the last few weeks I have been involved in an intense exchange of messages with his life-long friends, whom I've literally seen grow from little kids in kindergarten into family men. Dealing with them way more than usual over these last two months has brought up a new, strange sensation. I actually don't want to talk about this with anyone, and I don't even want to ponder it that much, because I'm almost afraid of what it could shine a light on.

I left Padernello, my country village with its two thousand souls, because I felt that view on life was too narrow for me. I couldn't stand the closed-mindedness I saw around me, or the racism, which wasn't even particularly hidden. I dreamt of exotic men, people with a completely different story from mine, jobs I had maybe never heard of before. I dreamt of the big city, with its thousand things to do every day, with all its incredible opportunities for fun and learning.

And so, I left when I was 28 years old, and I've never, ever regretted it. It has never come close to crossing my mind. I've never wondered what life I'd be leading had I stayed at home in Italy. I don't think in this way. That parallel world has not become reality because at that time I felt, for various reasons, a strong urge to leave, so the choice I made was the only available and possible one at that time. I like to think that everything happens in the best possible way. Everything is perfect in itself. Thinking about how things could have been has always seemed to me like a huge waste of mental energy and time.

Yes, I wanted a life in a metropolis, with all its implications, but I don't despise my origins at all. On the contrary, I always go back to Padernello with pleasure. But I've never understood how you can think that the world stops there, when by now everything and everywhere is so easily available.

In a way, I've always felt half-way. I love nature, yes, and people, but also metropolises and their anonymity.

Yet, at my brother's wedding, and the three bottles of Prosecco I drank probably had something to do with it, I found myself feeling nostalgic. Wow. Nostalgic for how we used to be as a family, all together, yes. Emotional and moved because my brother has found a cool and capable woman, a perfect partner who I feel I can trust. In her turn, she had the incredible luck of finding a peach of a man (an ugly one, okay, but still juicy and very tasty). Nostalgic because time is passing me by. Happy for my parents, who are getting to see at least one of their children marry.

Also nostalgic for all the friends I've lost over the years, or for my lack of really strong relationships here at home, apart from the one with Lucio. Whereas Mauro was celebrating the most beautiful day of his life surrounded by people who were at kindergarten with him. These are friends with whom he has shared so many experiences, some of which slightly outside the bounds of legality, and so many fuelled by alcohol levels that could have required a hospitalisation.

Here they are, in front of me, Ceccato, Bia, Beppuzzo, the friends of a life-time. As teenagers, these guys didn't feel like studying at all and were more interested in picking up girls. Back then (and still to this day, for that matter) they showed no respect to their metabolisms, subjecting them to 'Viking dinners' where they would drink and eat as if there was no tomorrow, with no need for a reason why. Also, they would often invest their time in small vandalic acts which, according to them, were socially acceptable. And here they are now, almost all of them family men, having more or less got their heads together, but they have not lost that carefree and exuberant side that I rarely find in the English guys I know. And that I like so much.

And while I was there dancing and singing at the top of my lungs,

I was visited by a sudden thought: what if I was wrong? What if I made a mistake, going away? What if what I've been always looking for is here, in Padernello, '*il paese più bello*', the most charming of villages, as my father has always referred to it?

I preferred to quieten the whisper of those thoughts by going heavy on the red wine, given that my beloved Prosecco was finished. I ended up spilling some red wine on the floor. I was about to kneel down with some paper napkins to clean the spillage when Bia screamed across the dance floor at me, 'Roby, leave it. I'll clean up!'

The madman came running at me and threw himself into a John Travolta knee slide, in perfect *Saturday Night Fever* style, mopping up the spilt red wine with his elegant trousers, which must have cost him a few hundred euros.

Exactly my point.

A beautiful wedding party indeed, which had me returning to London with a strange nostalgia that I had never felt before…

London, Friday 9th February 2018

Three days to go to my departure!

I'm a mixture of excitement and apprehension. Rightly so. It's logical that I should feel slightly anxious if I stop and think about all the things that could happen to me during my trip. If I then add everything that could happen to my house here in London and to my family in Italy while I'm on the other side of the world, it's understandable that yesterday I decided to have my tarots read by Mojana, a fortune teller I went to last year. In fact, according to her, I was supposed to meet the Brazilian man of my dreams before September 2017, so as far as I'm concerned, she doesn't come with this fabulous and encouraging CV. However, with my departure looming, any form of reassurance will do. I explained to her that I had just come back from Italy and that I am about to leave again.

'I'd like to know what to expect from the journey I am about to embark on', I asked her (so much 'no expectations'. Sneaky, sneaky mind!).

Mojana immediately got to work, surrounded by her own spirits, and started telling me that my trip will be a success, that I will understand my true vocation...

'I see you happy, serene, you will find a lot of answers to the questions that are tormenting you now. I also see you doing a therapeutic job, which will bring you much satisfaction. But, above all, I see so much love. You are surrounded by love.'

E la Madonna! Good God! Are you telling me that I have underestimated the relationship possibilities offered by Nepal? And just when I was about to get all excited, she continues, 'Yes, your family will give you so much love, and so will the people around you. Moving back to Italy is a choice that will do you so much good.'

....

WHAAAAAAAT? Italy?

'But I was talking about my trip to Asia. Italy has nothing to do with it!', I explained to Mojana.

Oops! A small misunderstanding, but never mind. Looking at all the tarots again, and adding some new ones, my trip is confirmed to be a success, nothing bad will happen to me or to my family.

'Trust the Universe, and you'll see that you will have everything provided for you. You will be given whatever you need', continued Mojana in her beautiful warm, soft voice.

That would be exactly my objective, and it's no coincidence that she has reiterated it to me.

Something that has really resonated with me is that I have to stop giving my power away to those around me. I give away too much power by allowing people to influence me, paralyse me with their judgements and hurt me with their words. Actually, putting it like this gives the wrong impression. I am not a defenceless victim of people who are stronger than me. I am the one giving them this power. And that is not all: I often compare and draw conclusions about others myself. In other words, I judge, and, by judging, I only hurt myself.

So: no attachments and possibly no judgements during this trip, even if the latter seems even harder than the former.

Unfortunately, I won't meet My Love, according to Mojana, but I will nonetheless have a fling with a very rich, spiritual man, who will teach me a lot. Okay, so no need to cry and despair too much, it looks like I'll have some sex. That's something, at least. Whoop-whoop!

Anyway, I don't want to linger on the fact that Mojana, the tarots, the spirits and all their neighbours ended up somehow feeding into that strange nostalgia which has lingered since my brother's wedding. I mean, as if I didn't already have my brain in overdrive! As if I didn't have already a lot of things to think about! I surely don't need this new idea creeping up on me, taking me totally by surprise.

Moving back to Italy.

Yes, I was just missing one more huuuuge thought to distress myself with.

Sure, I would receive more daily love than I get here, working alone in my sweet little house in Honor Oak Park, but I am aware that workwise it would mean my death. I know that after a while, I would feel so under stimulated. I know I would always feel as if there was too little to do.

Roby, set off on your journey, and don't think about this. Stay in the present. You are already thinking about what comes later, the future.

Answers will come freely on their own, even without the questions.

Trust yourself.

You have to stay in the now, and in your specific case it's a beautiful now. A colourful question mark with flowers, elephants, rice and curry, trekking boots, beaches, mountains around it...

What else do I visualise? Dark eyes staring at me curiously, warm, bright smiles, sun cream, baggy trousers, snorkelling mask...

Oh, man. Rats, too. And mosquitoes, those bloody bastards. And probably diarrhoea.

Okay, then. Sun cream with a 50 SPF, cortisone cream for insect bites, insect repellent with 90% DDT (so if they don't die from coming near me, I will from poisoning) and kilos of Imodium in my backpack.

Asia, here I come.

I can't wait to leave. I'm so looking forward to some respite for my brain and my heart, which seems stuck on a loop, going over the same things. What a load of shit, I tell myself. Besides, Valentine's Day is around the corner, which induces a mini depressive breakdown in me every year. I always have discussions about it with my friends, who have been in relationships for decades, and who repeatedly assure me that it's just a day like any other. Sure, my birthday, too, is a day like any other, but I still want to celebrate it. What's more, Valentine's Day doesn't have to stand for big expensive gifts. I would be happy with a red Lindor chocolate and a big hug. A small gesture to make me feel loved by my partner, on that day like all the others. The hearts, the teddy bears, the special offers on dinners for two, the boxes of chocolates, not to mention the thousands of smiling, hugging couples you see all around the city, seem to be screaming at me, 'You are still single, for another year running!'

This year, however, with my departure to Colombo on Monday 12th February, I'm gonna catch you out big time, Valentine's Day! I will not gorge myself on chocolate watching *Bridget Jones's Diary* for the 73rd time. Who knows where I will be, and with whom. Universe, we are almost there! And remember, I trust You!

DAY 2

'Mosquitoes, bring it on, you bastards!'
-Mount Lavinia, Tuesday 13th February 2018-

… May this month full of question marks begin!

I'm writing from the Lavinia Beach Hostel, the only hotel I've booked for my whole trip. I thought that for the first two days I would have preferred to stay by the sea and relax a bit, before venturing out to explore the country. So, for this reason, I came to a beach near Colombo called Mount Lavinia, which doesn't take its name from some mountains rising above the sea, but from the famous Mount Lavinia Hotel: a modern tourist complex for 250 guests, situated at the top of the rocky promontory where this beach ends, and the official residency of a British governor more than two centuries ago. In turn, the hotel name was inspired by a local dancer–Lavinia, surprisingly–who broke the governor's heart.

Of course, I have left the resort to the others and instead chosen the Lavinia Beach Hostel, which in fact is not a hostel at all, but rather a cute little hotel. It comes with a beautiful garden, full of colourful flowers and birds. When I arrived here, around 10am, my room was not yet ready, so they offered me another room in case I wanted to sleep, while waiting for my actual room to be ready. And man, did I want to sleep! With all my heart, truly, given that on the plane I watched one movie after another. The room they have given me as a replacement has a single bed, which I haven't slept in for years, all wrapped in a mosquito net. Which reminds me of my task for this first day in Sri Lanka: fighting mosquitoes. First, though, I gave in to Morpheus's embrace. I basically fell asleep wondering why in this part of the world people are so in love with bright colours, like phosphorescent green and shocking pink, lemon yellow, smurfy light blue. *Mah*. God knows.

The flight went well. Once I had landed in Colombo and left the airport, I took a big deep breath. Asia, here I am in your chaos of colours and sounds.

My smile grew.

How are you, Asia? What do you have in store for me this time?

I look around: a great many (short) men and a few women are on the streets. It is already too hot despite being only 9am.

From the very beginning, the country of Serendipity looks very different from that collective folly that is India. No cows or monkeys in the street, fewer gaudy clothes, nobody honking loudly like there's no tomorrow just because they are alive today, and not dozens and dozens of eyes on me (though local men do stare, straight into my eyes. Making eye contact like that would be reported to the police in London).

I had organised with the hotel to have a driver waiting for me, and it's definitely been a good move. After that long flight, and having been awake for 28 hours, I wouldn't have had the energy to haggle the price with a local taxi driver. Yes, because haggling is my favourite Asian pastime.

Once I woke up, I asked the hotel owner to use her washing line, and I took out of my backpack all the clothes I had brought with me in order to spray them with a magical anti mosquito liquid I prepared myself following some online instructions. Every time I've travelled in Asia, my trip has been ruined to some extent by bites from various (best identification I can manage) insects, and the consequent allergic reactions I've had. In Thailand I was saved by a crazy, hyper-cool Canadian girl who gave me her cortisone cream. In Indonesia, instead, I had to go to three doctors, each of whom gave me different advice, whilst all agreeing on making me pay a hell of a lot for any medicine they gave me. This time, not only did I equip myself with a serious cortisone cream to contain the damage.

Not only did I buy an insect repellent with 90% DDT, which should protect me against mosquitoes at the price of turning me radioactive, if used for a long time. This time I even bought a liquid to spray every five-six weeks on my clothes, and I have made myself a lotion with almond oil, some drops of lavender and eucalyptus essential oil to apply on my skin after showering. Mosquitoes, bring it on, you bastards!

In the evening I finally went to the beach, which is not that great, to be fair, and no sooner had I set a foot on the sand than a guy came up to me. Not even with all my best efforts and verbal techniques could I manage to get rid of him. Anyway, I know that this is included in the Asia package. There are always so many people who want to talk with you, either because they are really genuinely interested (a few), or because they want something from you (money, most of the time, either directly or through purchases from their shop or their uncle's or cousin's). Time doesn't have the same value that it has for us Londoners. To local people, time seems to be something to kill, and they are quite happy to come up to a stranger who is peacefully strolling on the beach and ask her all about her family and her life.

In the end, partly to give some meaning to our forced interaction, I asked him to recommend a place where I could eat something local, and so I ended up sitting in this dive on the beach, eating a fish curry, with this guy sitting in front of me trying in every possible way to find out how long I would be staying in Mount Lavinia.

Back at my hotel, I have moved into my real room, which had been nicely prepared, and I've come across the first novelty of this new Sri Lankan world for me. The bed, another single one, is inside a big rigid mosquito net, which looks like a proper camping tent you could almost stand up in. You see how these Sri Lankans are ahead of the game?

I then went out in the garden to enjoy the balmy evening, and I started talking with a nice couple. She was from Mexico, and he was Irish, and they met in Argentina (a classic). They are at the end of their month in Sri Lanka and, given that tomorrow is Valentine's

Day, they are treating themselves to a night in a four-star hotel, just before they fly back to Mexico.

I almost forgot that tomorrow is Valentine's Day. My trip is already starting to have the desired effect.

They gave me some tips on which places I should definitely see. Since Colombo is basically halfway up the island, on the west coast, I could choose to travel north, which is more natural and wild, with centuries-old temples and historical cities, then moving clockwise around the country. Or, second option, I could start my journey going south, which is more touristy, with plenty of lovely beaches, to then move inland. The weather is currently nice on the west coast, where I am, while monsoons will soon be arriving in the eastern part of the island. This detail, together with the fact that I left London quite tired and would therefore prefer to relax a bit on the beach, has made me lean toward option number two.

There you go. A chat with two people in the garden and I already have a draft of my itinerary.

Movies I watched in total on the plane: 4
Temperature upon arrival: 32 °C
Time it took my hair to explode on my head because of the humidity and become like Monica's in *Friends* when she went to the Caribbean: 7 hours
Mosquito net models seen so far: 2
First Sri Lankan meal: rice and fish curry
Name of the guy I wasn't able to shake off: Tanishka
Time Tanishka spent with me: 1 hour and 23 minutes
Attempts I made to close the conversation with him: 7
Attempts which failed: 7

DAY 3
'What boy do you think I am? I don't touch'
-Mount Lavinia, Wednesday 14th February 2018-

Wow. I wasn't expecting this, I swear. Can it be true, as the Italian hip-hop group Otierre put it back in the '90s, 'When you least expect it, (things happen) like a bomb'?

Well, the only bomb we can actually talk about right now is the one that has just blown up my hair. Nothing to be done. I already knew my hair undergoes a transformation in Asia, but I wasn't expecting it this soon. What with the humidity and the sudden heat that dries it a lot, I am also obliged to physically take on my backpacker persona by using hair accessories that in my London life have no place whatsoever, like bandanas or headbands. Let's cover this head, come on, not so much out of solidarity to Muslim women, but rather to avoid subjecting the people I meet to this visual abuse.

And yet, shitty hair or not, just when I was absolutely not thinking about it, I pulled. On my second day! I should be in *The Guinness Book of Records*. Actually, I should just start my own version: *The Prosecco Book of Records*.

I woke up with the goal in mind of exorcising my paleness by beaching myself on the scorching sand like a swooned cetacean. I arrived in Sri Lanka really exhausted, physically but above all psychologically. I've read somewhere that extreme tiredness and fatigue are not really due to doing, but rather to constant thinking, analysing, living in doubt or fear, stewing in negative thoughts. And I've been top of my class, lately, in all of the above.

So I went to the beach. Seeing it in daylight confirmed my

opinion from yesterday that it's not a picture-postcard beach. The small wooden boats dotted here and there are picturesque, and so are the groups of local guys playing football on the water's edge, but I was expecting something better from Sri Lanka.

There you go! Those damned expectations again.

There was this local guy, wearing black shorts and a white polo shirt, who was cute, but quite thin and not that tall. He was barefoot and raking the sand to clean up the garbage that unfortunately ruins the seaside here in Mount Lavinia.

After his initial 'Hello, madam', to which I respond with a smiley 'Good morning', he literally assaults me asking if I want 'A coffee a cappuccino a fruit juice a smoothie a sandwich a pineapple cut in pieces', and I explain him that no, for the time being I'm not hungry but would probably think about it at lunchtime.

'Yes, madam, please you come to our restaurant, the food is very good, and we take care of our clients. As you can see, I'm cleaning the beach in front of us.'

And you are right to clean it, because the beach is sadly quite dirty.

I quickly said goodbye because in the distance I could see a magical scene unfolding, one that I have seen many times on TV, but never in real life. I'm talking about fishermen pulling the fishing nets all together, engaged in an exhausting tug of war with the sea. There were around 15 men (for maybe a total of... 750kg maximum?), together with some tourists who had joined them, with several more people gathered around to photograph this picturesque scene. I obviously ran towards them and cheerfully joined the collective effort, and when the fishing nets had been pulled onto the beach and were jumping full with fish, I studied the dark skinned faces of the fishermen, with some of them curious, others bored, others expectant.

We were there, waiting for the dance inside the net to calm down a bit, and the whole scene seemed almost surreal to me. Instead of being sat at my laptop with a cup of Nescafé, as I generally am around 9.30am, I was there, surrounded by Sri Lankan fishermen, waiting to find out if their fishing had been a success. Dire Straits lyrics were blasting in my mind: *There's so many different worlds, so many different suns...* Man, is that true.

When the fish finally surrendered to destiny and the nets were opened, I felt so sorry. I felt sorry for the fishermen, who lead extremely poor, tough lives, going out to sea at 3am to throw their nets then waiting until the morning to see how it went. This is their only source of income, and today they were faced with a not so abundant haul, which also had to be shared among all of them. More than this, I felt sorry for us humans and for how we are treating the environment. There were plastic bottles, caps, crisp packets, even pens and so much more, in those nets. And I quickly felt anger rising amid the sadness: how can you possibly treat your sea in such an obscene way, when your livelihood depends directly on it?

There is a sewer dumping its trash straight into the sea, trash on trash, a view that breaks your heart. Some tourists and I went in the sea to retrieve the floating plastic bags, which we then gave to the Coast Guard policemen. Back and forth like that at least a dozen times, each time with some wet plastic bags to put in the policemen's black bags. Absolutely disgusting. We were literally surrounded by dozens and dozens of bags, and the more we gathered and dropped into the black bags, the more we'd see floating in the water. This less than pleasant dip, with all that litter, was ameliorated by one of the two policemen, quite handsome and with a big, nice smile. The fourth time I went to him with the trash I had retrieved, he told me, 'Now I get ready, and I come swim with you'.

Can you believe these Sri Lankan men? Wow, I don't remember any other local man in India, Thailand, Laos, Vietnam or Cambodia being so direct.

I'm trying to hold in my laughter. Picked up while litter-picking. Fantastic!

Once I had fulfilled my environmental duty, I went into the

water for a proper dip, along with many others, including the local guy from the restaurant I had talked with before.

'You have a nice job if in your coffee break, that we would spend by the vending machine, you can swim', I tell him.

'Yes, it is. My name is Shanaka. Today is Valentine's Day', he answers. Like that, in this order.

Oh boy! I had forgotten about that! Me, obsessed as I've always been with this celebration. And, although happy that I hadn't remembered, I was also surprised that it's celebrated in this part of the world, too.

'I had no idea you celebrate Valentine's Day here, too', I tell him, and he answers, 'I cannot celebrate it because I don't have a girlfriend'. I don't have enough time to smile about this logical and simple remark, before he asks, 'Would you like to swim together?'

Clearly, this must be the most in-vogue invitation in Sri Lanka.

The. Sweetness. I don't remember the last time I received such a direct, pure and warm invitation, and I feel a wave of tenderness.

'Ehm… Okay, but I get scared if I don't touch', I explain to him. I'm really crap at swimming, and if I don't touch the sea floor with my feet, if I get out of my depth, I am prone to mini panic attacks. I just felt like he probably wouldn't have understood the expression 'out of my depth', so I stuck with a colourful translation from Italian, which seemed to convey the image better.

We move away from all the others, and after two minutes of swimming (well, swimming in his case, and floating while propelling my body forward slightly with each move, in mine), Shanaka stops and tells me, in his insecure English, 'What guy do you think I am? I don't touch'.

#misunderstandings.

#blesshim.

First Big Misunderstanding, which makes me laugh with gusto. And who knows how many more there will be.

We talk a bit, and he tells me about his job, and immediately, 'I have four days off and I think to go to the south. Where you go?

We can take the bus together (how sweet), so I show you the best, most beautiful beaches, and then we can go together to a beach party on Friday (oh, yes, music to my ears!). Maybe we can take a room together (another one to file under 'Here in Sri Lanka we take things slowly') and share the expense'. Uh, so many things we could do...

'Okay, Shanaka, thanks for all the offers. Maybe I'll think about them. For now I'm saying goodbye, because I want to go and get a bit tanned. See you later at the restaurant where you work. I'm coming there for lunch.'

Indeed, when the sun becomes too strong, I go and look for shelter under the sun umbrellas outside the restaurant and ask him to exchange numbers, even if I haven't really decided what I want to do.

While I'm there half asleep on the sun bed, listening to the Russians next to me and realising with pleasure that I still remember something of that amazing language I studied at university, I receive the photo of a sunset by text.

Ta-da! Our Shanaka is making his first move. Actually, it's the third one. And it's another sweet and romantic one. Later on he brings me my watermelon juice, and he lays it on thick with a fourth move: 'If you like beer, we can have a beer together tonight on the restaurant terrace when I finish my shift'.

Ah, the things we could do! And, for the second time: can you believe these Sri Lankan men? I'm pleasantly surprised. And also slightly worried, because if I have a whole month of attempts to pick me up ahead of me, I don't know if I'll have the energy to handle them all.

I go and take a walk on the beach, which on a positive note is long and in theory you could walk all the way to Colombo along it, and I find a marvellous shell. When I get back, I give it to Shanaka, telling him, 'Happy Valentine's Day! Love is all around us, you see?'

Very hippy and trite, okay, but always nice to hear.

I then entertained myself talking a bit with the Russians, who were pleasantly surprised by the fact I can speak their beautiful and complicated language, albeit with several mistakes after all this time, and then I said goodbye to Shanaka.

'But you come back, yes?' he took the pains to enquire.

'Yes, I'm going to take a shower and pick myself up a bit, and then I'm coming here for dinner.'

Under the (cold) jet of water, I ask myself if I really want to get entangled with a local guy, travelling with him and even possibly sharing a room with him. I don't know, and I tell myself to see how the evening goes, without planning too much. No expectations about how things might develop. Let's go with the flow.

I went back to the little restaurant on the beach, and Shanaka recommended the fish curry, which was indeed way better than the one I had last night. First big difference from the Indian food I've tried: I can handle the spice level. God, thank you.

Curry is a bit like the main dish for many Asian cuisines. A dish of Basmati rice accompanied by one or more little bowls with ingredients that vary depending on the type of curry. In my case, the bowl contained a fish stew prepared in coconut milk with an abundance of spices, including–unsurprisingly–curry powder, which is itself a mixture of spices.

I have a feeling that Sri Lanka is a bit like the USA: the portions are huge, both last night and today. And I also have a feeling that I will be eating rice for the next three months, in every possible form and with all kinds of sauces.

I'm there, eating alone, listening to the sea, rather than looking at it, given that it's dark. I'm there thinking about what I should do tomorrow, and whether this Shanaka is a blessing or more like a potential nuisance, when a guy arrives wearing a T-shirt with 'Choose love' written on it. Sure, there are probably millions of T-shirts with that slogan around the world, but the fact that I've seen one right when I'm undecided on what to do next, is not by chance.

Over the years, I've often been able to seize messages like these, interpreting them as if they were addressed to me: words printed on T-shirts or tattooed on the skin, or incredible coincidences, which make me think that there is someone watching over me and giving me guidance when I need it. Message number one, then.

Shortly after, the Russians arrive and sit at the table near mine, inviting me to join them. They offer me beer and *Samogon*, a diabolical Russian grappa, and we toast to the *krasotà*, the beauty of this world.

It's a toast that touches me inside. Yes, our world is indeed marvellous.

While I'm there, Shanaka arrives to tell me that he has finished working. A mere 14-hour shift, I realise.

'You come on the terrace with me?' he asks, with two beers in his hands.

And, for the third time, can you believe these Sri Lankan men? Small and a bit thin, very sweet, with no qualms whatsoever about casting their nets and seeing what fish they manage to catch. Some of my girlfriends who complain about the lack of initiative shown by the men they meet should come here on holiday. Definitely.

And so, without necessarily blaming it on that deadly Russian grappa, I go to the terrace with him.

We talk, we talk, sipping this beer that I don't even like, but which I know one way or another will be the only available alcohol for the next months.

'You are… 28 years old', he tells me at some point.

Yes, but 11 years ago.

'No, I'm older.'

'Older? No! Then you are 30', he continues with a serious face. 'Thirty, right? I guessed.'

Let's say that you are as good as guessing my age as I am at swimming.

'No, I'm older.'

'Then you are 31', he pontificates. Okay, then, I'm 31.

'Yes, exactly. Well guessed.'

On my side, I don't want to think about how old he can be. While he rolls a cigarette, he explains that he wants to take care of his parents, who have paid for everything for him, and what with what he's saying, along with the trouble he has in finding the right subjects and pronouns, I feel a lot of tenderness towards him. I think that in fact he's quite cute. He has a handsome face, short black hair, dark smiling eyes, a scar on his eyebrow, straight white teeth, plump lips which are just of the right size and a nose that suits the rest quite well.

We start smoking and, in the distance, there are red Chinese lamps soaring up into the night sky. 'For Valentine's Day. It's the people in love that throw', Shanaka explains.

What a show. The sea melts into the night's darkness, but we can still hear its never-ending chant. The lanterns, like flying red roses, carry who knows which promises of love. My journey has just started, and I'm already sitting in a terrace in front of the sea with this guy who has suggested we spend a few days together. I have three months of absolute freedom ahead. And London seems four light years away. I'm relaxed and soft inside, a condition which generally goes well with some cuddling. He is detailing all the things we could do over the next few days.

'Whatever you want, you just ask', he tells me.

'Really? Whatever I want?'

'Yes', he confirms.

'Okay, so let's say that now I want...'

'What?'

'No, you have to guess', I tease him a bit.

'No, you tell me, how I can know?' he asks, clearly not gifted with telepathy.

'Some things, you don't have to ask for', I continue, remaining in this limbo where flirting blossoms wildly.

'Okay, but you ask' he insists flatly.

'Okay. Roll me another cigarette', I say, wriggling out of it. Shanaka rolls it, passes it to me, but in doing so he takes my hand and starts kissing it.

Ohi ohi. Long live the men who take the initiative.

And a longer life to those who are good kissers.

Done.

We kiss like that, sweetly, with the lazy waves in the background and these small red dots above the sea, which remind me that in the end it's still Valentine's Day, and that it's going better today than it ever has in the past six years.

When his colleague comes upstairs to tell us that the restaurant is closing, Shanaka tells me, 'We have to go. I sleep here, but room is small. Now I take you to your hotel because it's too dark and you don't know the way'.

True, both of his observations. And how sweet, to offer to walk me home. Once we get to the hotel, where luckily enough there was nobody around, Shanaka unveils his plan, 'Now I come in room with you, yes?'

For the fourth time: can you believe these Sri Lankan men? Before answering, I think about it for ten seconds, during which I try to come up with any good reasons for saying no. None comes to my mind.

'Yes' is all I say, accompanied by a cheeky smile.

Spending the night with someone in a single bed surrounded by a rigid mosquito net resembling an igloo? Check. Done.

Shanaka left early as he didn't want to be reprimanded by the hotel staff in the morning. Hugging in front of the mirror before he left, we looked quite comical. I seem twice his size. He's very sweet. Definitely an unexpected surprise from destiny.

Yes, I definitely want to spend some more time with him, even if I have to use all my interpreting skills to understand exactly what he means sometimes, so broken and shaky is his English.

Anyway, tomorrow I'm going to Colombo, so we'll probably see each other again during the weekend, after I've explored the capital.

While I was there on the terrace drinking beer with Shanaka, I took advantage of his trip to the toilet to check my mobile. To my surprise, I found a message by Antonio: 'Did you arrive? *Tutto bene?* All good? How is this Sri Lanka?'

I replied, 'Everything's great, I'd say. I'm at the beach drinking and smoking'.

To which he replied, 'How I wish I could be there with you. Instead, I'm home alone'.

How come? Did the girl you liked so much, with whom there was 'an incredible energy', prefer spending Valentine's Day with her boyfriend? Oh, my God, what a weirdo!

I put the mobile away with an even bigger smile, without answering. It serves you right, Antonio. Keep choosing the cheaters. Instead, 'I choose love'.

Hours it took me to get my first mosquito bite: 26
Plastic bags I took out of the sea: 29
Average number of mistakes Shanaka makes every time he says something: 7
Minutes it took him to roll a cigarette: 4
Sweetness of this local boy from 1 to 10: 9
Bikinis I brought with me on this trip: 2
SPF of my sun cream: 50
Samogon's alcoholic percentage: more or less my dad's age
Romantic proposals received so far: 2
Glasses of Prosecco I will see this month: 0

DAY 4

'How blooooooody hot...'
-Colombo, Thursday 15th February 2018-

Finally some air, for Coolness' sake! Here we are sweltering and besides not being a heat lover, I left 11 degrees in London to suddenly find 32 degrees here. It will take me some time to adjust to this.

I'm writing from the rooftop bar of the Colombo City Hostel, a hostel recommended by my travel Bible, the Lonely Planet guide. I arrived here this morning by tuk-tuk and exhausted the rest of my energy trying to put up my mosquito net around my bed. An Egyptian guy tried to help me, and really did his best but, like me, he had never put one up before. The result? Despite the great efforts of both parties, soaked in sweat, the mosquito net is a fucking disaster and I will probably be attacked by a hoard of disgusting stinging and bloodthirsty insects straight out of hell.

Given that I had not yet sweated enough and the heat had not quite killed me, I decided to take part in the city walking tour offered by the hostel and led by a South American guy called Manu. During our walk, Manu explained that he has been travelling for a year, and now he has stopped in Colombo to work because he needs some money to continue to India.

Every time I hear about people who have been travelling for six, nine, twelve months or longer, I initially feel a spontaneous pang of envy, because I wonder how much mental freedom must be behind such a life choice. Economic freedom does not come into it. It's a myth that you need money to travel and, by the way, one that really irritates me when I hear it. What an average person spends during one weekend in London... Well, it's actually quite hard to establish

82

what 'average' means, but let's say 40 pounds on dining out and a drink. As I write it, I realise this definition does not cover all those English people who make a habit of destroying themselves every weekend with expensive alcohol, or who take a taxi home, or who go to stylish clubs... Okay, never mind. But let's assume that the average expense for a night out in London is around 40 pounds. With these same 40 pounds I guarantee you that I am able to live for like five days in Asia, including food and accommodation, and I'm not necessarily talking about a bunkbed in a hostel.

So, as I was saying, these people you meet who have been on the road for months if not years both inspire and intrigue me. My first instinct is to admire and envy them, as they are so free, unshackled from all the other things or fears that block the rest of us from doing the same.

On second thoughts, however, I wonder if they may be escaping from something, or if they don't have absolutely anything worth going back home for. And I know, deep down, that I don't belong to this category. The last time I travelled for a relatively long time was in Vietnam and Cambodia. During that trip I learnt that, even though I love getting away from my habits and routine, there comes a point where I feel like going back home and am really glad to return to my normality. Further proof of the fact I often feel like I'm in between two worlds, suspended between Asia and the Western world, dreams and reality, being a hippy but grounded at the same time. Let's see if this journey will confirm this or rather another truth I feel quite strongly within me: the fact of being in a state of constantly evolving, ever changing.

Anyway, I was the only one doing the walking tour. Talk about 'Let's do this tour so besides seeing Colombo I will also meet a crowd of other travellers who might be my next travel buddies, yahoo!'

Not only did I not meet anyone, apart from Manu, but I also didn't understand half of his explanations. This was due on the one hand to his strong accent and, on the other, to the fact that being a tour guide was not exactly his vocation, and so he wasn't doing it with the enthusiasm necessary to entertain me. And please bear in mind that, with the oppressive heat all but body slamming me to the ground, and the lack of caffeine for the last two days (welcome to the land of tea), some energy and vitality was needed in order to hold my attention.

One thing worth mentioning is one of those coincidences which I already know will become a regular and frequent occurrence, because now I am able to recognise them. For a few years now I've been viewing coincidences as God or the Universe winking at me, telling me, 'You are doing well, baby' (Yes, sometimes God calls me 'baby').

Basically, while walking, one of my flip-flops literally opened up like an oyster. The bit between the big toe and the little toe came out, so it was impossible for me to walk with it. Now, out of all the places in Colombo where it could've broken, out of all the kilometres we've walked today, where did this happen? Right in front of a lady who was exhibiting, on a dirty sheet placed on the ground in front of her, shoes of different sizes, along with tools more or less blackened by usage. Do your flip-flops get broken? Don't worry, the Universe will immediately send you a Sri Lankan cobbler.

You could debate that, were the Universe really protecting you then It wouldn't have your flip-flops breaking in the first place. However, thinking in this way is typical of a mind focused on the negative. Also, how can you develop the belief that everything will work out, always and in every way, if you don't start seeing anything, situation after situation, as proof that the Universe is always taking care of everything?

The lady silently and quickly fixed my flip-flop under my attentive eyes. I was fascinated by her skilful handiwork and kneeled down to get a better look at what she was doing. And that's when the fascination I was feeling was abruptly replaced first by shock and then by a degree of disgust. I tried to keep a straight face while a question in capital letters violently superimposed itself on my other thoughts: in order to have such obscenely long hairs on your legs, madam, have you never shaved in your entire life, or have you simply refrained from doing so in the last few years?

That was the first cultural shock with Sri Lanka.

Poverty all around?

Whole families on a scooter?

A very different conception of time?

Men who continue to make advance after advance, contrary to what is the norm in the other Asian countries I've visited so far?

No. Leg hairs, around 4cm long. My heart skipped a bit when I noticed it.

Having seen many of them today around in the city, I have to say that I find Sri Lankan women a bit unkept. There are some beautiful women, of course, but they tend to dress in clothes that don't really do them any favours... And poverty has nothing to do with it. India is the poorest country I've seen, and yet Indian women are a triumph of femininity and attention to detail, colour and accessories, and have this dignified beauty which would take more than a few lines to describe. Given Sri Lanka's proximity to India, I was expecting women here to be quite similar, but my first impression is that we are quite far removed from the type of femininity I saw there.

Wow, man, I've never thought about whether under those saris and shalwar kameez women shave their legs or not. I had never really pondered the issue. Bollywood movies always show you these gorgeous women who look perfect, dripping in jewellery, with shiny hair, elegant make up and perfectly manicured hands decorated with intricate henna drawings. If a woman spends like two hours getting ready before going out, and if she pays attention to matching her bangles with her sari colour, showing extreme attention to detail, in my naivety, I take for granted that she has already dealt with the basics. But in fact, now that I think about it, I've never seen any female legs exposed to sight, so it's quite possible that I've had it wrong all these years.

For sure, it's a culturally specific practice. For sure, as a relatively wealthy Westerner my values and priorities are very different from those of Sri Lankan women. For sure, I am conditioned by Western beauty practices and ideals. For sure, even in my Western world many feminists and hippies would wholeheartedly welcome the freedom to be as natural and hairy as possible. And yet, even with all of this in mind, my reaction was revulsion. Her husband might well appreciate the softness of all those hairs. Or maybe he then goes off to pick up foreign ladies with shaved legs as soon as he can. We will never know (unless he turns out to be the policeman I met at the beach yesterday).

To be honest, I didn't find Colombo particularly inspiring. No monument left me in awe. It's a big city, but it seems to me to be quite relaxed, or at least by Asian parameters. For sure, waaaaaaaaaaaaaaaaaaaaay more peaceful and less noisy than the Indian cities I've seen. Here, I don't have the sensation of being constantly observed, though I have to admit the eyes I do have on me feel like they are devouring me with their gaze.

Coming to Colombo today sounded like the most reasonable choice, despite the fact that I woke up with Shanaka on my mind, because:

1. I absolutely don't want to plan my time around a man. Actually, around a boy. I haven't inquired about his age, but I don't think he can be over 28. I'm on the other side of the world, and I don't think I should follow and repeat the behavioural patterns I've so far adopted with men given that, clearly, they turned out to be intrinsically wrong. So my priority is to fully live my journey, not fully live the fling.
2. I kind of have to see the capital, even though I know straight off that I always much prefer the little villages and countryside to the big cities. Given that I live in a metropolis like London, when I go away, I prefer to see something completely different, so normally I'm not that interested in big cities.

Anyway, I have Shanaka's number now, and he had to work today, so let's see if we manage to catch up in the next few days, hopefully on a beach.

On a positive note, Manu had me taste what I think is the national specialty here, *kottu*: a dish based on shredded *roti*, a bread that somehow reminds me of our amazing *piadina*, with cheese, scrambled eggs, onions, leeks and chicken or fish as alternatives to the vegetarian version. All these ingredients are then stir-fried with spices. Manu explained that *kottu* is probably the youngest street food in Sri Lanka, given that it first appeared on the scene in the seventies. Mmm, it gets the seal of approval from me, especially given that all the ingredients are simple but combined in a lively mixture.

I'm now sitting in the hostel rooftop bar. As is always the case in such places, the walls are covered with inspiring and more or less philosophical writings. In terms of other people sitting here and enjoying the breeze, of course there has to be the ever-present yoga girl, with loose trousers, a tribal tattoo on her shoulder blade, long, straight hair, and a lean, sinewy body. There is also an American guy, who is drinking his beer while Skyping with a friend, and a Japanese guy who is minding his own business.

Given that Colombo has not excited me, and considering that I'll probably spend another night here before flying to India, I think I will go back to the beach tomorrow. Actually, not 'I think'. I am definitely going. But I'm not going back to Mount Lavinia. I'll move to the next beach southwards. And let's see if Shanaka is free, as he told me he would be.

State of my hair: out of control
Temperature in Colombo: 36 °C
Population in the capital: around 755,000 inhabitants
Price of a *kottu*: 100–250 rupees (between 40 pence and one pound)
Km I've walked today under a bloody scorching sun: 7
The nationality of Manu, my tour guide in Colombo: Colombian (and no, I haven't made that one up)
Length of the cobbler's leg hair: 4.1cm
Length of my leg hair: shaved to perfection
Messages that Shanaka has sent me today: 2
Types of fruit seen so far: 19

DAY 5

'The world is full of hhhhhot guys'
-Hikkaduwa, Friday 16th February 2018-

How many things can happen in a day!

Or not. It's up to you to decide what to do with this marvellous day that, once again, the Universe has gifted you upon waking: a pristine new thread in its tangled tapestry of infinite twists and turns. Some time ago I was listening to a podcast by Sadhguru, an Indian yogi and mystic, and he said that every morning thousands of people all over the world do not wake up at all; they die during the night. If we were able to contemplate this truth, we would naturally feel immense gratitude simply for having woken up to see another day (I mean, as long as your life isn't overly shitty), and we would try to live this day, so generously presented to us, to the best of our ability.

I'm writing from Hikkaduwa, a lovely seaside resort, the name of which strangely puts me in a good mood, reminding me somehow of a hic-cup. Hik-kaduwa. Many sea turtles come here to lay their eggs, and I got here by taking my first Sri Lankan train.

The whole thing has been quite picturesque. I bought the ticket directly at the train station in Colombo. At first, I was adamant that the guy at the ticket office had misheard my destination, given that he was only charging me 160 rupees for the ticket, which is like 50 pence (yes, pence). Two and a half hours by train for 50 pence. Asia, I love you.

At the station, however, there was so much confusion. On the one hand, there were hordes of people running up and down the stairs connecting the platforms, dragging behind pieces of luggage and packages of considerable sizes. On the other, trains were arriving extra full, with many guys literally hanging outside the open train doors, as I've seen before in movies. As if this was not enough, some of them were jumping onto the platform while the train was just slowing down, meaning before it actually stopped. It must be one of the national sports, jumping from a moving train.

'Okay', I told myself. 'Let's get ready.'

I managed to identify which train I had to take, even though there were only a few signs in English, and was able to board it–while it was stationery–and make my way to the compartment. The idea of staying pressed against the train doors, squeezed among all those men and guys, didn't seem particularly alluring.

By some mysterious process of train-based discrimination, or more simply because we have no idea how these things work, we tourists were all left standing and were on our feet for the whole two-and-a-half-hour journey to Hikkaduwa. The time, however, went so enjoyably. On the one hand, I was curiously admiring the several sellers relentlessly going back and forth through the train selling practically anything: from samosas, to nuts, to sandwiches, to boiled eggs, to other snacks I couldn't begin to identify. On the other, I was starting to gather anecdotes and stories from the other travellers, which is indeed one of my favourite pastimes while travelling. There was a guy who was there to take part in the Iron Man in Colombo, and he had just been joined by his beautiful girlfriend, a medical student, who was there both to support him and to have a holiday. There was an English couple who will be going to Delhi to volunteer for six weeks with an NGO called 'Tender Hearts'. I want to do some volunteering myself on this trip, but I definitely won't be paying for it. As if it wasn't enough that I paid my own plane ticket to come here and give my time! Piper reassured me that when the right time comes, everything will happen smoothly, without stressing over researching and thinking, so for now I am simply gathering information, writing it down here and seeing what happens.

I started talking with an English girl about *Shantaram*, one of the best books I've read in the last few years, and which regularly comes up in my conversations as soon as they touch on India. Something tells me that I'll be having many more exchanges like this one on this topic.

On an ultra-sweet note, there was this local guy who helped me put my backpack up on the luggage rack. He told me that he got married in January to a German nurse met five years ago in a hostel in Colombo (There you go. It always happens to others. Yesterday, in my hostel, there was nobody interesting. In his hostel, instead, this guy found his wife. And, therefore, she has found her husband. Okay.)

He explained that the wedding had been logistically quite hard to organise and manage. 'I am a Buddhist, and according to tradition the parents were supposed to do some specific things, but her parents didn't understand why we had to perform those rites. It was hard to explain it to them.' Oh, how sweet. I wanted to tell him that maybe the reason why the parents couldn't adapt to something different was not because of the different religion, but because they were German, but it didn't seem appropriate.

The journey went well. The only thing that worries me is that my backpack is quite heavy, even though I thought about it so carefully and at length, and it's already bothering me on my fifth day. I only have 77 more days to go! Basically, if I don't wear my heavy trekking boots while moving from one city to the next, I need a third bag. I don't think I want to have to do that every time. I'm already loaded up like a mule, and I don't think the temperatures will go down, so the idea of travelling for hours and hours by train or bus with these heavy boots on doesn't appeal either. And yet, I know I have only packed what's essential. It's not even the few old rags I brought to wear that make my backpack heavy, but all the extras, like medicines, the sleeping bag, the mosquito net, the several adaptors… I really wouldn't know what to take out.

Once I arrived in Hikkaduwa, I set off on foot to find a hostel near the station, ending up at the Traveller's Hostel where, for 800 rupees, which is around three pounds, I get a night in an eight-bed dorm plus breakfast. At the moment there are only four of us in the room, all girls.

One of them is covered in astonishing mosquito bites, and man, do I feel her pain. I gave her some cortisone cream, as two years ago a crazy Canadian, Ali, did with me, at a time when I really needed the kindness of strangers. I was in Thailand with obscene buboes on my arm, neck and shoulder, probably inflicted by some insects that were not of this planet, and which had happily and repeatedly dined on my live flesh.

Here is one sense of the word 'karma'. What you receive, you give. What you do, will come back to you. Or at least so they say.

On the other hand, something that nobody says is that organisational skills here in Sri Lanka seem pretty shitty thus far. Last night I exchanged a few messages with Shanaka. He said he would join me in Hikka, as the locals affectionately call it, given that he has some days off, as he had indeed told me when we were in the sea.

'Great, but around what time do you think you will be arriving? And do you already know which hostel you will be staying in?'

'I don't tell you. Last year I worked in Hikkaduwa. I know many places. I want surprise you.'

What a sweet thought, thanks. But there are moments in life when romanticism is of secondary importance to pragmatism.

'Okay, but if I check in in a place and put my backpack on that floor, the above-mentioned backpack then stays there for three days. There's no way I am going to move out of there, bag and baggage, and come to the hotel you've chosen. Isn't it better if you tell me straight away where you are going?'

My efficient, pragmatic and hyper-organised London mentality versus his more relaxed, vague, loosely-defined and romantic Sri Lankan one. I mean, how much better would it have been if he had given me an address, and we simply met there tonight? Well, maybe in a parallel universe, things are going this way. In this universe, however, they aren't, so, given that I don't know the guy, plus the fact I don't know how far I can take him at his word, and considering that I am completely ignorant of how things work here, I've decided for the time being to organise myself independently, and so that's what I have done.

'Okay, then. Text me when you get here', and I said goodbye.

I go to the beach, and I'm immediately happy about my decision to come here rather than stay on in Mount Lavinia for another day. White sand, a pleasant and welcoming atmosphere, several little restaurants and bars, as well as numerous wooden huts selling day trips or boat tours and renting out snorkelling equipment. It is clear that there is more tourism here than in Mount Lavinia, and the long beach appears at first glance to be very clean. And the sea is that inviting blue that I had so anticipated in my pre-departure fantasies. I throw myself enthusiastically in the sea, wearing my full-face mask in order to do some snorkelling without the usual mini panic attacks I get every time I put my head under water.

In fact, the snorkelling was nothing special (once again, expectations…), so I came out of the water quite quickly. While I was sitting at the water's edge to take off the flippers I had rented, a small and inconsequential but equally vicious wave not only pushed me backwards, making an ass of me, but also stole my snorkel, which was clearly not well fixed to the mask!

Noooooooooooooooo!

A largely peaceful search and rescue mission followed, walking slowly back and forth with the water at my knees, trying to find the lost snorkel swallowed by the wave. Right when I had calmly accepted the situation, telling myself that sooner or later the waves would spit it out again, two local guys came to offer their help.

'Have you lost something? We dive and look for it where the water is deeper (oh, how kind of you!). How much you pay for this service?'

Ah, ecco. 'Zero', is my smiling answer.

I stay there for a bit, and then I accept that the sea seems to want to keep that precious piece of plastic, which might come back to the beach tomorrow in one of the nets dragged in by the fishermen.

A short bald man, who manages one of those wooden huts renting out the snorkelling equipment, and who has followed the whole event, asks me, 'So do you give me the mask as a gift? You cannot use it without the snorkel, while I can build a new one'. Do you hear this guy? Blessed are the resourceful.

And I'm also referring to myself. 'Okay, I give you the mask, since for me it's now useless, and in exchange tomorrow you give me the snorkelling equipment for free.'

Exchange accepted. I always wonder if my cheekiness would be accepted and indulged in the same way if I were a man ('Roby, quite often you ARE a man', I hear Mauro's voice saying). Probably not. Well, if on the one hand being a woman makes us subject to a lot of male attention we would often rather go without, at least it also has some positives. Wasn't I worried this morning because my backpack was too heavy, and I was feeling bad at the idea of carrying that weight up and down three countries for the next 80 days? There you go, Roby. The Universe has listened to your desires and made your trip lighter. #Carefulwhatyouwishfor.

In the end, I mean, how many days do I think I will snorkel during my trip? Five? Seven tops? And is it really worth carrying around this big mask which, as a matter of fact, takes up a lot of space? And so, quite easily, I'm happy to report, I let it go. From now on, I'll be travelling lighter.

At the end of the beach is Turtle Point, where sea turtles come to eat. There were three of them, nice and big, and though it was beautiful to see them, it was not as exciting for me as it had been in Gili Trawangan, in Indonesia: I was serenely snorkelling on my own when, turning my head, I saw this peaceful giant blissfully minding his own business, eating seaweed a few metres from the beach.

Here in Hikkaduwa, unfortunately, Turtle Point was full of idiot tourists who–and it's not clear what great achievement they were ticking off by doing so–absolutely had to touch the turtles while it's written everywhere not to. Standing with the water up to his mid-thighs, was the self-proclaimed Turtle Man, another resourceful local who has come up with the role of protector/manager/feeder of the turtles. He kept repeating to all the people there not to pat or touch the turtles, while simultaneously filling their hands with seaweed to feed them with (in exchange, of course, for a tip).

It was way more exciting later on when, on my way back to the hostel, I saw a small commotion of people who were all looking at a small cemetery, filled with crosses, on the beach. When I got closer, I discovered that in fact the crosses and small heaps of sand were not graves but rather the opposite. They were marking the spots where turtles had laid their eggs, and each cross showed the date and the number of eggs laid. Right when I was there gazing in fascination at this cemetery that was in fact a cradle of life, a beach warden came out with a bucket full of tiny new-born turtles.

Wow, I arrived at the right time! Five minutes earlier, and I would have gone away, smiling at having understood that the cemetery had nothing to do with death. Five minutes later, the turtles would have all been in the sea already, and I would have missed the whole thing.

Instead, by being there in that precise moment, I got to witness the baby turtles' release, this sweet and poetic event, which was so special that it moved me to tears. The beach warden emptied the contents of the bucket onto the sand, and the race for life started immediately. Here they are, these defenceless baby turtles, born in large numbers because unfortunately only 5% will make it. The remaining 95% will get eaten by seagulls or big fish or end up entangled in fishing nets or killed by boats' propellers.

Here they are, a bit confused and lost, but instinctively heading towards the sea, some quicker than others. Some of them hobble along, others take a long time to make their first step. And then there is always one who wins, one who hears the sea's call louder than the others.

This should be an event to admire in silence, marvelling at

nature's perfection and at the instincts we are all born with, instead, once again, tourists prove themselves to be a bunch of half-wits. Some people are touching and confusing the turtles, some block their way with their feet, some take photos and blind them with the flash while others stun them with their excitement and screams of encouragement.

A few metres to cover between the bucket and the sea and, once they reach the water, there they float, without wondering too much about what they will be swimming off into. Seeing these little creatures born without a mother and trying their best to move away from that chaos of noisy people to reach the immense ocean, filled with dangers of its own, has saddened me a bit. They must feel so lost, bless them. Good luck, baby turtles.

Once back at the hostel, Shanaka confirms what I intuitively knew. 'Excuse me, Roby, today I cannot come. For sure I come tomorrow.'

Okay, no worries. Thank God that, as I said, I had organised myself independently of him. And it's great that I'm living this whole thing without any expectations, or Shanaka standing me up might have altered my mood.

My mood has instead remained quite high, thanks to the beautiful day on the beach, and I'm ready to face my first Sri Lankan Friday night. I dined in a seafront restaurant and, to end my day in style, I thought about treating myself to a massage.

Let the party begin! When I travel, whatever I save on accommodation I spend on massages. The problem here is that quite often, rather than 'massage', we are actually talking about a strong and vigorous body rubbing, administered with a certain commitment and strength, sure, but often lacking in technique and basic anatomical knowledge. I left a tip for the masseuse anyway, a trend I started the moment I took the taxi from the airport, given that I have to give back to the world some of the money Destiny gave me at Heathrow airport.

By the way, the receptionist at the massage centre was quite hhhhhhot. I was almost ready to be cheeky and tell him something, had he not been so very professional and dry. I have to admit anyway that, on first impression, I'm more attracted to Sri Lankan men than Indian men. More than anything else, they seem to spend more time exercising, given that I have noticed more biceps and athletic bodies here in two days than in whole weeks of travelling around India. An Indian friend of mine once joked that they are too absorbed in spirituality to be bothered with muscles. Also, let's not forget the way Sri Lankan men look at you, straight in the eyes and for a long time. Something unthinkable in London.

Welcome back to Asia, Roby.

So I found myself on the street, having been shown the door by the hhhhhhot but indifferent receptionist. I was debating whether to go to bed, feeling fairly relaxed and very oily, or instead go to the beach party that Shanaka had praised so much and attended regularly last season. Considering that I am on holiday, that it's Friday night and that I won't be spending many days by the sea, I decided to take the plunge.

I start walking and a tuk-tuk immediately stops. 'Are you going to the beach party at Vibrations?' the driver inquires.

Ehm... How does he know? The Fourth Secret of Fátima. I don't think I have 'I'm going to the beach party' written on me anywhere. Or maybe it's the only event of the evening, so necessarily, if you see a tourist walking around, you assume s/he must be going there.

'Indeed I am, but I prefer walking, thanks.'

This is an answer which always leaves the local people gobsmacked, as they clearly cannot grasp it. How is it possible that someone who can afford a means of transport doesn't want to make their life easier? As far as I'm concerned, I love walking, especially in new places, because it allows me to see much more and to interact with the people I meet on the street.

'Don't worry, it's for free. I have to go that way anyway.'

Perfect, then. Another little gift from the Universe. By the way, once I got to the party and got off the tuk-tuk, another driver who was waiting there outside the venue remarked, 'Ah, you came here for free, right?'

Fifth Secret of Fátima. How could he know that?

Sri Lanka: a country, a question.

Anyway, I get into the garden of this venue, Vibrations, which really is beautiful. Open air, of course, divided into different areas. From the bar, where dozens of people are clustered, to several tables and deckchairs scattered around the big garden, at the end of which I can see a swimming pool. To the right, the dance floor, with a mixture of local guys and Western tourists, all busy dancing to the rhythm of music which calls me almost violently to join in.

I've come to a conclusion: flip-flops are not exactly the best shoes to dance in. But never mind. I close my eyes and I let the notes take me away. The music sounds really good, and a guy who looks quite good is sitting with a friend at the edge of the dance floor. We exchanged a few looks, but when half-way through the evening he finally stood up to start dancing, it all came crashing down, as he was completely out of synch.

How sad! Hhhhhhot guys with no sense of rhythm! A girl gets all these images in her mind, and then the guy looks like he's dancing at one of those silent discos which are quite common in London, where they give you a pair of headphones and you choose which channel to listen to and to which music to dance to. The result? Hundreds of people moving at different rhythms in a completely silent room.

Sadness indeed. The hhhhhhot guy's got as much rhythm as a sack of roti flour.

Or divine justice. It's a matter of points of view.

So I let that one go, and sit and drink up the whole scene with my eyes.

The dance floor was super busy, and despite the venue being quite stylish, most of us were backpackers who, like me, had not exactly come equipped for a night out in a trendy club. Several girls were dancing barefoot, others were still wearing their bikini under their top. I was at least wearing a nice black short dress with butterflies, albeit drenched in massage oil.

I am there looking around, thinking that my journey has just started and I'm already at a packed party, when I am struck by the First Great Epiphany.

THE WORLD IS FULL OF HHHHHHOT GUYS.

Of all ethnic backgrounds, ages, shapes, typologies. There is a nice, varied display at the party, though no one seems to be taking any actual interest in me, and in fact I can't exactly be bothered either. I'm feeling so good just at dancing for a while and then go back to the hostel early, so that tomorrow I can go on a catamaran trip with Turtle Man. With the snorkelling equipment for free, let's not forget that.

Given that epiphanies are often connected to each other, I immediately make another unexpected discovery, thus getting to the Second Great Epiphany. EVEN IN SRI LANKA THEY PLAY *DESPACITO*.

I cannot believe it. I smile, somewhere between amusement and resignation, and off I go, dancing and singing:

Ya, ya me está gustando más de lo normal
Todos mis sentidos van pidiendo más
Esto hay que tomarlo sin ningún apuro
Despacito
Quiero respirar tu cuello despacito
Deja que te diga cosas al oído
Para que te acuerdes si no estás conmigo

Good. I've given vent to the Latin spirit in me, too. I'm there thinking of going home when, in absolute contrast with the music played until now, the DJ surprises me by putting on *The Eye of the Tiger*, one of the iconic Rocky songs. And Rocky Balboa has been my idol since, like, forever.

I smile to myself because these things don't just happen by chance, and by now I am absolutely certain about this. I am able to read the signs. They are all messages and reassurances that I'm doing well, that I'm on the right path, and that I just have to trust the Universe. Since I started paying attention to coincidences, the world has become a huge book to read.

My brother Mauro, whom I presented this theory of mine, had the following to say, 'Thinking that the multiple things that are happening are a message for you is indicative of an egotistic view of the world typical of many mental illnesses'.

Thank you, little brother, but I know I'm the one who's right.

Okay, Universe, I'll stay at this party a little longer. Let's see who I have to meet.

I'm there looking around while this short, cute guy, with nice dark eyes but in extreme need of a haircut, comes to talk to me. Agreed, I'm the last one who should be casting judgement on other people's hair, but he has got me here. I'm always surprised by the way some short men are not in the slightest perturbed by our clear size and height difference and try to pick me up anyway.

'You are not dancing anymore?' he asks.

'Let's say I'm taking a break. It's too hot.'

'Where are you from? I come from Afghanistan', he continues. A question, an answer.

There we go. I was missing an Afghan in my list, I think to myself.

I go back to dancing anyway because I'm not that interested in him, though I'd be curious to hear his opinion on stoning. He starts dancing close to me, a technique practised in both London and Kabul, clearly.

In the end, when I have basically been reduced to a sweaty (and oily, let's not forget that) mass, I tell him goodbye and that I'm leaving.

'No! Why? Come on. I'll buy you a drink and we can go and get some fresh air near the swimming pool.'

And okay, alright. It would be rude not to accept. Plus it's Friday night, I'm on holiday, *evviva la vita*, let's have this drink.

Sitting by the pool with my feet soaking in its clean, refreshing water, I discover that his name is Mujib, he is 29 years old, works as a reporter for the New York Times and, more importantly, he too thinks I'm 31–32. When I disclose to him that I am seven years older, he asks me, bewildered, what my secret is.

'My love for life', I answer him.

Mujib plays his cards very well, I have to admit. He asks me a lot of questions, and he doesn't refrain from paying me compliments. 'I noticed you immediately. The way you were dancing was oozing a self-confidence that I always find so sexy in women.'

Roby, a small reminder for yourself, something to reread on days when you might feel like a walking toilet: remember that even when you were picking out trash from the sea, and even when you were covered in massage oil and as slippery as an eel, as sweaty as a lobster in a sauna, with your makeup halfway down your face because of the heat and hair one might reasonably assume had been styled using fireworks... you managed to pull.

Never underestimate your gorgeousness (nor the vastness of the hunger in the world, and I'm referring to a specific hunger).

Sure, Mauro would point out that this is a guy from Afghanistan talking, where many of the women are hidden (they'd probably like me to say 'protected', rather than hidden, but this is my journal, and I can write whatever I want here) behind voluminous black veils. It is quite logical that any girl exposing a few extra centimetres of skin here and there is bound to become a prime target for him, no matter how bad looking she is. Once more, thank you, *fratellino*, my little brother. And *fratellone*, my older brother, too, because I know that both Mauro, the younger one, and Alessio, the elder one, would agree here.

We talk about the situation for women in his country, how relationships work before marriage, alternative careers we could go for... The little mop-headed guy turns out to be interesting.

'I think you'd be a good journalist. You are asking me a lot of questions and chatting comes quite natural to you', he tells me.

Thirty-nine years of experience in the field, my boy!

I think back to the summer camping trips organised by my parish, when I was a teenager. I used to hide a tape recorder in my pocket so that I could record my friend Lucio and his bullshit, without him knowing. He would pretend to be Batman and tell me about some unsuccessful rescue mission, stretching his imagination and sense of humour to the max. Lucio and that whole muddle of feelings associated with him and his situation seem to belong to another life.

In the end our short, shaggy-headed Mujib properly takes the plunge, going all in, 'Fancy a second drink in my bedroom? I am staying in that hotel, literally across the road. My room comes with a giant terrace, so instead of looking at the pool we can look at the sea (and not see anything, given that it's the middle of the night)'.

Very good point, fair enough, but it's not his lucky day. It's not even about the age difference, given that I think the age gap is actually bigger with Shanaka. Mujib has played his cards right, I give him that, but he's missing a few too many centimetres because I can find him attractive.

'Opportunity never knocks twice', they say. Never mind. I'm not answering the door to this one.

Off I go to my hostel, this time paying for my tuk-tuk. Mattress, here I come!

Age they seem to think I am so far: 31–32 years
Countries in the world where 'Despacito' is an unstoppable hit: 87
Year when stoning was abolished in Afghanistan: sadly, that year has not arrived yet
Main reason for stoning women: if they are accused of sexual intercourse outside of marriage, and it doesn't matter if it was rape
Height of Mujib's tuft: 9cm
Height of Mujib: 170cm?
Fruit juices drunk so far: 3
Baby turtles released on the beach today: 102
Baby turtles still alive at the moment: I hope 102
Days it took me to have my first conversation about Shantaram: 4

DAY 6
'Every time I see that star, I will think of you'
-Galle and Hikkaduwa, Saturday 17th February 2018-

In the end, despite leaving opportunity out in the cold, I went to bed late last night, and I am also slightly jetlagged still, even though the time difference is only four hours, so I decided to take things easy this morning.

I had a relaxing breakfast, included in the 40 cents that I pay for my accommodation: kilos of bread, butter and jam, coffee and tea. Nothing fancy, but always good.

I then entertained myself with some other travellers, including a guy who vaguely resembled Ryan Gosling, already bare chested at 10am. I gathered more tips and recommendations on what to see in the south from those who are about to finish their holiday.

With one thing and another, it became too late to go on the snorkelling trip with Turtle Man as I had planned so, flexible as a reed, though not as thin, I've changed my plan: sightseeing around Galle Fort, which is a UNESCO World Heritage Site and, according to many, a real little jewel.

I went there by bus, and let me take this opportunity to say a few words on Sri Lankan buses. They are quite psychedelic, although way less than the Indian ones. The drivers always express their personality through the choice of colours, all various degrees of bright, and the images or objects with which they furnish their buses. By 'images and objects' I am referring to plastic flowers (which prove my point about local men's romanticism), photos of Bollywood actors, as well as images of Jesus, the Buddha or one of the host of deities worshipped in Hinduism. To complete the picture, there is often a radio blasting inane songs from Bollywood movies or, in the case of better equipped buses, maybe even a TV showing these movies on loop. The ticket, however, costs next to nothing.

Galle is indeed a little gem, protected by walls and surrounded by the ocean on three of its four sides. When a Portuguese fleet made a navigational error and ended up here in the 16th century, they decided to settle down, building a fort to protect themselves from outside attack. Despite being reinforced a century later with other walls and bastions, the fort failed to protect against the Dutch assault. The Dutch defeated the Portuguese and took up residence in Galle, making it the most important harbour in Sri Lanka. It was only in the 19th century that the Port of Colombo overtook it in importance, remaining the island's main port to this day. The fort we see today was rebuilt by the Dutch in 1663, after they destroyed the original to defeat the Portuguese.

Walking around Galle feels like stepping back into the past, but of another country. The cobbled lanes of the historical centre ooze elegance and tranquillity, while the old colonial buildings exude decadence and peace. I don't feel like I am in Asia at all.

Unfortunately, I've chosen the hottest hours of the day to visit the fort, between 12 and 4, and the heat is really putting me to the test. I visit several temples, mosques and churches, and then dive into the city's colonial past by enjoying an iced coffee in the hall of the beautiful Fort Bazaar hotel, which dates back to the 17th century.

I then enjoy a long walk on the bastion, admiring the English lighthouse, the sea on one side and some local guys playing cricket on the other. When I start walking towards the bus station in order to catch the bus back to the hostel a tuk-tuk stops in front of me. The driver tells me, 'Hello, I know you. You stay in Hikkaduwa'.

How do they know? Either I am more memorable than I think, or nobody has hair as obscene as mine in the whole of Hikkaduwa. In either case, this is the Sixth Secret of Fátima.

'I'm going back to Hikka. Do you want to come with me?' he suggests.

'Oh, okay, but I was going to catch a bus, so I pay you what I'd pay for the bus.'

'No, 800 rupees are okay?' the driver replies. Ehm, I mean, what am I missing? You offer me a lift I'm not remotely interested in, and you want me to pay for it as well? You can drive home alone and thankyouverymuch.

I don't yet know what Shanaka is up to tonight, so I've come to have dinner on my own in this little seafront restaurant, Mamias, where I've just had an excellent grilled octopus. How I love these places! Fish and seafood for a fifth of what you'd pay back home!

Right when I am writing my journal, I receive a text from Shanaka: 'I arrive now. Where are you?'

'At Mamias restaurant. Do you know it?'

'Yes, I know. I am there in five minutes.'

Okay, my dear Diary. Let's go meet the night and its many surprises.

The morning after

Well, let's say that organisation is not at all the specialty of our human puppy Shanaka. Yes, human puppy, both because he is slender, and probably no taller than 170cm, and because he adopts these forced behaviours to look like a Man. I don't know how to explain it clearly, but when a man is self-confident, he just is and that's that. He has nothing to prove. He doesn't have to walk in a certain way, or smoke in a specific way. His being emanates clearly from his various gestures and behaviours. Shanaka, on the other hand, seems to study his moves to some extent, wanting to appear in control of a situation which, in my opinion, scares him a bit. When he came into the restaurant he was walking with springy steps, touching his full lips and scarred eyebrow, maybe taking some inspiration from a movie scene. He sat at my table, looking around first and then saying, 'Ciao, Madame Roby (Madame Roby? Really?). How are you? My tuk-tuk is outside. We go?' I am basically laughing to myself: his efforts to keep my interest in him alive are so sweet, and his idea of courting is kind of funny.

So we went together to this Yula, the hotel-restaurant where Shanaka worked last year. They didn't have any rooms available (did calling beforehand to check their room availability sound like a bad idea?), so we tried two other places, like Mary and Joseph in a Sri Lankan Nativity. In the end we found a room in a place called Top Secret. What can I do? The names of some of the places here really make me smile. They gave us a room with the biggest bed I've ever seen, like a super mega king size, with mosquito nets everywhere.

'We go and drink something?' suggests Shanaka after putting his little black rucksack on the floor. The guy travels light.

So we go to the beach, where there is even a small bonfire and, once in a while, someone lights some mini fireworks. Just like that, for no apparent reason.

I'm happy to be with Shanaka. First Valentine's Day, and now a delayed Guy Fawkes Night with him, too.

'Do you want a beer? Let me buy you a beer', he offers. I don't even like beer, but he seems so eager to buy me something.

'For me a Coke and an *Arak*', he says to the barman, who immediately picks up this national liqueur and starts mixing it. Shanaka smokes quite a few cigarettes while he tells me about his life in Mount Lavinia. He buys another drink and, automatically, gets me another beer.

'No, Shanaka, this one is on me.'

'No, you don't have to pay. Never. I don't even want to share. I pay everything.'

Okay, I guess that in his culture, the man has to really be the Man and look after his woman (of the moment). I wish men in London would behave like this! But the whole thing makes me feel a bit uncomfortable because, while that sum is nothing to me, it is a big portion of his salary.

And so, with a beer in one hand and a cigarette in the other, we enjoy the bonfire under a beautiful starry sky, a few metres from the ocean, where some baby turtles are probably fighting for their lives.

London is a tiny little dot in my mind, as small as one of those stars, while in fact I've been on the road for only... six days. The whirlwind of dark thoughts polluting my mind for months seems to have lost intensity and speed. Right now, my attention is fully focused on the moment. Eckhart Tolle would be proud of me.

More specifically, all my attention is focused on trying to understand what Shanaka means, with his basic English. I almost get emotional when he repeats back to me, sentence by sentence, the exchange we had on that terrace at his restaurant; an exchange which culminated in our first kiss. Not many men would have remembered line by line what we had said to each other.

'Do you know the meaning of my name? It means 'star', and I'm the brightest star in the sky (obviously)', he explains, and let's not count how many grammar mistakes he made in saying all this.

'How nice! So every time I see that star shining more than the others, I will think of you', I answer, visualising myself covered in mozzarella, ricotta and Parmesan, I sound that cheesy. Although my cheesiness can be forgiven in the circumstances (beach, bonfire, starry sky and alcohol).

'We are making golden memories now. If I know that one day you think of me, I will be happy', continues Shanaka. Sweetness made into a boy. His way of thinking seems light years away from that of the men I am used to meeting in London. And he's right. This should be the point, but instead we love to create paranoia for ourselves by projecting our needs onto others, and our fears onto the future.

Oh, well. I'm getting teary-eyed at the purity of his heart. Shanaka's goodness, though, soon gives way to a somewhat Sicilian attitude, 'I'm a bit jealous if I think you meet other men, but I know that life is like that. You are on holiday alone, of course you will meet and sleep with other men'.

Well, I wouldn't say of course, but it's very likely, yes. However, this thought is projected onto the future, while our friend Eckhart Tolle, whom Shanaka has probably never heard of, wants us to stay in the now, in the present.

'Shall we go to the room?' I suggest, with a wink, to which he replies, 'Oh, my God. I wanted a lot you say it'.

In the room, it went well. I'd say twice as well.

There were some fearful moments, followed by silent inner laughter, when Shanaka, in the heat of a kiss, banged his teeth against mine, making a horrible sound and leaving me unsure whether he had broken one of my teeth. I immediately checked in the mirror, and–thank God–they are still all where I left them yesterday. I actually wonder how much experience a guy of his age can have. I know he has never had a girlfriend but surely, working in the tourist sector, he must have had several chances. Yet, the script he seems to stick to in terms of 'how a Man behaves' makes me think that he has never got past a few dates with the same woman.

I would like to say it was the ardour of all his enthusiastic kissing that led me, a little later on, to let go of all precaution, but I would be lying. Inside my head was an ironic voice going, 'Yes, just imagine. How cool would it be if, after all these years of struggle, all it took was a 25-year-old Sri Lankan guy, 5cm shorter than me, whose English is only understandable thanks to my patience and affection, for me to have a baby!'

And so, supported by this small glimmer of reason I intentionally stepped into lightness. Which, indeed, is not so light at all. Maybe that's what Kundera meant by 'the unbearable lightness of being', a concept I've thought about a lot.

Let it go.

Oh, my gosh, I'm fully aware that no self-help (or Disney) writer ever meant this, when they invited us to let it go. It's totally my personal interpretation. I have chosen to let myself go, in this respect, too. I've chosen to run a risk (in terms of diseases, I mean, but I think that Sri Lankan people have fewer STDs on average than English or Italian people, after a quick evaluation of their social and cultural scene) because the stakes totally justify it. And how marvellous would it be if a baby were to be born out of a moment of serenity, happiness, joy, fun and affection?

I'd say that this particular instance of 'letting it go' is definitely bigger than the one with the snorkelling mask. I'm making progress, and quickly for that matter.

He's sweet, Shanaka. During the night he kept me really close and hugged tightly, and it was a beautiful feeling.

He is sweet in what seems to me a very 'Asian' way, based on my experiences anyway. I sometimes wonder how these people have managed to reach adulthood with their soul's purity intact and an almost childlike innocence. Hasn't cultural contamination arrived here and ruined them, as it maybe did with us? Haven't the movies and the internet, with all its content, showed them how the rest of the world thinks and behaves?

Shanaka has just left. He has to go and see his grandfather who lives in Tangalle, and it's going to take him six hours by bus. I don't think we'll be able to see each other tonight. Again, he has insisted on paying for the room, despite my pleas to at least split it. Nothing doing. You cannot negotiate these things with Sri Lankan men it seems.

Meanwhile, I've just come back to my hostel, and sitting outside was the poor man's Ryan Gosling, who can't have brought any T-shirts with him because he was bare chested once again.

'Do you think you will be sleeping in your bed here tonight?' he asked me, smirking.

What a strange question. Could he be envious? I wonder what the Sinhala is for, 'How about minding your own bloody business?'

Instead, albeit with that question in my mind, I smiled back and said, 'It's great when things don't go according to plan'. And it's so true. It can be really great.

With Shanaka, I am indeed experimenting to see what happens when you don't have any expectations or attachments to the outcome. Two days ago he didn't manage to come and see me, and I had a great day anyway, filling it with loads of beautiful things, putting myself first. Yesterday he managed to come, and we had some really sweet and joyful moments. We made golden memories, as he said.

If we manage to make new ones, maybe tomorrow, it will be fab. But I'm not clinging onto this hope with all my might. If it doesn't happen, I will create other memories, either alone or with somebody who will be on my path tomorrow.

Teeth in my mouth that Shanaka broke with his way too passionate, or not so expert, kiss: 0
Teeth that Shanaka has in his mouth: all those intended by God
Age of Shanaka's grandfather: 81
Baby turtles that have died since yesterday: I don't wanna know
Abs I counted on the stomach of the poor man's Ryan Gosling: 6 sections
T-shirts that the poor man's Ryan Gosling must have: 1, and it's probably in the dirty laundry
The Sinhala for 'How about minding your own bloody business?': නමුත් ඔබේම කුකුළා සාදන්න, හරිද? (namut obēma kukuḷā sādanna, harida?)

DAY 7
'Excuse me, but how old are you?'
-Hikkaduwa, Sunday 18th February 2018-

During my mega feast of bread, butter and jam at breakfast, accompanied by some furtive looks at the poor man's Ryan Gosling's abdominals, always so conveniently on display, I've decided to stay in Hikkaduwa today and see how it goes. What do you have in store for me, stunning scorching-hot day?

The beach is pretty, as I already said. White and inviting. There is also a national marine park, with an entrance fee to pay, and one of the main activities people sell you here are snorkelling trips, given that there is a bit of coral reef.

Yesterday morning I missed both my tour with Turtle Man and my free snorkelling equipment. Today I've decided to kill two baby turtles with one stone (ehm, no, not the best wordplay of my life) and I've gone to the guy I gave my mask to, to see whether I could go on a catamaran trip with him. And you know what? He'd found the snorkel. Good for him. So he'll be able to make millions by renting it out over the next few years. I'm happy for him. I borrowed it one last time for my trip, so as to fully enjoy the underwater view.

I had never taken a traditional catamaran before. I don't know why, but it reminded me of a cartoon I used to watch called *Flo la piccola Robinson*, about a shipwrecked family. It looked like one of those boats castaways would build in order to leave the island: two hollowed-out logs joined together by a pole; a light boat that seems to slide on the water.

Let me correct myself: it is indeed one of those boats.

On board, it was only me and the local guy in charge of

110

the catamaran who I think probably spoke a total of 27 words in English. With gestures, I made him understand that I'm quite shitty at swimming and to please check on me once in a while, just to see if I am still alive.

In terms of fish, I didn't see anything unforgettable or particularly exciting, although there were some marvellous purple starfish. The simple fact of being perched on a catamaran was kind of fun. The whole scene became quite comical when, after I'd finished snorkelling, I wasn't able to get back on board. Did a small ladder on one side seem such a bad idea, for Catamaran's sake? How can I get back on board? I mean, they were obviously counting on me using my upper body strength, but my arms can take about as much weight as a couple of French fries covered in mayonnaise. What am I going to pull myself up with? I felt like a seal using her flippers to move, but now that I think about it, a seal in water is way more agile than me. I then tried to push up with my legs, bending like an Olympic swimmer turning in half a second at the end of the pool. This technique... didn't hold water either. Then the man tried to pull me up, but my (wet) 74kg and his 55kg (tops) made the whole thing quite a challenge. He then offered me the oar, but I still couldn't pull myself up. I was laughing to myself because from the outside the whole thing was as humiliating as it was comical. I looked like a whale struggling to free herself from a net. And the guy, a picture of earnestness, instead of laughing with me about the whole thing, was dead worried. And looking at his anxious face, I couldn't help killing myself with laughter.

God, I thank you for the immeasurable gift of self-irony you gave me. It simplifies my life and my relationships so much!

I suggested staying in the water and clinging somehow to the cross pole, and it wouldn't have been a bad solution, though surely not very orthodox. In the end, however, with many a 'Jesus Christ!' and a couple of 'Krishna's, I managed to haul my (toned) ass on board.

In order to support the local economy, I then bought a boat

safari tour of Hikkaduwa Lake from Snorkel Man. According to the leaflet, this tour should have been a chance to see many bird species and monitor lizards, quite similar to Komodo dragons but a bit smaller. In fact, much as the views were really pretty, I didn't see many animals. In the end–even the boat tours here seem to include a visit to a Buddhist temple–we stopped off at Seenigama Vihara, which basically takes up the whole of this islet in the centre of the lake (file under 'Wherever there are a few spare centimetres of land, build a temple'). As my Lonely Planet Bible informs me, it's one of the only two temples in Sri Lanka where victims of theft can seek retribution and revenge. Anyone who has been robbed can come to this temple to pray, but above all, to buy a specially prepared oil made with chilli and pepper. Once back home, they light a lamp with this magic oil and recite a specific mantra. Sooner or later, the bastard thief will be identified because they will be struck down with misfortune.

Mega idea for a potential business: I could sell litres of this magic oil in my region, Veneto, where thieves pillage homes continually! If only we believed in that! If only we had the faith of these Sri Lankan people!

Just for a change, I was alone on this tour, too. Just me and the boat driver, a plump 23-year-old with a big smile, who seized the moment to make his move. It's my seventh day here and hats off to the entrepreneurial spirit of these local men!

'Why don't you come and sit here, at the end of the boat?' Mr I Clearly Love My *Kottu* suggested, gesturing towards the seat next to the engine, which he was manoeuvring manually to direct the boat. And okay, let's go and sit next to him.

After the usual icebreaker, 'Where are you from?', came the other guaranteed question, 'Are you married?'

When I answered that I wasn't, I could see pure surprise and shock in his eyes, 'Why not, madam?'

Mah, I don't know, you tell me. For me, that is the biggest Secret of Fátima.

Then it was my turn to be surprised when he seriously asked, 'Do you want to marry me? We get married together'.

How sweet. But no, thanks. And so here we are, at my first wedding proposal. Seven days. Did I really have to go and live in London, wear myself out with all those men who didn't want to commit to me, to whom I gave myself hoping to be loved back? I should have moved to Sri Lanka! I would already have four children by now.

With a fisherman.

Living in a hut because our house was destroyed by the tsunami.

Oh, well. Life goes as it has to go. I made my choices back then. It's quite useless to stop and ponder parallel worlds now. I have to remind myself that everything happens for a reason, that the choices we made in the past were the only ones we could make back then, and that everything is perfect as it is now.

And the sun making the water shine with a thousand reflections, the wind on my face and the blue and green filling my eyes make this a perfect moment indeed.

The tour also included a quick visit to the devil mask museum in Ariyapala, at Ambalangoda, a small village nobody would stop in were it not for these masks with a magical meaning: they were once–and still are–worn in ritual dances to drive out evil spirits causing bad luck and illness. I would have loved to stay there a bit longer and check out the workshop next door where three local women were painting some masks while catching up on the latest local gossip.

In fact, by stopping such a short time in this museum, I was able to spend more time at the Tsunami Museum, where I experienced my own mini tsunami of emotions. There was no escaping all the sadness, anger and despair I felt there. It is not a real museum, but a shack made available by one local person who lost his whole family in that tragedy. The photos on display are raw, uncensored, even brutal, and they went straight to my heart. I was moved to silent tears looking at the images of that disaster, streets and houses destroyed by the fury of the water, amassed corpses, but also all the help that arrived from the rest of the world. The pictures were powerful enough, but the text, full of mistakes, made me cry even more due to its purity and simplicity. They were calling for us to share out the wealth of the world, maintaining the idea that the tsunami was God's punishment because people are greedy, and it was therefore in our karma to be punished like that. I would have liked to point out that if God wanted to punish people for their greediness, He could maybe send an earthquake to Wall Street, rather than a tsunami to the poor fishermen of Sri Lanka. Just saying. The fact that they had been hit by this immense tragedy and were seeing it as God's admonition filled my heart even more with tenderness and sadness.

I didn't know anything at all about the Matara Express train that was passing Peraliya a few moments after the first killer wave hit the beach. To date, it's the largest single rail disaster in world history by death toll, with at least 1,700 fatalities. I came to Hikka from Colombo by train, and I know that the tracks are only a few metres away from the sea. On that terrible day many people who were fleeing the beach jumped onto the train, thinking it a safe place to seek refuge. At the same time, dozens of panic stricken inhabitants ran towards the train, giving their children to the passengers on board, who almost seemed protected by being inside the carriages. Unfortunately, the water made the train lose contact with the rails, and the second deadly wave swept away all its 1,500 passengers.

More than 1,500 people died a few metres from where I was standing. Some estimate the death toll to have been 2,000, because, if there were 1,500 paying passengers, there would also have been an unspecified number of non-paying ones.

To commemorate this tragedy, a few hundred meters from the Tsunami Museum and Information Centre is a huge standing Buddha statue, looking out at the ocean. His hands are in one of His typical poses, indicating courage and protection. Which are both needed, I'd say.

Finally, reeling from the emotions stirred by this tragedy, which still baffles me–given its enormity, I struggle to properly imagine it–I was overwhelmed by the wonder of nature. Once again, I was lucky enough to witness the miracle of newly born lives. The final stop of my boat and tuk-tuk tour was at the Kosgoda Turtle Hatchery. They bring the turtle eggs laid on the beach here, so that they can hatch away from the danger of thieves (unfortunately turtles eggs are considered a delicacy and are eaten in the villages) or accidents. When you enter, there is a whole series of pools with turtles of different species, and I was quite intrigued by an albino one. There was also a turtle whose flippers had been cut off by a boat propeller.

In other words, if the tsunami doesn't kill them, you can be sure people will.

Then, for the second time since I arrived in Hikka, I found myself in exactly the right place at the right time, meaning that, once again, a hundred eggs had just hatched. The few other visitors and I went down to the adjacent beach to witness the release of the baby turtles. Right from the beginning, then, this event was way more intimate than the one I witnessed at Narigama Beach the other day. The founder of the centre drew a line on the beach, writing 'Good luck' between the line and the sea, then he freed these small creatures from the bucket. And I don't know, but what with the emotional burden of the Tsunami Museum, these turtles that live a hundred years and have to survive nets, boat propellers, predators etc, the sky turning sunset pink, our silent and joyful admiration of these little animals' first moments of life… Everything seemed so poetic and beautiful and intense. The gentleman allowed us to gently take some baby turtles from the bucket and put them on the sand. I took one and I wished her all the luck in the ocean, and to be sly and agile. And so we stood there, smiling in silence, watching to see which turtle would reach the finish line first.

A very special moment indeed.

Some of us were already leaving, given that half of the baby turtles were already in the sea, when, with a loud shriek, a seagull dived into the water. We all stopped and looked at each other, disappointed and stunned, wondering if any of those poor little creatures had already met their end.

And I complain that my life as a single woman in London is tough!

I was happy with the tour. I saw a lot of things. If I could drive a stupid scooter, I would be even more independent on my trips. Whenever I'm in Asia, I kick myself for not having learnt. Why was I swotting away at home, while my brothers were happily driving around on their Ciao mopeds? Why didn't I ever ask Lucio to teach me to drive his souped-up Vespa when he came to see me every afternoon?

Who knows? Maybe these three months are going to be my time to learn. Or to maybe find a man behind whom to sit, clinging to him sensually.

Roby, remember, no expectations, no attachments…

Talking of men, Shanaka didn't turn up until 8pm, despite saying he would be in touch before 1pm. But let's not get attached to these trifles. When he finally texted, it was to tell me, 'I have just left, I arrive late. I feel lonely'. Join the club, my dear. If it's true that it takes six hours by bus between Tangalle and Hikka, it means he will arrive around 3–4am. 'Oh, don't feel lonely. Since you arrive late, it's better if we sleep separately and we talk tomorrow morning. I'd like to go to Unawatuna, so write me when you wake up'.

Tomorrow morning I'll decide on what to do but yes, I'd like to go to this other beach.

Once back in the hostel, I started talking with this big girl, Pien, taller and bigger boned than me, and it was such a pleasant conversation that it felt natural to continue it over dinner. Topics: our trip so far and men. Obviously. I may be on the other side of the world, but I have brought a good chunk of myself with me.

'I arrived one week ago, and so far, I've seen three beaches, but my plan is to rent a tuk-tuk and do the whole tour of Sri Lanka by tuk-tuk alone.'

....

And they call *me* crazy.

'In Holland there's a TV program where a guy toured the whole of Sri Lanka by tuk-tuk, so now many Dutch people want to copy him. I already have the one-month driving license, and I have looked into tuk-tuk rental prices.'

There it is: a kind of trip I don't think I'll ever do.

Moving on to the other subject, men, she confesses, 'I want to take a break from the dating apps and all the dates. I've already been let down too many times. I've suffered too many disappointments.

'Tell me about it!', I think to myself.

'As a matter of fact, I have no interest in meeting anyone during this trip', she continues. 'I want this trip to be almost a watershed between the life I've led so far, and the beginning of my university chapter.'

University? This throws me a little. 'Excuse me, but how old are you?' I ask her.

'19.'

....

This song starts blasting in my mind at 10,000 decibels. It was in a Chicco advert a few decades ago, possibly before Pien's parents even met, and went something like, 'Oh little child, you have to go around so much to understand how the world works'.

The fact that at 19 she says she has already lost all hope of meeting someone, and wants to do that 'going around' she has to do by tuk-tuk, makes me a bit Pien-sive and brings me to the deep and delicate conclusion that she is totally out of her mind.

'19???????????' I ask her, with a shocked face and an incredulous tone of voice, to make sure I've heard right. She then asks me the same question, and rightly so.

'I'm 38', I answered, and she burst out laughing.

'Wow, you are twice my age!', and she continued laughing with gusto.

Man, I had not thought about it. Wow. And these situations happen often during my trips. Part of the reason is I am in good shape and am aging well (well, until now). Another part of the reason is that when we are travelling, we are all dressed in cheap clothes, wearing no makeup, maybe sleeping in the same hostel, and so we all assume we are in the same economic situation. Finally, it is also because when travelling you are so focused on enjoying everything that you really don't bother with judging things, people and events. I consider it quite unlikely, back home, that I would end up having dinner with a youngster fresh out of college (but never say never, especially knowing me).

This is probably what scares a lot of the people who ask me, 'Three months travelling on your own? But don't you get bored? Don't you tire of always being alone?'

The truth is, in my experience, it's actually really hard to stay on your own. Of course, when you want to, you can mind your own bloody beautiful business and keep to yourself. Equally, when you want to, it's 100 times easier to find company. We are all more open to sharing, not judging, enjoying the moment with whomever is there with us.

An emotion-packed day, then. And let's see what tomorrow has in store. Goodnight, Hikkaduwa!

Time it took me to get back on board the catamaran: 17 minutes
Times I laughed trying to get back on board: 6
Times the guy laughed: 0. Bless him, he was terrified
Purple starfish I saw while snorkelling: 5
Sharks I saw while snorkelling: 0 (thank God)
Wedding proposals received so far: 1
Day of the Indian Ocean tsunami: 26th December 2004
Time the Matara Express train was struck by the seaquake: around 9.30am
Matara Express passengers who survived: 150
Estimated global death toll of that tsunami: 230,210 people
State of my hair: liable to prosecution

DAY 8

'Sorry, I don't feel much like talking'
-Unawatuna and Hikkaduwa,
Monday 19th February 2018-

I know I'm on holiday and I should take things easier. Well, first of all, I'm not 'on holiday', but travelling, which are two very different things. Secondly, I'm one of the most relaxed people on our amazing Planet Earth, but this doesn't take away from the fact that bad organisation irritates me a loooot. Plus, something I've been promising myself for years is to stop depending on others, especially men.

When I woke up, I found a text from Shanaka: 'Hi, Madame Roby. I come to the beach with you. Where is your hostel?'

I sent him the name and address of my hostel, so he could reach me here, and we would leave together by bus, but didn't receive an answer for over 30 minutes, so in the end I told myself, 'Fuck it, I'm going on my own'.

I understand he may be busy, I understand he is from another culture, but I don't want to postpone my plans and maybe end up losing out on such a beautiful day just because he has a Sri Lankan sense of time. He can keep it. I have my London one, and I've waited for this trip for so long that even waiting an hour for someone feels like a crime. Especially as this somebody is not of great importance in my life. At least, not for now. So I text him, 'Okay, so I'm going to Unawatuna, and once I'm at the beach with some wi-fi I'll send you my position'. Yes, because, so far, they've had wi-fi everywhere. Many people are missing a few teeth, I've noticed that, but everybody has wi-fi.

Something not everybody has is common sense. Common sense is actually not that common. Or maybe this isn't the problem. I don't know. These Sri Lankan men throw me a little. When I got off the bus in Unawatuna, I started walking towards the beach, and this man came up beside me. Probably around 50 years old, he was wearing a beige, short-sleeved shirt, black linen trousers and black flip-flops. He was slender, with shiny eyes, not exactly a Colgate smile, and of course jet black hair.

'Where are you from?' by now seems to be the most popular icebreaker. Having obtained his answer, he moves quickly to the second most common question, as per the script, 'Are you married?' I'm an idiot and am still providing honest answers. Many women would quicken their pace, pretend not to hear or nip it in the bud immediately. Instead, I am intrigued by the cultural gap, and I'm curious to see how far he'll go. In response to my answer, he very seriously announces, 'If you want to marry me, I can think about it'.

....

Shouldn't I be the one thinking about it? I don't know, maybe I'm wrong, but it seems to me that you approach me, you offer me something I'm not remotely interested in, about which I was not thinking at all... I should be the one who, faced with such a proposal, takes the time to think about it. It's not like this was my idea.

Mah, I may be wrong. Anyway, in eight days I've already received my second wedding proposal. Both from very desirable candidates and based on unshakeable foundations of mutual knowledge and trust, by the way.

Unawatuna beach is pretty with all its palm trees stretching towards the sea. It's well equipped and serviced, with clean water and white sand. I've settled at a beach café, ordered my watermelon juice, now my daily treat, and sent my position to Shanaka. Not even half an hour after I texted him, here he is coming towards me, wearing black shorts and a Hawaiian-ish, short-sleeved shirt, apparently focused on assessing the environment around him. He made me smile because, once again, he had that 'Man of the world' walk that

I noticed at the restaurant on Saturday evening. Be yourself, please. Why are you acting like that? Or, for all I know, the fact he's with an older foreigner has him feeling full of himself (almost a tongue twister, this sentence!).

'Everything are ok?' he asks me. I smile at his almost record breaking ability to make a mistake in a three-word sentence. By the way, this seems to be his favourite expression, and even though I've corrected him five times already, he doesn't seem interested in getting it right.

We get a juice together, he insists on paying once again, and then we finally take some photos together because we have none so far.

'At 1.30pm I have to go. Work called me. I must go back to Mount Lavinia. I start at 6pm', he tells me, between sucks on the straw.

What? 'I don't understand, Shanaka. You are going away in half an hour? But if you knew that you had to go away by 1.30pm, why did you spend two hours on that hot and dusty bus to come here for such a short time?'

'I want see you', he answers.

Like that. There is no easier answer.

The first comment which pops up in my mind is, 'Oh, *piccolino*, how lovely…'

And, immediately afterwards, others bubble up quite assertively. I know many women fall for the exotic dating game. Sure, these men throw a little tenderness and sweet words our way, practices which are almost gone in our Western world. And Sri Lankan men are handsome, with beautiful complexions, dark eyes, captivating smiles (when they have all their teeth). Some of them even have a hint of muscular definition on their slender frames, like Shanaka. Without resorting to the usual sarcastic joke about what really motivates them, I realise that I am judging a Sri Lankan gesture by London standards. 'A man travels two hours by bus to see me? Wow, he's really interested and really cares for me.'

I'm not saying this is not necessarily true. I'm only saying, and I am so sure about this, that two hours to him are nothing. Time doesn't have the same value that it has for me. I'd be the first to think 953 times before setting off on a two-hour journey to see someone for half an hour only. And by the way, I don't think I've ever done such a thing, because it is completely incompatible with my prudent sense of time management (Roby, the ice-hearted woman). So yes, a nice gesture, but I have to keep in mind that here I'm in a totally different culture, and acts of love can be so culturally specific.

For example, let's say I fancy a coconut. In Sri Lanka, a man would climb on a tree (I have a feeling that many of them do it regularly), grab one and offer it to me as soon as he gets down. In London, a man has to go out, and maybe it's raining and even cold. He has to go to a specific shop where he knows he can find coconuts, and probably has to take a few means of transport to get there. The gesture is the same, but the effort required is different. So there you go, Roby. Don't be blinded by details, and always try to put things in context.

'Okay, I understand. Thanks for coming for such a short time.'

I put aside the slight disappointment I'm feeling. I had imagined a different day, where we would swim together and walk along the beach or, indeed, where he would show me how quickly he can climb a tree. Here we go again. Expectations, those bastards...

'Where do you go tomorrow? If you stay in Hikka, maybe I can come back in the evening', he tries to suggest. But no, it's time for me to continue my journey southwards. Other beaches, other people, other adventures are waiting for me.

'No, tomorrow I'm going to Mirissa... So is this the last time we see each other?'

'No, I try to see you before you leave. You leave from Negombo, yes?' he asks me, with a sudden organisational lucidity that surprises me.

'Yes, of course, it's the only airport.'

'So I come to Negombo to see you.'

'Okay, we'll see about this later. Or, instead of staying in Negombo, I could stay again in Mount Lavinia. It's not that far from the airport', I continue. I could, but then again let's see. Let's see what happens in the next three weeks.

'We spent many beautiful moments together, Madame Roby. I hope you don't meet other local men, or I am jealous' (hooray for the honesty). Strangely, he doesn't seem to object to my going with men of other nationalities, almost as if he couldn't do anything about it.

Kind of cute, this competition with the other Sri Lankan men.

Two small tears roll down my cheeks, Shanaka's purity and simplicity are so... refreshing. For 12 years, I've been living in a nation of emotionally challenged people who can most of the times only open up once they are under the influence of alcohol and then, most of the time, return promptly to their shells when sober. Apparently, talking about one's feelings is not in the top 95 things that children are taught in England. Here, instead, I have a guy who sits on a bus for two hours just to see me and say goodbye, and who tells me frankly about his jealousy and how beautiful it was to meet me.

I wiped one of my tears with a fingertip and gently pressed it on his hand, saying, 'This gift is for you'.

Hahaha, now that I'm writing it, it makes me laugh. So cheesy! You wouldn't even find this on a Baci Perugina chocolate wrapper. But it's as if, faced with all his feelings, quietly laid out on the table, it seems natural to adopt his tooth-decay-inducing romanticism.

'I want to make a gift for you before you leave', he announces, with this broad smile, an explosion of whiteness and perfect teeth.

'No, Shanaka, I don't want you to spend more money for me. Already, the time we've spent together was the best of gifts.'

'No, I do a gift anyway. I want', he insists.

Having understood a bit about how he is, and that trying to dissuade him would be a waste of breath, I accept, but my practical voice chimes in with, 'Okay, but it can't be expensive, heavy or big, because I would have to carry it around for 73 days'.

And so he goes away, with a chaste, quick kiss because we are in public, and maybe even that much affection amounts to a mini scandal, especially between a local man and a white woman. I look at him walking away in that bouncy, slightly self-conscious way. He turns towards me, smiles and passes a finger along his eyebrows as if to say goodbye.

I think he's watched a few too many boyband music videos.

I'm left with a bit of sadness and poetry inside. I've only been travelling a week, and it seems that so many important things have already happened. On my previous trips, changing hostels and cities almost every day, or at least every two or three, it was hard to truly connect with anyone beyond a simple dinner or a drink together. With Shanaka, I have created some memories that I know will make me smile with tenderness. And I wonder how long I will have to wait before meeting somebody else, be it a man or a woman, with whom I can feel a bit at home. *Mah*, Universe, I trust You. You've been amazing so far, thank You.

This mini depression lasted for about half an hour. I've made myself take things as they come, without forcing anything. Will we see each other again? If so, fabulous. Will we never see each other again? I've already received more than I could have imagined, only a week since my arrival. No attachments and no expectations, Roby. And make sure, above all, not to fall into the old pattern you've been following for years, where your moods and happiness depend on men.

I'm there giving myself this wise self-persuasion speech, when a beggar leaps towards me. He is basically sitting on the sand and pushing himself forward with his arms, and I understand why when I see his feet, which are almost non-existent, as though they stopped growing when he was still a baby and sort of turned in on themselves. He wears flip-flops on his hands to keep them clean and, especially, to stop them burning when the sand is too hot. To make his 'steps' even more difficult, he is carrying a basket in his lap, full of incense sticks. I buy a packet from him, thinking I could maybe give it to Shanaka. Lightweight and practical, albeit probably not very original. I then start talking with the beggar and, after a while, still touched by what I saw yesterday, I asked him to tell me about the tsunami, where he was when the waves hit the beach.

While I was in Cambodia, I asked many local people to tell me about Pol Pot, the Khmer Rouge and the genocide they committed. I remember an English guy telling me he found my questions insensitive and unfair, as I was making people relive such horrible memories just to satisfy my curiosity. Well... points of view. There are some who find talking cathartic, like me, for example. Indeed, had I survived something like that, I would want to talk about it as much as possible to as many people as possible, so as to prevent it happening again. Here in Sri Lanka, I have the chance to hear first-hand stories about an event that I only saw on TV, the images of which made me cry so much and for so long. Curiosity? Yes, but not superficiality.

'When I saw the first wave arriving, I was near the beach with a friend who was working on his boat. He picked me up and put me on his shoulders and started to run as fast as he could. We were lucky, very lucky.' He doesn't offer any other details, and I don't ask for them. Maybe someone else will provide them another time. 'I don't want to beg for money, that's why I go around selling stuff', he continues, pointing at the basket in his lap.

'Do you have a cigarette?' he asks, and I offer him one, lighting one for myself. He tells me about his life, which is hard, but he doesn't complain about it, and inside me, an emotional tornado is whirling. Sadness, because he clearly doesn't have an easy life. Anger, because the world is so unfair. Admiration, because I have no idea if I could stay that positive were I in his shoes. Shoes which he can't even wear, given the state of his feet. Shame, because we Westerners ruin our lives over such bullshit, unaware of how immensely lucky we are. A sense of universal brotherhood, which I always feel towards the poor. The desire to help, somehow, even if only by listening and smiling, sharing a moment like smoking a cigarette together.

'Thanks for the cigarette. I go and sell my stuff', he says by way of farewell after talking with me for ten minutes. I buy another packet of incense sticks, even though I don't exactly know what I'll do with them, and give him three more cigarettes and some money.

'God bless you', he says, with a somewhat gap-toothed smile.

'God has already blessed me', I think. 'God bless you, too. Thank you. Good luck', I smile back.

Back at the hostel, I join the travellers sitting outside on the porch, including the now ever-present poor man's Ryan Gosling. Once again, bless him, he had no clean T-shirts to wear. The conversation moved from one subject to another before settling on meditation, specifically the silent Vipassana meditation retreats I have heard about a few times already. That November afternoon I spent with Paola enjoying an enormous cup of ice-cream, the very day I told her about my decision to go on a three-month trip, we were talking about this. She has done two such retreats and was suggesting I try it, 'Because yes, Roby, putting your life on hold and going to the other side of the world to put some distance between you and your problems is a great solution, but not always easy to do. With this kind of meditation, instead, you learn to be less affected by everything. You learn to stay more centred and grounded, seeing and experiencing everything with more detachment'.

Two years ago, while in Vietnam, I met a Canadian girl, Michelle, who had just come out of a silent Vipassana meditation retreat, and she was telling me that she would recommend it to everyone. 'Having ten days to spend with oneself in such a brutal way, disconnected from the whole world, is basically a real privilege', I remember her telling me. I wonder if it was during those ten days sitting with her own thoughts that Michelle had a glimpse of the mega company she would go on to create, back to Montreal, and which I sense will become a million-dollar success. Kind of weird to think that meditating silently for ten days would give you the idea of setting up Bellesa, the first online porn platform especially for women. Who knows what ideas I might come up with, if I were to have such an experience?

I'm there, sitting in the garden with this bunch of people, sharing my opinion on this meditation retreat, which is that it fits in perfectly with the overall travelling. Paola did her two in England–Herefordshire if I'm not mistaken–while I would envision having such an… exotic and strange experience when you are also physically removed from your everyday life. After you've been on the road a while, or at least it's always been like this for me, you sort of enter 'the zone': a state of heightened mental presence, where you are fully focused on the moment and only asking yourself what you want to do in the next few hours. All the worries associated with what you've left at home, be it your work, house, family or friends, become so much smaller. You start putting so many things in perspective and realise how much we overcomplicate our lives.

Exactly.

One of the biggest lessons I've learnt from travelling is that life is inherently so simple. It is very simple indeed, because at the end of the day you just need to satisfy your primary needs and be able to enjoy the small things. The backpack I've taken on previous trips, my faithful travel companion on night buses, dusty tuk-tuks, overcrowded trains and wherever else I dragged it, silently reminds me that we only need 10kg of stuff to experience months of amazing adventures. A few old things to wear, some books, plenty of Imodium, a bikini, trainers, flip-flops, a sleeping bag et voilà.

'It's complicated', we love to say. Actually, others love to say, because that phrase really annoys the shit out of me. It's not the situation that's complicated. You are the one who wants to see it as complicated. And the more we tell ourselves that it's complicated, the more we complicate it, for Choose Your Words Carefully's sake.

I know that when we are travelling we are way more open to introspection, to finding messages here and there scattered on our path. We are more prepared for it. And we have more time for new experiences. Since we have already physically come so far from our everyday normality, why not take one extra step out of our comfort zones?

I throw myself into this loooooooooooong conversation about silent meditation retreats, and everybody is quite fascinated. Some have already heard about Vipassana meditation, others think it's a crazy thing to do and they could never ever do it, others know someone who did it and tell us what they've heard.

I then leave the garden and go back to my room, and there's a new and very cute guy under my bed. That is, we're sharing a bunk bed, and I'm sleeping above. Not in a horror movie kind of way, where the woman goes to bed and, in the middle of the night, an evil shadow creeps out from under her bed.

'Hi, welcome. Where are you from?' I start the conversation. How easy it is to start talking with anybody when you are travelling!

'I'm Swiss. You have to excuse me, but I don't feel much like talking. I've just come from a silent Vipassana meditation retreat in Kathmandu, and I'm still in my own world a bit.'

....

Va beh, Universo. Okay, Universe. Why don't You just come out and say it?

Actually, there's no need.

This coincidence is just too huge to ignore.

Can you believe that outside in the garden we were talking at length about quite an unusual and intense experience, and twenty minutes later, under my very own bed, a guy appears who has just been through it?

Going against this is pointless. Here, it's really a matter of going with the flow and, even better, going with the soul, warmly embracing what has been put on my path for a reason. Come to think of it, I could do it in Kathmandu, as well, given that I might be tired towards the end of my trip. Staying in one place for a few days, meditating and pondering all the things I will have seen and done over the previous months seems like a beautiful way to close the circle before going back to London. Like taking stock of the situation. Fuck me, that's an awful lot of stock I'll be taking, meditating for ten hours a day.

'Wow, I was just talking about this with the guys outside! How was it for you?'

'Oh, it was very hard. Some days I just wanted to quit. I've lost a few kilos, but, sure, I've learnt not to be so emotionally affected by things. Anyway, I think that the real benefits will be more long term. I can't really tell now. But one thing is weird: I thought I would be so happy to be able to talk again, after ten days of silence, but it's not the case. I feel as if I'm in a bubble, a bit detached from everything.'

Needless to say, I get online, and would you believe it? (Totally.) There are still some places available for women at the Vipassana retreat in Kathmandu when I will be there in April.

Good. I'm enrolled. As talk-show host Renzo Arbore said in an Italian beer ad from the '80s, before raising his glass to enjoy a refreshing sip, 'Meditate, people. Meditate'.

Wow. Who knew, this afternoon at the beach, that I would be taking such an important step right afterwards? This is in fact the first thing I have planned, the first fixed point around which my Nepalese experience will unfurl. And this is exactly what I was hoping for, which my friends found so strange as they listened, incredulous, about my lack of plans for this trip. 'Things will turn up on their own. No need for me to stress myself out with research. You just have to pay attention to the signs and be open to adventure. No attachments, no plans.'

When I went back out into the garden, I found this Dutch guy Jorge, who was celebrating his 500th day on the road. Well, that would be too much for me. Five hundred days travelling... A year and a half away from home. Apart from the fact that travelling wears me out physically, I also have beautiful things to go back to. I'm not trying to escape my life.

Well, maybe I am, but only temporarily.

Jorge was telling me about all the countries he's seen, when some guys from a nearby hostel came to tell us they had bought too much food for a barbecue and ask whether we wanted to join them and share the cost. Barbecue? Of course I want to join you!

In this other hostel, we found the usual range of dreadlock dudes, yoga freaks, highbrows with their noses in books, keeping a bit to themselves, the ever-present guitar player and some other characters less easy to categorise. And I think I belong in this last group. A bit hippy, but grounded and practical. A bit spiritual, but just a beginner. A backpacker, who might be a bit old to still be backpacking (but who gives a shit?)

Sitting next to me at the table was this English guy who works as a counsellor for people with mental health issues. He was telling me that his dream would be to open a café where people with different sorts of problems can work, just turning up when they want, without any stress. A sweet idea, but probably not the best in terms of staff management and shift organisation, I'd say.

Tomorrow I continue onwards to my next stop, Mirissa. More sun, sea and sand, and hopefully another beach party.

Dates of my upcoming silent Vipassana meditation retreat: 14th–25th April 2018
Hours of daily meditation on a Vipassana retreat: 12
Total hours I've meditated in my life so far: around 40
Movie-industry job offers received so far by the poor man's Ryan Gosling: 0
Days on the road for Jorge: 500
Days on the road for me: 8
Mosquito bites so far: 2
People with whom I talked about *Shantaram* at the barbecue dinner: 2
Year *Shantaram* was published: 2003
Rats or mice I've seen so far: 0
T-shirts or tank tops I've seen so far on the poor man's Ryan Gosling: 0

DAY 9
'This is from the DJ'
-Mirissa, Tuesday 20th February 2018-

I'm writing from a teeny-tiny bedroom, which nevertheless comes with a very loooooong bathroom. In Mirissa, I ended up at the Sandula Homestay, and I'm the only guest. Basically it's the house of a family with two children, and the parents (although the name suggests the mastermind is the mother) have separated the part of the house they live in with a curtain, renting out the little bedroom immediately to the right of the entrance. Sandula, the mother, must be a lot younger than me, and is a very smiley, interested woman, whom I liked immediately. She asked me about everything, from my job, to my family, to the weather in London, to the cost of living in England, to my travel plans, etc. I like curiosity in people; it shows an active mind and an engaged spirit.

But let's start from the beginning. I arrived in Mirissa by bus, and thank God I found a direct one from Hikkaduwa, which cost me the beautiful sum of 70 rupees, around 30 pence. I know I am repeating myself, but I have to reiterate this: public transport in Sri Lanka costs next to nothing! So far I've been using a technique I'm calling the 'Mary and Joseph': I basically arrive at a place, pick up my backpack and start going around asking if there's a room and how much it is.

I have friends who organise everything down to the smallest detail, even creating Excel spreadsheets with the addresses and phone numbers of the hotels they have booked weeks in advance, adding transport timetables for travelling from one city to another, finally reserving a column for notes on evening shows or entertainment.

Honestly, for me, that's where organisation borders on neurotic and paranoid. To be fair, a few years ago I was a bit like them, in the sense that I too would book the accommodation in advance, but now I know that you always find something, and often cheaper than what you'd find online, especially as, once you are there, you can always haggle a bit.

I walked down a lane brimming with signs for hostels and restaurants, a clear indication that we are entering *Backpackerland*, and after asking in four places I found a nice big single room with a bathroom all to myself for 1,100 rupees, around five pounds. I was about to open my backpack and arrange my stuff when the owner came back, saying that he had made a mistake and the room was already booked through Booking.com, and so he was going to take me to his friend's homestay instead.

Okay, no problem. And that's how I came to Sandula Homestay, half hidden down a narrow lane. Who knows? Maybe there is a precise reason why I had to end up in this room, rather than the one I was starting to settle in to.

I spent some time talking with Sandula and her eldest son, Thiranya, who is 13 years old and spent the whole time standing next to her, silent. He studies English at school, but he is very shy, bless him, so it was difficult to get a word out of him. His mum explained that he was going to have a dictation exam at school in a few days, and she has asked me if I could maybe help him a little. Of course, I couldn't ask for more! So we arranged to meet up in the evening, in that very living room, to practise some dictation. And then off I went to see Mirissa.

And Mirissa is a dream! I fell in love with it immediately, at first sight. The beach is long and wide, and the sand is light coloured. About halfway along it stretches out into the sea, making a point, before sweeping back to form another long beach. These two crescent shaped beaches, so clearly separated from each other, are connected by a strip of sand, opposite which is a small hilly island that you can climb to the top of to admire Mirissa from a height. The intense blue of the sea, in its various degrees of transparency, the gold of the sand, the green explosion of the palm trees scattered along the beach that, thank God, offer some protection from the scorching sun...

It happens sometimes that you immediately get a good feeling about a place. The initial impression. You set eyes on a landscape for the first time, and you just know that you like it. Love at first sight doesn't only happen with hhhhhhot guys.

It happened to me with Capri, for example. Even from the boat, approaching the island, I felt serious joy building up inside me. Then, once I took the cable car to the main square on top of the hill, my heart just opened up wide. It felt like being in a movie. There were people everywhere on that May morning, sitting at café tables, sipping their cappuccinos in peace while reading a good book or enjoying a friendly chat. At the small white church nearby, several jubilant women in fancy hats gave it away that the bride and groom, who'd just come out to much applause, were foreigners. And they were so right. What better place to get married? Wherever I looked was sun, sea, flowers and beauty.

What really conquered my heart in Mirissa is this tiny tidal island, which is only accessible at low tide, and from which you can gaze back on the opposite shoreline. Something quite unusual for me. It's almost like climbing up a castle made of soil, and, once at the top, you either look out to sea, in front of you, or back at the mainland. Something I don't remember seeing in other places.

On top of that, as if I hadn't been open enough about my feelings already and told Mirissa how much I like her, this seaside town bewitches me with my first truly spectacular Sri Lankan sunset. An orgy of pink, orange, red and stretching shadows. A priceless display that leaves me sitting there, admiring it in stunned silence, feeling immensely lucky.

Little by little, the beach livens up and the evening transformation begins. Whole groups of friends, families or couples flock to the beach, inaugurating the evening with a cold beer. The cosy seafront restaurants put whole crates of fish out on display, so you can choose which ones you want. The sand quickly fills up with little tables, each one with its own candle. I feel a bit sorry that I don't have anyone with whom to sit and enjoy this evening, which is set to be a good one. At the homestay, by the way, it's not even possible to meet anyone, given that I occupy the only available room. I consider sitting down on my own, and maybe one thing will lead to another and someone will ask me to join them (or, more likely, I will start talking with the people sitting at the next table), but then I decide to go back to the homestay and take a shower. The feeling of, 'Oh, what a shame, it would be lovely to have someone to share this moment with' only lasts a minute, anyway, and in the meantime music from all the restaurants starts filling the air.

Yes! Music! Because Mirissa is like a beautiful flower standing proudly with its straight stem, impeccable and strong, emanating perfume, charming in its bright colours, almost telling you, 'Oh, you thought pretty petals were all I had to offer? No, I also give out this incredible fragrance, especially at night. Oh, you thought I would only last a few days? No, I can keep this up for weeks, if I want. If you cannot handle all this beauty, it's your problem'.

Which, by the way, is what I should have learnt to say years ago to all those men who told me I was 'too much': 'You are too honest, too intense, you give too much, and you do it too quickly, you do too many things, who can keep up with you? You love too much, you open up too much and too soon, you are just too much! Who can handle you?'

It took me years, and many tears, to understand that the problem was not mine, but theirs. The point is that I wasn't too much for them, but rather they were too little for me. If you are not able to handle all these beautiful things, that's your problem. Step aside, thank you, to make way for those who won't be afraid, who won't feel inferior and will instead say, 'Wow! This lady intrigues me big time'.

Anyway, we were talking about Mirissa. Not only does it have this really beautiful beach, not only does it offer sunsets that are ablaze with poetry, not only does it come with all these seafront restaurants where, with your grilled fish and the waves in the background, you can tell yourself that life really is special, but Mirissa also hosts my beloved beach parties! Yes! Tonight we're going to dance!

I went home and took a shower in that bathroom which could be a mini football field, and then I spent an hour doing dictation practice with Thiranya, who is actually quite good. He reminded me a lot of myself at his age, and how much I wanted to get good marks at school to make my parents proud. When I corrected the dictation and praised him for all the words he spelled right, I could see his eyes light up with that little satisfaction that his shyness allowed him to show. What I liked even more is that his mum, Sandula, wanted to take part in the dictation exercise to see how her English was and learn something new.

This is something I've seen a lot in Asia, especially in Cambodia. People's desire to learn, taking advantage of any possible resource to do so, especially us travellers. I still think back with so much affection to my tuk-tuk driver in Seam Reap, whom I had hired for three days to take me around that triumph of trees and temples that is Angkor Wat. While I was visiting the temples, he would stay in his tuk-tuk and do some English homework, which I would then correct while he was driving me to the next temple. Not to mention that boy in Battabang, Cambodia, who came to knock on my hotel room door at 10pm, leaving me quite perplexed because I clearly had no idea who it could be at that time. I had arrived at the hotel that same afternoon, so I didn't know anybody. When I opened the door, there was this guy I had seen working at reception. He passed me his notebook, saying, 'You check, please, madam?'

After all, most of these people haven't had the chance to go to school for long and, even if they have, they have studied in their language and are well aware that English is somehow key to survival.

I told Thiranya and his mum Sandula to rewrite every word they misspelt five times, as I used to do myself and which always proved very useful (#veryeightiesteachingechniques), and then I headed to the beach for the long-awaited beach party. Sandula wanted to know

135

what time I'd be back because, unfortunately, and this is the only downside to this homestay, they cannot give me a spare key, which means that when I get back home I'll have to ring the bell and wake them up. It's a bit of a drag, having to depend on them, plus the unavoidable feeling of being checked up on. I don't think I'll stay out that late anyway, given that tomorrow morning my alarm clock goes off at dawn.

Indeed, because I haven't said everything about Mirissa. Going back to my flower simile from earlier, this enchanting little town would say, 'Not only do I have this hyper-cool little island, not only do I show you amazing sunsets that you will revisit with your eyes closed for years to come, not only do I throw fabulous beach parties every evening, but... you also get to see blue whales!'

Yes! Mirissa is the best spot for seeing these giants of the sea, 30 metres and 200 tonnes of pure majesty. This is the main reason people come to Mirissa. Wherever you go, they sell tickets for blue whale tours, and I've bought mine from Sandula. Her husband will take me by tuk-tuk to the harbour tomorrow morning, where the boat departs from.

So, as I was saying, I don't think I'll be home late, but you never know what can happen at a beach party...

Basically, in Mirissa, there is a beach party every evening, but always at a different venue. Since these venues are all on the beach, however, it's quite easy to figure out where to go. You just have to follow the music, as well as the huge beams of light splitting the night. On Tuesday night the beach party is at this venue right at the end of the beach, to the right, and when I arrive there is already a small crowd, even if only a few are actually on the dance floor. I immediately take the plunge and start dancing, since the music is gorgeous. Can you believe these DJs in Mirissa? They could work at the Ministry of Sound if they came to London! The house music is blasting and gaining momentum, and I start exchanging looks with the DJ, but simply because he is wearing a baseball hat. What with it being dark, and my being quite far away from him, plus the fact that I'm half bat, in terms of eyesight, I can't really see his face, but I instinctively like men in baseball caps. They're a bit like stilettoes for some men if we want to go for a cliche. I see a baseball cap, and I immediately think the guy is cool, sporty, relaxed, easy going, genuine, adventurous.

Also, I've always been intrigued by DJs. They have their own charm. DJs stand there like preachers, in front of their faithful followers, devoted to house music, and they take them on a trip for a few hours, elevating and animating them, giving them strength. Sure, quite often it's the drugs that elevate, animate and give them strength and energy, but music plays its part, too. And anyway, if I had to guess, I wouldn't say there are many drugs going around at this beach party.

I'm there, either exchanging glances with the DJ or closing my eyes and surrendering to the music. I want to be right inside those notes, where there is so much life, a moment brimming with its own presence. Eckhart Tolle, how am I doing? Were you also referring to this when you spoke about the power of now and being fully in the moment you are experiencing?

When I open my eyes, the DJ salutes me, touching his baseball cap and then pointing his finger at me, as if to say, 'Dance, baby, dance!'

I smile back at him, give him a thumbs up, and go back *in the zone.* In one of my previous lives, I must have been a podium dancer, since dancing really takes me to some wonderful places. I am gently called back to this world by a light touch on the arm. I open my eyes, and there's a guy with a beer in his hand. I had seen him earlier taking care of the lights. 'This is from the DJ', he tells me with a big, pretty smile. Ohhhhhhhhhhhhhh, how sweet!

And also, 'Ohhhhhhhh, now I have to drink this crappy beer that I don't even like'.

I look at the DJ, touch my heart with my hand (my heart, not my left breast, that would have been a different message) and raise the bottle towards him. I know right from the start that I won't be able to finish it. Firstly, I don't like beer and secondly, it's like a half-litre bottle, so much for puny London measures! I dance and I sip some beer, and I think back to the person who last bought me a drink. Never mind Shanaka, I mean in my world. Was it maybe Nick, the guy who will have to go to prison in a few months, having been caught with his little MDMA home laboratory? Possibly, although he bought me a drink in a pub, and I paid for the second round. No, I don't think I've been in this situation before, where I am happily minding my own business, and the waiter (or the lighting engineer) comes over and tells me, like in the movies, 'This is from that guy over there'. It's also true that I'd need to have a proper think about this, because I have over 20 years of flirting behind me, and that's a lot of material to go through. Anyway, it doesn't matter.

I also wonder whether accepting the beer makes me look like a bitch, given that I cannot stay long. What was I supposed to do, not to accept it? I would have looked like an even bigger bitch. Ah, the unknown dilemmas of a sensitive soul, for Paranoia's sake!

At 1am I really had to go. I went over to the DJ, who maybe read those steps as the beginning of an explosive night of fireworks.

'I'm sorry, I have to go now, but thank you so much for the beer. You have been so kind. It's still half full, so please finish it. Toast to my health. I can't drink anymore.'

'No, come on. Stay a bit longer.'

'No, tomorrow morning I'm going whale watching. I have to wake up in four hours, basically', I explained. He then took my hand. First he kissed it, then he said goodbye by gently squeezing it and intertwining his fingers with mine. Once again, can you believe these Sri Lankan men?

Walking back home along that dark beach I was initially quite alert because it was pretty late, after all, and I don't know the place at all. However, I soon relaxed because I saw that I only had the black and peaceful sea around me, a few couples sitting a little further up the beach, smoking their spliffs quietly, and just an infinity of stars to crown our thoughts. Once more, I felt a small pang in my heart, wishing for someone to share that incredible starry sky with, sitting on the sand and listening to the sea's whisper, laughing and talking, but then I caught myself. No attachment. Stop it with these 'It would be so nice if...' ideas. Let it go. Let all these expectations fade away, as they diminish what is in front of you, which is already a lot and so amazing.

Today has really been a top, top day. Mirissa has bewitched me. I'm going to bed happy, and at 6am tomorrow (ehm... today... ehm... in a few hours, for Blue Whale's sake) I have to wake up. Despite the initial desire to sleep for longer, I already know I'll wake up all excited. Let's hope I see one!

Couples smoking a spliff on the beach: 5
DJ's height: around 170cm
Writing on the DJ's baseball cap: Adidas
Percentage of local people at the beach party: 30%
Companies organising the blue whale boat tours in Mirissa: countless
Mistakes made by Thiranya in his dictation: 7
Mistakes made by Sandula in her dictation: 5
Level of appreciation I'm receiving from local men: medium to high
Shades of orange and red in Mirissa's sunset: too many to count
Biscuits eaten so far: 0
Teas drunk so far: 15

DAY 10
'But I never talk about me, only about whales'
(or 'I've never eaten out')
-Mirissa, Wednesday 21st February 2018-

What. A. Strange. Day.

And I add: it's a crazy world.

Wow! Today I have so much to tell you! So, the alarm clock went off at 6am, and I travelled to the other side of Mirissa by tuk-tuk to get to the 'Raja and the Whales' ticket office. Not only did Sandula sell me the ticket promising me that they offered one of the best boat tours ever, but my Lonely Planet Bible seems to be of the same opinion. When I arrived there were already a lot of people, and the staff gave us all a pill to prevent sea sickness, given that the weather forecast said it might be a bit rough today. My stomach is quite strong. Not even when I was caught in the perfect storm, going to Albania by boat, did I vomit. I was green in the face and crawling along on my elbows, but I didn't vomit.

The boat is quite big, and I settle on one side. We leave the harbour, and the staff, all guys in light blue 'Raja and the Whales' polo shirts, immediately set to work. They start running up and down, in and out of the mini kitchen, in order to provide all the passengers with biscuits and coffee, given that the ticket includes all meals. Right when the sunrise is exploding silently in front of me, I receive a nice dish full of fruit to complete my breakfast. Definitely a good beginning. The boat sails on towards the open sea, and they explain that whale sightings can happen at different distances from shore, so they never know how long the boat tour will be. One of the staff members, whose gorgeous skin tone goes particularly well with

140

his light blue polo shirt, starts telling us random facts about whales. Although he talks in a slightly automatic way (I would too if I had to say the same things every day), he does display some passion for the topic. 'The blue whale is the largest animal ever known to have lived on Earth. These magnificent marine mammals rule the oceans, at up to 100 feet long, which corresponds more or less to three buses in a row, just to give you an idea. Living in water, where they are not subject to gravity, they can grow far larger than animals on dry land, whose skeletons have to bear their weight. A blue whale can remain underwater up to 11–12 minutes before resurfacing to breathe. Gestation lasts from ten to 12 months, and at birth a calf can already measure up to seven metres. Every day a calf drinks around 200 litres of its mother's milk, putting on between 3.5kg and 5kg per hour and growing up to 90kg a day'.

Astonishing data. He reels it all off so quickly, that I can't even digest it properly. A calf can grow up to 5kg per hour? And there's me worrying after eating a lot at dinner! Only now that I'm writing it all down am I being properly blown away. In fact, the information that stuns me most is yet to come.

Looking around at each one of us, standing in a circle around him, the whale expert continues, 'It's possible to measure a blue whale's age by its layers of earwax.'

....

See what I mean? Not only 'What?????' but also 'Blue whales have ears?????'

After a few more explanations, and some good chats with the other passengers thrown in, it's time for a sausage sandwich, and I have to admit that this service is way better than I expected. The sun has now started to burn, and thank God I had the foresight to bring a long-sleeved top with me, otherwise after a day on the open sea I would be burned to a crisp and delirious with sunstroke. The wind is obviously strong, and to keep my hair from becoming even more of an eyesore, I've protected it under a wide hairband. Sunglasses, factor-50 sun cream all over my face, flattened hair... Well, let's say I've been more gorgeous in 85% of my other life experiences.

But the whales won't care, and the others on the boat are either couples or elderly people, with whom I happily exchange travel anecdotes, but everything stops there.

Around 11am we catch sight of several other boats, all stationary and almost forming a circle. If they have all stopped there, it means that they've spotted a whale. So we stop too. And here it comes, out of the blue (literally!). The queen of the sea surfaces, amidst excited shrieks and stupefied gasps, and with hundreds of cameras and mobiles pointed her way from the surrounding boats. She blows out some water, heads back into the depths and, with her tail following suit, finally disappears.

What a feeling.

I've seen the largest mammal alive, a few metres away from me. How many times have I seen that tail beating the water and then disappearing into the sea on TV? And when I boarded my flight one week ago I hadn't the faintest idea that a few days later I would be witnessing the exhilarating sight myself.

The whole amazing event repeated itself seven times. Basically, when the whale goes down it is understood that it will surface again around ten minutes later to breathe, and so the boats move forward trying to guess the whale's course. The boats were usually right, but twice the whale came up quite far from the spot they had all sped to. Around ten minutes after the dive, all the boats engines are switched off, and we wait and see which boat will be the first to spot the whale.

Each time, pure magnificence.

Nature moves me to tears. It is so majestic, so perfect. I read somewhere that human beings are the only species to have declined as it evolved, losing certain physical abilities, slowing down its metabolism, etc. Also, in a spiritual podcast, they were pointing out that human beings are the only imperfect species on the planet: we are the only species that lies, cheats and hurts others for the sadistic pleasure of seeing people suffer. And right there, in the middle of the sea, with the blue whale's water plume and tail still imprinted on my retinas, I felt this so intensely.

Nature is perfect.

So perfect that it also sent us some playful dolphins, a nice big school that performed leaps and even serenaded us with chittering noises. Then, on the way back to the harbour, we met a large, solitary sea turtle, who was floating peacefully, minding her own business in that big blue expanse.

The whale expert starts giving us some more information. On the one hand, I am carefully listening to what he is saying, on the other I'm thinking that, no, he is not bad at all. When he smiles, his white teeth emphasise his beautiful deep brown complexion, and through the sleeves of his polo shirt, I catch a glimpse of biceps definition, which always suits any man so well. Although 'man' is a big word because I don't think he is even 30. Anyway, I take a photo of him, more as a joke than to flirt. Honestly, I feel like a walking toilet and I'm crappily dressed. I feel like shit and look like it too. I've only slept four hours, I am not wearing any make up, my face is all greasy and there are probably still smears of sun cream I haven't rubbed in. I am basically dressed like a handyman, and my hair has been admitted on the boat by God's grace alone. The idea that this guy could somehow find me attractive is not even a physical possibility, for me. And if a woman is feeling like this, it's really hard for her to flirt, so I was seriously only joking.

He sees that I've taken a photo of him and smiles at me. He then carries on with his explanations, which unfortunately I cannot hear because there is too much wind, and I am far away from him. So, I have the bright idea of taking another picture, and he gives me a thumbs up.

Once he finishes talking, I go over and ask him if he can basically repeat everything he's just said, given that I couldn't hear him, and so Chamath (that's his name) gives me a private lesson on the queen of the sea. A French couple joins us and, like me, they listen to Chamath eagerly. I then start asking him questions about his job. 'What a strange job you do! Do you like it?'

'Yes, I like it a lot. I love whales.'

'So do you wake up every day at dawn?'

'Yes, we need to be on the boat by 5am to start preparing everything for the passengers' arrival. But it's not a problem for me, I got used to it, and also before working for Raja I was a sailor. I like this life. My dream is to go to New Zealand, my favourite country.'

That's a bit weird. 'But have you been there before?' I inquire.

'No, I've never travelled outside Sri Lanka.'

'So how can you know that it's your favourite country, if you have never seen it, and you haven't seen any other countries?' I ask, trying to understand.

He answers me calmly, 'Because they have cheese and snow'.

....

They sound like two good reasons.

Again: and they say *I'm* out of my mind.

Chamath's oddities continue. 'Every morning I brush my teeth for around 20 minutes (#howtowipeoutyourgumsintwoyears), and I change toothbrush every five days. I really love brushing my teeth.'

....

Okay, good for you, even if this doesn't seem to me like a normal topic of conversation, and I don't even think brushing your teeth that much is healthy.

We talk a bit more, with the French couple still there with us. He tells us that he has a sister, what job his parents do, and that he loves the sea. Then, slightly out of context, Chamath drops the fact that he has never had a girlfriend and that he is 25 years old.

'What do you do when we go back to the harbour?' he asks me, slightly embarrassing me in front of the French couple.

Can you believe these Sri Lankan men? They continue to surprise me. In a week I've received more direct proposals from local men here than in all my months in Vietnam, India, Laos, Cambodia, Malaysia and Thailand put together. I tell him that I'd like to go to the Secret Beach, a little tucked-away beach that Sandula recommended.

'Oh, yes, it's very beautiful. Can I come with you?'

'Well, it's not my private beach. Of course you can join me.'

'Do you want more food?' he then offers, and indeed I'd love another slice of chocolate cake. It's the first real cake I've had in ten days! Said and done. Not only does he bring me a double portion of cake, but also another dish full of fruit. I look around to see if everybody is getting their fruit, as an afternoon snack, given that it's almost 3pm. No one is, so I ask the French couple, 'Do you think that he's giving me a preferential treatment?'

'You've made a splash', they answer me, laughing (and I can't help but hear Mauro's voice in my head: 'Yes, just like a whale').

....

Is this true? Really? With today's face and outfit? Looking about as attractive as a sea cucumber? I cannot believe it. If it were true, I should definitely start writing myself a list: 'Dear Roby, remember that you pulled when you were immersed in trash, when you were oily all over, with your mascara on your cheekbones and scandalous hair, covered in sweat, and now even when you look like a builder trying (and failing) to pass as a woman'.

And in any case, my boy, you are 25 years old, come on, I could be your mother in Sri Lanka (or in South London, too, for that matter: I've read somewhere that it has the highest percentage of teenage mothers in Europe).

When we return to harbour and moor in the berth, Chamath tells me that he has to take care of a few things on the boat before leaving and will come and join me later on, but in the meantime he'll ask one of his friends with a moped to give me a lift to the Secret Beach. All these favours embarrass me a bit. I can go on my own to the beach.

'No, it's not a problem at all. My friend is happy to take you there. You cannot walk. It's quite far, and the road to get there is long with many ups and downs.'

Okay, then.

I get to this little beach, which is indeed secret, tucked away at the end of a looooong uphill then downhill trail. Walking all that way under the scorching sun wouldn't have been pleasant or fun at all. The beach is also really small, not even 20 metres. It's more like a small cove, with a little restaurant nearby. I arrange my towel and stuff and go into the water for the first swim of the day, but the seabed slopes away pretty steeply, and since I'm a crappy swimmer, I don't feel confident in the water.

I go back to the beach and lay on my towel, and after a while I feel something stinging me, or nipping at my foot. I leap up faster than Usain Bolt off the blocks, terrified at the idea of having been bitten by a bloody insect. Instead, I discover that it's just a little hermit crab! I then realise that I am surrounded by them, each one busy running its own errands, complete with bag and baggage. Oh! Hermit crabs have always put me in a good mood. The fact they immediately withdraw into their shells at the first sign of danger, and move around with the whole burden of their homes on their backs...

It's definitely a species that could work a bit on attachment, I think. The fact they never let go of their shells. I laugh to myself imagining a comic strip where a hermit crab is lying on a psychologist's couch and says, 'Doctor, you talk about attachments, but I don't really understand what I could be attached to. What do you think?'

An animal species that would cease to exist if it started letting (its shell) go. But this is us humans overthinking, overanalysing and worrying. Animals live in the moment, they follow their instinct, they are aligned and live in harmony because they do what they feel.

After around an hour, which I spent reading, Chamath arrives. He comes right up to my towel, but remains standing in front of me, while I look up at him from below.

'Hello. Did you swim?'

'Yes, a bit, but the water gets deep too soon, and I'm a bit afraid. I'm not a good swimmer' (big overstatement), I explain.

Still standing, he inquires if I'm hungry.

'Not really. I ate loads on the boat.'

Still looking down at me, he investigates further, 'Until what time do you want to stay on the beach?'

'I don't know, I've just arrived. For sure, a bit longer. I'd like to see the sunset, anyway.'

'Okay, then I go', he answers.

....

Ehm... I'm a bit confused. This guy has come after all this time, all this way, just to say these three things? What am I missing here?

Mah, something is not quite right here, but what do I know about how his culture works? I distinctly feel I lack the knowledge to understand this exchange which, by my Western standards, seems very odd. But also let go of the need to understand everything all the time, Roby.

'Okay, then', I answer, a bit baffled, still looking up at him.

'Okay... but can I have your number? So you can correct my English and teach me new words.'

'No problem. It will be a pleasure for me', I reassure him.

And so off he goes, leaving me a bit puzzled about exactly what just happened. In my confusion, I end up laughing at myself: dumped even by one of the local guys, who are apparently so keen. If my brothers were to hear about this, they would use this anecdote to take the piss for the next 25 years at least.

Maybe he found me repulsive in a bikini. As long as I looked like a builder in bad drag, it was okay, but once unveiled, I was less appealing. 'And yet he said he loved whales', I already know that my brother Mauro would drily remark.

Oh, well. With the entire episode promptly classified as the Seventh Secret of Fátima, I try to leave this mysterious and almost tragicomic sketch on the beach, where, by the way, the sunset is not even particularly visible.

When I get back to Sandula's and connect to the wi-fi there is a hailstorm of beeps from my phone. Among all the other messages, there's one from Chamath.

'You can get something to eat and drink at the café on the beach. The owner is my friend. I will then pass to settle the bill for you', he writes.

147

Now, okay. I know I'm more corpulent than all the Sri Lankan people I've seen so far, but how much does he think I eat? He stuffed me with food on the boat, he offered me some more on the beach, and now he's still making sure that I'm fed?

Look at that. How chivalrous these Sri Lankans are! They don't stop to talk with you, but you can stuff your face at their expense.

'Thanks, but I only received your message now that I'm back at the homestay. You are very kind. It would have been nice if you had stayed a bit longer', I answer him, although well aware that you cannot have it all.

And here, another one to file under 'Intercultural Misunderstandings', the Second Big Sri Lankan Misunderstanding is unveiled: 'But you didn't ask me to sit on the towel with you. Plus you were reading, and I didn't want to disturb you'.

....

I mean, did I have to invite him to sit on my towel? Well, I find that excessive. How about bringing one himself? Maybe that's not how it's done in Sri Lanka? Oh well. The afternoon at the beach is gone now. 'Listen, I'm about to go out for dinner. I am alone, so if you want to join me, maybe we can practise some English', I suggest.

'Oh, I have never eaten out', he confesses.

....

'Excuse me? What do you mean? Not even with your friends?' I insist. I find it impossible to believe. Come on. This guy is 25 years old, and he has never eaten out?

'No, never', he assures me.

Oh, Jesus, we are entering very delicate territory here. I am talking with someone whose life experience is waaaaaaaaaaaaaaaay more limited than mine, and therefore very likely has a narrower world view as a result.

'Okay, don't worry, we can go to a very simple place, nothing fancy, and I'll explain how it all works. How does that sound?'

'Okay. I am so happy', he confides. The sweetness. A little boy in a grown man's body, basically. Okay, then, I'll be a baby-sitter

148

tonight. Before going out, I do another dictation with Thiranya and Sandula, and the boy gives me a drawing he did for me to thank me. Blue, green and orange flowers. Oh, what a sweet darling!

I then go to this little restaurant near my homestay, where I told Chamath to meet me. I get there before him, and when he arrives on his black moped I can clearly see how fidgety he is, and that he doesn't really know how to behave. I feel a smile tugging gently on my lips at his sweetness, but I wouldn't want him to think that I'm taking the piss or laughing at him. Basically, what we are dealing with here is a restaurant virgin. But what do local guys do when they go out?

I explain the abstruse concept of a menu to him: 'So, we choose what we want from this list, we tell the waiter and after a while they bring us what we asked for'. I feel like I'm on another planet. Then, the same behaviour that I've noticed in Shanaka manifests in Chamath. He also wants to play at 'being a Man' without knowing the proper etiquette, and the results are quite comical. 'What do you want?' he asks.

'A mango juice', I answer.

'Okay, you can have it.'

'I know. Thanks anyway.'

While I'm drinking my mango juice with Chamath's kind permission, he confides, 'My heart is beating so quickly. I am very happy'.

....

Oh, piccolino! What a puppy.

And also: fuck me… Who on earth have I stumbled across, for Cetacean's sake?

I'd never have believed that anybody in real life over the age of 12 would utter such a sentence. I understand that, faced with such purity and naivety, 'kind-hearted Roby' needs to step in and leave her more lively and shamelessly saucy counterpart, 'Roby the flirting queen', at home for the night watching Netflix.

'Nobody has ever talked to me like you did today', he explains.

149

'What do you mean? Every day you meet hundreds of tourists from all over the world, and you talk to them', I point out.

'Yes, but I only talk about the whales. Nobody ever asks me any questions about my life. Nobody has ever been as kind as you and got interested in my life. I never talk about me, only about whales', he clarifies.

Good point. He's knocked me sideways.

And yet, how is that possible? 'Chamath, probably you don't give people much of a chance because you are always very busy with your work... I don't think I've done anything special. I'm sure that if you are open and smile, then many people will come and ask you about your life', I insist.

'I don't know, maybe it's true. But I was a bit disappointed when you didn't invite me to stay with you at the beach', he continues.

'But Chamath, if I had told you earlier that you could join me, what else did I have to tell you? Besides, the beach belongs to everybody, I don't have to invite you', I try to make him understand.

'But I don't know how you women think (don't worry, you're not the only one). I have never talked with girls. I don't know how you think about things.'

....

'What do you mean, you have never talked with girls?'

I feel more and more as if I'm in a parallel world, further and further away from what is my normality. To think that anthropologists seek out isolated tribes in the furthest flung corners of the world... when they could just come here and study the mentality of some of the guys working in tourism in Mirissa!

I cannot even say it's a cultural thing. Shanaka is more or less the same age as Chamath, but he's definitely a step ahead with people in general and with girls in particular. I listen in stunned silence as Chamath insists that he has never talked with girls.

'Not even with your sister's girlfriends?' I inquire.

'No, we always stay quite separate, as groups. Guys and girls don't go out together.'

150

As a matter of fact, I've been here for a week, but I haven't noticed any local girls out and about.

It must be that his heart was not beating fast enough already, because Chamath decides to take the plunge. 'I don't know if I can tell you, but you are so beautiful.' ('The most beautiful of all the cetaceans', my brother Mauro would chip in yet again.) And then he adds, following a train of thought that's derailed and is heading off at full speed God knows where, 'I have never kissed a girl'.

Oh, Dio. Voglio morire. Oh, my God. I want to die.

The whole thing is almost comical. I don't understand if he's saying this as a strong point and something to be proud of, or rather as a warning and justification for what he may be anticipating in his mind, and exclusively in his mind, needless to say. Indeed, while his wildest romantic fantasies are all promising to come true in one evening, I am thinking that I don't like where this conversation might be going. Plus, there is a beach party where I'd rather be in this very moment... and I absolutely cannot bring Chamath with me. This walking emotional block, left more or less inviolate since birth, could end up having a heart attack if he were wild enough to combine two new and intense experiences in one evening! A restaurant AND a beach party? No, it could send him over the edge. Plus, imagine how someone who's never been to a beach party or a club would (not) dance. Either he won't dance, kind of ruining the vibe for me a bit, or he will go to the opposite extreme, and throw some furious and possibly medically alarming moves and embarrass me.

No, it's my last beach party, given that tomorrow I'm moving to the next beach, Tangalle, and I want to enjoy it, so I do something low, but necessary.

I lie to him.

'I'm sorry, but I'm a bit tired. Aren't you sleepy, given that you wake up so early every morning? I really need to go and sleep after this morning's very early start. I want to go home, sorry.'

I apologise to you, little pure and candid heart, but I had to do it.

'I understand. I pay.'

'No, absolutely no way, but thanks for offering.'

'Okay, but then I give you a lift to your homestay', he insists. And okay, let's give him this memory of my hands on his hips. I now understand all those damned men from the past who told me I was too much. Maybe they meant that I stirred up too much emotion in them. Here we go, pure adrenaline rush! Who needs rollercoasters? When we arrive at Sandula Homestay, I get off his moped and thank him. He offers me his hand, and I find the whole thing so sweet.

'How do you say goodbye in Italy?' he inquires.

'We exchange two kisses on the cheeks. Like this, look', I say, and I place two uber chaste kisses on his face. He probably blushed, but what with the darkness and his complexion it was difficult to say. 'Oh, this is the first kiss I give to a girl.'

Oh, Jesus Christ. Please help me.

If he sees that as a kiss, his journey into the emotional and sexual world will be extremely long (but also bursting with thousands of strong sensations). Maybe for him a handshake qualifies as heavy petting. Oh, man, I don't even want to think about the kind of dreams he'll be having tonight.

And, finally, off he goes. A whole evening of cultural shock for me. Besides the compliments and the nice things he might have said, I feel like I've been with a child, and behaving so differently from normal has kind of drained me.

The beach party is exactly what I need right now, and I so deserve it. I wait for five minutes, then I slip into the night armed with my little darkness-splitting torch, headed for the beach. I think back to all those friends of mine who told me to be careful, that men here play all nice and flatter you just to get the papers.

With his innocence and purity, Chamath has taken me back 20 years. Well, not even, because when I was 20, chaste and pure as I was, I was much more mischievous than him.

This is exactly the kind of pure, innocent souls that surprise me. I wonder how they can reach the age they have and remain so... intact, unpolluted by the world. And yet TV, Western movies, all the books available to the whole of humankind, they all depict a reality with such a tangle of feelings and thoughts and considerations, and cheating and sex and corruption... How have they escaped the influence of all this? The problem is that, on one hand, this candour of theirs definitely inspires affection and sweetness but, on the other, takes away a degree of... masculinity maybe. Or, at least, that vein of douchebaggery that, in my eyes, is always a bit cool in men and which, unfortunately, I like. So far, these local men seem to have a much narrower perspective than mine, and I see the Grand Canyon between our ways of behaving and thinking. On the other hand, I'm sure that plenty of women would literally melt in front of all that unadulterated Chamathness. As my grandmother used to say, 'There's a lid for every pot'.

The beach party was nothing special, so, given that I actually was tired from having got up at that ungodly hour, and considering that the average age there was probably around 26, I went home early.

And. Here. The. Folly. Begins.

As soon as I connect to the wi-fi, I receive a flood of messages, all from Chamath. He is so happy. I'm such a good person (a bit of a liar, but good). He would have liked to spend more time with me, but he saw that I was tired. He will never forget this day for the rest of his life (a line straight out of a Bollywood movie). I will live forever in his heart...

Oh, Jesus Christ of the Universe and of all Its creatures...

... He thanks me for having given him the first kiss of his life... He likes my smile. I'm a beautiful lady with an amazing smile. There are no words to describe my beauty. I'm different from all the other foreigners, closed off in their own world...

Oh, Angel of God, my guardian dear, to whom God's love commits me here...

And then he takes the plunge big time, 'Please, can you wait one more day before leaving? So we can go and have dinner again. Now I know how to behave. Tonight I was very nervous'.

OUR FATHER, WHO ART IN HEAVEN, HALLOWED BE THY NAME...

I felt stressed just looking at all those messages. This Chamath is talking nonsense, totally out of the blue (whale), and I don't feel like seeing him again just to hear about how much I've impressed him. I thank him for all the nice words, but I explain that I cannot change my plans, as I would lose a day from my itinerary, and that's not possible. Then I try to talk to him in this corny way he seems to like, adding, 'Don't be sad for this refusal of mine, but be happy for the memories we've created. There are so many kind and nice people in this world. You just have to be open to meeting them. Besides, Chamath, I'm much older than you. Actually, thanks for making me feel like a teenager again' (without the spots, though).

I sent this message and switched off my mobile, otherwise there was no chance in hell this guy was going to let me sleep.

For Raja and the Whales' sake, I only wanted to see the whales... ('You could have just looked in the mirror, sis'.')

I go to bed, smiling at Mauro's hypothetical joke and at the absurdity of the whole situation.

Go to bed now, Roby. Tomorrow we're heading southwards to Tangalle!

Weight that blue whales can reach: 200 tonnes
Quantity of krill a blue whale can eat in a day: 4 million
Distance at which you can hear a whale's song: 8km
Age of the oldest blue whale ever found: 110 (who knows how much earwax that is)
Times I've been sunburned so far: 0
Hermit crabs sighted at the Secret Beach: 6
Kinds of fruit in the dish served on the boat: 7
Mistakes made by Thiranya in his dictation today: 5
Mistakes made by Sandula in her dictation today: 4
Messages that Shanaka sent me: 2
Messages that Chamath sent me after dinner: 21
Distance between my thoughts and what I was actually telling him: 2,453km
Time I stayed at the beach party: 40 minutes

DAY 11
'Break his heart gently'
-Ah, yes, still Mirissa, Thursday 22nd February 2018-

Ah, yes, my dear Diary, I've ended up staying in Mirissa, showing zero attachments to the plans I made yesterday, letting go of the itinerary I had in my mind. Let's go with life's flow and accept its surprises.

Let me explain a bit.

I woke up with the idea that I had to pack my backpack and go and catch the bus to Tangalle. I had told Sandula I would be gone by 10am, also because I knew she already had another guest booked in.

When I switched on my mobile, however, I received a machine-gun round of messages. Beep, beep, beep, beep! With every 'beep', my anxiety level rose. They were all from Chamath, all with the same tone, and I would like someone to explain to him, in Sinhalese so he can understand better, and very gently, that if he thinks he can win over a woman in this way, he is very much mistaken. He is having the opposite effect, meaning that he is irritating me quite a lot.

Not least because what he is saying sounds completely crazy to me.

'I will never find another girl like you. I am not like the other boys (I hope not, for their sakes!), I only want your happiness, but not only that (I think it's clear what you want). I want to see you again even just for one last time to say goodbye properly. I don't care about your age. Age is just a number. What matters is one's heart...'

Someone please help me. Universe, come to my aid. What have I got myself into, totally unintentionally?

Yet, even though Chamath is completely out of his mind with his delusions of love, I, Roby, don't have the heart to hurt him. I'm not able to be that selfish. At the end of the day, this lunatic, raging in his own special way, is only asking to see me one last time. I would feel too much of a human shit to deny him what seems to have become his new raison d'être.

'For fuck's sake, why didn't you make me more insensitive, God?' I wonder as I text Chamath, 'Okay, I can postpone my departure to the afternoon. I'll wait until noon, in case you manage to get back to the harbour by then'. Indeed, yesterday he explained that sometimes the tours finish sooner because they find the whales early in the morning, without having to go out into open water, so every shift can end at a different time.

Meanwhile, I empty my room because the new guest is supposed to arrive in the morning. I check out, and then I sit in the living room writing and reading. At some point, this white guy laden like a mule with three big backpacks arrives at the door. He is tall, quite thin, has short brown curls, a wide forehead and blue eyes that slope downwards slightly, although without creating the sad expression that often accompanies this eye shape. On the contrary, his eyes are lively and kind. A nice warm smile and light brown stubble. He must be more or less my age, given that he has some laughter lines around his eyes and mouth. My mind immediately registers that he's cute, facially, but that his body falls quite far short of my athletic, muscular ideal. It also registers that, with all those backpacks, his girlfriend must be joining him soon.

'Are there problems with the room?' he asks me, with a slight German accent.

'Oh, no, don't worry. I've just postponed my departure a bit, but the room is all yours. I'm simply waiting until it's time to catch my bus.'

While Sandula changes the bedsheets, he introduces himself. Andre, from Leipzig, and we start talking like old friends. He also went to see the whales yesterday, but his experience was quite different from mine, on an overcrowded boat with really bad service

156

on board. I therefore offer to forward him the pictures of whales and dolphins that Raja and the Whales sent us all last night.

'But... are you travelling alone?' I ask him, with elegant nonchalance.

'Yeah. You wouldn't think so, judging from my backpacks, right? Yeah, I don't travel light.'

'No, you don't, but I'm expecting hyper organisation from a German, so who knows what you have inside there.'

He laughs at my oh-so-subtle mockery and explains, 'On one hand, I have a lot of equipment to draw and paint, because I am an artist, and on the other, I have many tools and things that other backpackers don't have. Like these two', and he takes out two big cups in which you can insert a metallic bar that you plug in to heat the water. 'This way I can make myself a tea whenever I want.'

How German can you get?

In fact, he is also carrying around half a supermarket in those backpacks, because after we talk for a while he takes out a bag of bananas and offers me one. Then, when Sandula makes us tea later on, Andre produces a packet of biscuits, which are always so welcome.

He's cute and kind, this Andre, and the conversation flows so naturally that is a pleasure. We talk about our travels, first and foremost.

'I'm happy to have met someone more or less my age', I tell him.

'No, come on, how old are you?' he inquires.

'Older than you think. I'm 39', and indeed he is surprised. He is 38. Yes, it's nice to find someone of my generation. Even nicer to find someone who has travelled quite a bit. All the things and tools he's carrying around are the results of years of travelling and lessons learnt.

'Tupperwares, for example, are so useful! If you don't manage to finish your meal because the portion is too big, you don't necessarily have to leave it there.'

I have to admit that the idea of packing Tupperwares has never crossed my mind. It must be because, after awful experiences with ants and mice in my hotel bedrooms in India, I avoid keeping food in my backpack at all costs.

He's interesting, this Andre. He has lived and seen a lot. And he's really cute, though I've never been one for blue eyes.

The exchange that confirms that yes, I like Andre, is when I happily and excitedly show him the huge bathroom attached to his new bedroom. 'Look at the size of the bathroom! Isn't it fab? You can do some jogging in the morning, if you so wish!'

He looks at the bathroom with a serious face and drily remarks, 'What a waste of space'.

Italian enthusiasm versus German pragmatism. Fabulous.

I am keeping my mobile in front of me, waiting to hear from Chamath, and in the meantime Andre and I have already had two teas each.

'So you will be travelling for three months? I go home in July. I am at the end of my trip in Sri Lanka now (great, so you can give me loads of tips!). On Monday I'm leaving for India (oh, wow, really? I'm going to India, too, after Sri Lanka!) and then I'll decide what other countries to visit. There's plenty of time. I love doing long trips (tell me about it). Actually, I'm so happy. I've just spent a few days with my Canadian friend Jacob, another artist whom I met three years ago in Mexico. Listen to how we met. I was in Oaxaca, and I had put my backpack in the trunk of the taxi. When I arrived at the hostel and got out of the taxi to get my wallet from my backpack to pay for the ride, that bastard of a taxi driver sped away (oh my God, what a story!). I couldn't believe it. I had my passport, my credit card and all my money in the backpack. I lost everything. I was basically left with only the clothes I had on me. In the end I had to wait in Mexico for a month for my parents to send me some money and a copy of my passport, and I ended up working as a chef in that hostel, in exchange for food and accommodation. Jacob was there, too. He ordered dinner every evening and still to this day affectionately calls me 'chef Andre'. He even gave me some of his T-shirts because I had nothing to wear. We then stayed in contact on Facebook, and when I posted my pictures from Sri Lanka he wrote to say that, amazingly, he was here, too. Fantastic coincidence, right (well, not really, but it would take a while to explain...)? So we met up and spent some days together. You don't often get to see people again that you met while travelling.'

Eh, I know. I sometimes wonder if and when I will ever meet up again with people I've shared such special moments with while travelling. Maybe our lives only crossed paths for a few hours, but it would be so cool to see them again.

Andre explains that he is an artist who specialises primarily in bookmarks, which he shows me, but he also does watercolour paintings and centrepieces which he then sells at the Christmas markets in Leipzig. He shows me his websites, www.firlefanzen.de and www.etcetera23.com. He seems to have an Instagram account for every different artistic thing he creates. 'For example, Jacob taught me back then to print on T-shirts, and for the T-shirts I create a separate Instagram account.'

One man, one account, you might think. Or maybe 23 in total: as Andre explains, 23 seems to be a recurring number in his life, hence his choice to include it in his website.

In fact, Andre is a chef, so cooking and art are his two life passions. Besides travelling, of course. He tells me that he normally buys fish and vegetables in the market and cooks his own meals, where his accommodation allows. Nice! A chef. I like him more and more.

'But what time is your bus?' he asks me. I explain that I don't really have a precise time, and that I've got bogged down in this weird situation with a local guy. 'I couldn't live with myself if I denied him the chance to see me again.' I tell Andre the whole story in detail, and we laugh about it together.

'This is an aspect of solo travelling that, as a man, I've never discovered, since it's practically impossible that a local woman would approach me, or at least be this insistent.'

Indeed, I've never thought about it. Of course every traveller has different experiences based on their character and perception of the world, but it's equally true that there are situations which, for better or for worse, can only happen to a woman. For better or for worse, because I doubt that Andre has ever been offered a drink by a DJ, or the occasional free ride from tuk-tuk drivers.

Meanwhile, a banana and some biscuits later, it's suddenly 2pm. Unbelievable. Andre and I have been talking for four hours, still sitting in that living room.

'In your opinion, would Sandula and her children be perplexed, if not downright shocked, by this? They must find it so weird that two strangers of the opposite sex, who have never met before, spend hours talking, laughing, showing paintings and pictures to each other and sharing food.'

How special, when two people click immediately.

Finally, I receive my first (of several) messages from Chamath, and he says that he can be here by 4pm.

Mmh... This means taking my bus at 5pm and arriving at Tangalle in the evening, when it's dark, without having a hotel booked. I'm not that excited about this prospect. 'Listen, if you want to stay here one more night, I'll look for another homestay', Andre suggests.

'Can you imagine how shocked Sandula and her children will be for the rest of their lives if we end up sharing the room?' I say, laughing.

Which I wouldn't even mind, to be honest.

'No, don't worry, the room is yours. Worst-case scenario, I'll see if there is a room available in the house next door', I reassure him.

It's finally 4pm, so I say goodbye to Andre. 'It's really been a pleasure meeting you. Thanks for all the chats and food. JesusMaryandJoseph, let's see what this guy has to tell me now. Why do I put myself in these situations? Okay, wish me luck with Mr Crazy in Love. I'm going to need it all.'

'Good luck. Break his heart gently.'

How beautiful to understand each other, to find someone on the same wavelength as you. Man, not only did I get the chance to see a blue whale yesterday, but today I've found a German with a sense of humour! Unbelievable.

In truth, I would rather have stayed there talking a bit more, maybe relocating to the beach for a drink, than go and face a situation that I already know will make me feel uncomfortable. You see what a pain it is being kind? Why wasn't I born an insensitive bitch?

Oh, well. Chamath is there, wearing black shorts and a black T-shirt (why do local people insist on wearing beige, brown, black, grey, when their complexion goes so amazingly with bright colours? *Mah*, Secret of Fátima Number Eight). When he sees me, his face lights up with shiny eyes and a radiant smile.

He immediately starts with the same old story the very moment we sit down. 'Roby, age doesn't matter, it's just a number. You are so beautiful. I have decided ('I have decided!!!!!!!!!!') that I will wait for you all my life. Will you be back in five years? In ten? I don't care. I will wait for you.'

My first thought is: BASED ON WHAT, FOR BLUE WHALE'S SAKE?!

My second thought is: 'What the fuck has this guy eaten for breakfast?' I'm sorry, but he is really starting to irritate the shit out of me.

'Chamath, from a tiny thing like our conversation on the boat, you have been crafting this gigantic story. It's absolutely inappropriate. According to my culture, I haven't behaved in any extraordinary way, instead you come out with words that you have no right to use here. What I gave you was not a kiss, and it's not love that you feel.'

'Yes, it is. I know. For me this is love.'

Oh, fuck that.

I really feel like I'm trapped in a low-quality Bollywood movie, where the two protagonists look at each other, and from that one glance understand that they have to stay together forever and will fight against their families who, of course, oppose their love. But what do you know about love, if you have never even talked with a girl?

'Listen, you can believe what you want. It definitely isn't love for me, and it bothers me that you are abusing such an important word. Maybe one day I will be back, but who knows when, so get the idea of waiting for me out of your head. I don't want you to wait for anything. We can stay friends (I found it atrocious to tell him that even the word 'friend' has a different meaning for me), but you have to stop thinking about these things, that you'll wait for me, and you won't find anybody else like me.'

It's almost fascinating how the people who need your patience and understanding the most are the very ones who drive you to the edge of both. But this Chamath landed two days ago from another planet.

Fuck me. Ten days ago I was on the tube in London, looking around to see if by any chance the miracle of eye contact with another passenger would happen. Now I'm sitting with these two burning eyes staring at me in silence. And to think that this meeting was born out of my desire to be kind! I feel like a total shit. But I also feel trapped and uncomfortable, and that's not fair either.

I want to move away from this parallel universe and go back to mine, where my words and jokes are understood by Andre, and not terribly and seriously misunderstood by Chamath.

I take a deep breath, I soften a bit and I repeat everything again calmly.

'Do you understand, Chamath? I am happy to have met you, and we can stay in contact so that I can help you with your English, but you cannot start mentioning love just because you have talked with a woman for 20 minutes. I'm saying this for you. And I'm sure that if you are warm and open, then so many other people will ask you about your life. I haven't done anything special.'

'No, you have a golden heart. I see it.'

Again, Jesus Christ. Can you also see my two balls that you are breaking into smithereens with all this rubbish?

'Okay, thanks. You, too, very clearly. And one day you'll find the right woman for you', I reply, somewhat sharply, cutting him short. 'That's enough now. I have a bus to catch.'

'Can I give you a lift to your homestay?'

'No, thanks, I prefer that we say goodbye here.'

I don't want him to take me back because I don't want him to see Andre, who could be sitting outside, and I also don't want Sandula to see him and think she's been unwittingly harbouring a *Slutta Totalis*, a new species of irreputable woman, talking for hours with a white guy first, and then getting a lift from a local one. I'm almost 40 years old, I live in London, where no one gives a shit about anybody, and yet I care about what people think of me. I want them to think well of me. Even if I won't see these people ever again. Who knows what a psychologist would say. But I know what I'd say, which is: 'What a douche you are, Roby'.

Anyway, it seems our first kiss (okay, let's call it that) has emboldened Chamath somewhat because he asks, 'Can I say goodbye with a hug?'

Yeah, cool, the world is not going to fall apart over a hug.

The only thing is that he has clearly never hugged a girl before.

Let's say that his hug reminded me of that famous footballing incident where Zinedine Zidane headbutted Marco Materazzi in the World Cup 2006 final. Chamath threw himself head first against my shoulder, without even involving his arms which, at least in Western hugs, usually play a fundamental role. But, at the end of the day, what the hell do I know about how people hug in Sri Lanka (actually, do they hug at all?)?

Anyway, a super, mega clumsy hug, but he quickly overcomes the embarrassment and plants a kiss on my neck. Can you believe this Chamath? Five more dates and he'd be lowering my bra strap.

I say goodbye to him with a sigh of relief. My God, I'm drained. I feel like I've done the right thing, both in waiting for him and in talking to him so openly and clearly, but I know that I hurt him anyway, and so I still feel like a bit of a shit.

I don't even feel totally good within myself. For this trip, I had promised myself to remain free, detached from any external conditioning, instead here I am, having changed my plans, according to which I would have already been on the beach in Tangalle. I changed them because I was somehow pushed by another person, while I only want to listen to myself here.

But, in the end and in truth, I have actually listened to myself. I know I would have felt worse if I had left without giving him a chance to see me again. Lesson learnt, anyway (or at least so I hope): these local guys are really way too intense for my tastes. I should try to contain myself, but how can I do that? I've managed to pull while looking more or less repulsive! But yes, here I definitely smashed right into a huge cultural wall, and I will be more careful from now onwards.

Earlier on I was talking about this with my friend Piper, who is still totally immersed in the magic of her own three-month trip in Latin America, where she seems to have found a special man. I say 'seems' because we all know by now that countless things of all sorts can happen before we really reach the happy ending. I was telling her about how Chamath turned out to be crazy, and all the shit he was coming out with, and I asked her, 'But who is the one that is really out of their mind? Chamath, so quick to use the word 'love' and so certain that what he was feeling was love, or us Westerners, who think that love has to come with a totally different set of requirements?' Piper replied, 'Love is so simple in itself, but we are so afraid to experience it'.

....

Mah, I think I preferred her in her sarcastic and caustic phase, rather than with these heart-shaped pupils.

I'm there, walking back home in this strange mood, and I think that deep down everything happens for a reason... And maybe the reason is that I have to postpone my departure by a day and spend the evening with Andre. Sure, no expectations, but equally I cannot ignore the signs that the Universe has sent me today. What if Andre were the embodiment of serendipity?

164

Serendipity is the faculty or phenomenon of finding valuable or agreeable things not sought for. The origin of this word comes from Serendip, which is the ancient Persian name for Sri Lanka. This word was coined by the writer Horace Walpole on 28th January 1754. In a letter he wrote to his English friend Horace Mann, Walpole explained an unexpected discovery he had made thanks to a Persian fairy tale, 'The Three Princes of Serendip'. In that story the three protagonists were 'always making discoveries, by accidents and sagacity, of things which they were not in quest of'.

Serendipity is at the basis of so many discoveries, not all of them scientific, when people were studying something or trying to prove a theory, and ended up with something else entirely. Dynamite and penicillin were invented by chance. Christopher Columbus was looking for a direct sea route west from Europe to Asia, and we all know what he stumbled upon instead. The popsicle was invented because Frank Epperson, who was only 11 years old, accidentally left water with soda mix outside to freeze overnight with the stick used to mix them. Even the famous Tarte Tatin was born out of a simple mistake, when the Tatin sisters overcooked the apples and then decided to hide them by putting the base on top of the pan. So what if Andre were the unexpected surprise I was destined to receive while trying to behave well with Chamath?

Strangely, I don't believe that Shanaka is himself an example of such serendipity. For sure, it was a brilliant encounter that happened at the right moment, meaning both at the beginning of my trip and on Valentine's Day. Now that I think about it, this whole thing has really showed me that when you stop trying to force it, these things come to you with ease. If I think back on all the years I sat through this cursed celebration feeling varying degrees of unhappy, lonely and unlucky... I can only smile at how easily things flowed this year, when I didn't even remember that it was my beloved and equally dreaded Valentine's Day. Okay, Universe, I've learnt my lesson.

But Andre is completely different from Shanaka. We understand each other so well in so many ways. That was clear from the first minute.

I go back to Sandula Homestay to get my backpack, and Andre is sitting in the garden. 'How did it go? In how many pieces have you shattered his innocent heart?' he teases.

'Shut up. I feel bad enough already. No need to rub it in, thanks. Listen, it's too late to catch the bus now, so I've decided to leave tomorrow morning. Do you fancy having dinner together?'

'*Oh, Scheisse*', he answers, as if I had given him the worst piece of news in the world. It seems I've found myself a grade A smart-arse (or does he qualify more as a moron?). 'I've already asked Sandula to cook me dinner, but you can join me. She said it will be ready by 8pm.'

So we agree to see each other then, and I take the opportunity to make peace with the world and myself in front of another blazing sunset on the beach. I'm sitting on the sand, enjoying this incredible show on my own, when a local guy arrives and says, 'Hello, do you remember me?'

'No', I reply bluntly, attempting vainly to nip the exchange in the bud.

'I was at the beach party last night', he continues.

'Okay, but did we talk?' I mean, I admit my memory isn't the greatest, but I am generally able to retain faces and conversations for 24 hours.

'No, I was behind you, and you never turned round.'

SO HOW THE HECK COULD I REMEMBER YOU?

'I thought of talking to you now. I want to know about you.'

....

Please, someone help me! Or help him, because he is coming to me on a day where my patience and tolerance towards suffocating people are well and truly spent. What is wrong with these Sri Lankan guys? Why don't they learn from the Vietnamese or Laotians to mind their own damned business?

Sandula was quite surprised to see me for dinner. I explained that I didn't want to leave when it was dark, and that I have found a room at her neighbour's. It's good to see how resourcefully the families around here round up the fathers' salaries. There are so many homestays and guesthouses in every village, and I definitely prefer them to staying in a hostel.

I try to reassure my friends, who tend to exhaust themselves with organisation and preparation before a trip: you will always find a place to stay. Especially if you want to do sustainable tourism and properly see the real, local life. Get to a place and have a walk around. By staying at a homestay, you get a more authentic experience, in close contact with the locals, and you also know that your money is really going to those who need it. Unfortunately, however, sleeping in such places makes it harder to meet other travellers, which is the big advantage of hostels. But, okay, what matters is quality not quantity. And I'm quite inspired by Andre, with his sense of humour and the variety of topics we can talk about, plus the fact he is such a seasoned traveller.

For dinner we have (guess what?) rice and curry with potatoes, spinach and coconut milk. It's very good actually, with quite a delicate taste and, once again, the portions are humongous.

'Fancy a walk to the beach to digest?' Andre suggests.

Universe, You did listen to me. One day after thinking that it would have been nice to have someone to enjoy the beach and the starry sky with, talking and laughing, You send me someone with whom to do it. And never mind if he pronounces 'people' as 'pipl' and if he is a bit on the thin side. He makes me laugh, has no problems sharing his food and is even good at cooking. Perfect.

Obviously, as per my usual script, I start having romantic thoughts. And how can you not have them? The magic of an encounter which lasted six hours, the waves coming to say hello peacefully one after another, the profusion of stars above us, so bright...

In other words, the Italian is there with half an idea to kiss him, but the German is probably thinking about what spices Sandula used in her curry.

Our bladders have distracted me from pondering whether to

167

make a move and if so what kind. As we both desperately needed to pee, we go to the beach party (three in a row, hip hip hooray for Mirissa!). After emptying our bladders, we took care to fill them again. Since Andre gave me a beer over dinner, and he brought another one to the beach for me, confirming that yes, he is carrying half a supermarket in those backpacks, it was my turn to buy him one.

Anyway, we left quite soon. The music was not really to our taste, and what with the abundant dinner and the relaxing after-dinner stroll and chat, we were both ready to hit the sack.

When we take the turning leading to Sandula's, which is completely unlit, Andre produces from his rucksack an actual magic wand, long and thin, with a light at the tip. The Harry Potter of the backpacking world. He could have used a crappy little torch like mine. He could have had one of those round flashlights you hook to your belt. He could have even sported one of those lights you wear on your forehead.

But no, Andre had a torch shaped as a magic wand.

This seemed a marvellous thing to me. 'This is so cool. You look like a magician who has magically summoned some light!', I comment, laughing.

'It's a laptop light, working with any external USB. You can fold it up and it takes up minimal space', he explains, always dry and pragmatic, making me laugh even more because while I talk about magicians, he is super grounded and practical.

And that's when I thought that maybe, maybe… Why not? It's clear we have fun together, it looks like we are compatible travellers in terms of costs and tastes, I have no plans I am attached to, apart from two minor things I had in mind… But why should I necessarily stick to them? Let go of all your plans, Roby. No attachment to how you envisioned things to be. The Universe is giving me another chance to practise these two things that I want to learn.

The fact is that when you travel on your own you become very protective of your own space and time. I know this so well. When I tell people that I travel on my own, everybody looks worried and asks me how I cope with the loneliness. I wish I *could* be left on my own, even just sometimes! You always meet new people, and some of them sometimes cling to you, other times you join them, but given that the time we are taking for travelling is ours, and we have made sacrifices to carve it out from the rest of our life, it must be defended and well managed.

I don't know what Andre is looking for. I don't know if he is up for spending a whole day with me. It's one thing to be together for a few hours, it's another to be together the whole day.

Anyway, there is always and only one way to get rid of all these pointless worries. Ask.

Linking back to one of the many topics we talked about in the afternoon, which is the fact that I feel limited by my inability to drive a moped, I tell him, 'But listen, Andre, do you think you were sent by the Universe to teach me how to ride a scooter?'

To which he replies, 'I hope not'.

We both burst out laughing. Laughter that is an answer in itself.

Slightly hesitant, I continue, ' I mean... But please tell me to my face if it's a problem. I won't get offended... But I was thinking... What do you think if... I mean, I could leave for Tangalle tomorrow morning, or...'

'Or?' he echoes, right on cue.

'Or we could rent out a scooter together tomorrow and go and see new beaches and places.'

'It's not a problem. I know the benefits of being on your own, but I'm happy to spend a day with some company.'

Probably, the most German answer I've ever received. And the problem is perhaps that, for them, this qualifies as an 'outburst of enthusiasm', whereas in reality it is quite contained. But it's exactly this contrast between our two ways of being and doing that I find amusing.

We then say goodnight in front of Sandula Homestay, and I give him two kisses on his cheeks.

'Oh, my God, those are the best kisses of my life!', he mocks me, imitating Chamath.

How wonderful. I've found myself a proper smart-arse and a moron all in one.

Kgs that Andre seems to be dragging around in those three backpacks: 25
Instagram accounts that Andre has in reality: just the 6
Tupperwares owned by Andre: 2
People so far who have asked me to take a picture with them: 0 (further evidence that Sri Lanka is very different from India)
Erotic dreams that Chamath might have had last night: let's not go there
Messages from Chamath I found on my mobile this morning: 12
Messages received from Shanaka so far: 5
Messages received from Antonio since my departure: 3
Messages from Andre: 0

DAY 12
'What are you doing tomorrow?'
-Matara, Dondra, Dikwella and Hiriketiya,
Friday 23rd February 2018-

'Life is a beach' could be today's title. My brother would probably find an alternative; something like 'The beached whale', delicately emphasising my tonnage, rather than the places I've visited. Anyway, let's move on.

At 9am I meet up with Andre, who literally delights me by demonstrating the best stereotypical traits of his nationality. Not only has he already worked out an itinerary for us, but he has rented a bright yellow scooter with two helmets. Well done, Andre.

So here we go towards adventure, with that enhanced sense of freedom that a scooter affords. I cannot even say 'with the wind in my hair', firstly because my hair is trapped under the usual bandana, and secondly it is further flattened by the helmet. It's not like this is ruining a perfect blow-dry anyway. There's nothing to be done: my hair has morphed into something alien. Mega dry, it seems to have exploded on my head and is even curling slightly at the ends... And it's only my 12th day on the road. I wonder whether they'll allow me to board my return flight, or arrest me beforehand for visually disturbing the public peace. Or maybe just my hair, for disorderly conduct. (Or could they even stretch to a minor charge of hairesy?)

Anyway, yes, being on a scooter fills me with joy, not least because it means that I have found a travelling companion, albeit a temporary one. And maybe the time has finally come for me to learn to drive one myself!

And who knows what memories I will create with this Andre.

Young and carefree, we flew through the Sri Lankan countryside, visiting one temple after another. One of them was on a tiny island in front of Matara Fort, which we visited just to be able to say, 'Okay, we stopped as it was on our way', but which in fact was nothing special. We then continued towards Dondra, Sri Lanka's southernmost point, marked by its beautiful white lighthouse standing 49 metres high: it is indeed the tallest in Sri Lanka, and among the tallest in Southeast Asia. It had even been pointed out to me on the boat during the whale tour.

Here, for the first time, a group of women asked us to take a picture with them. It almost came as a relief. I was getting a bit worried that nobody had asked me for a photo thus far. At the end of the day, we are in South Asia, right? In my past travels I've been repeatedly asked by local people to be photographed with them, and I was starting to worry I had lost my allure.

I once watched a movie where a guy looking through his photos focused on a person behind him, sat in a café. He asked himself, 'How many pictures have I unknowingly been captured in? All those photos belonging to people we have never met and never known, but who nevertheless have our image in the background of their photos, a fleeting presence immortalised forever.'

Well, I must be in at least 2,000 photos belonging to strangers I met while travelling in Asia. At least. We're talking mostly men, usually shorter than me, of various ages. All of them wanting a photo with me. Why, I've never been certain. I suppose my height must be a factor, likewise my fair complexion. Add to this the fact that I often wear a *salwar kameez*, because it makes me feel more connected to the community I'm visiting, and generally look friendly and smiling... In any case, especially in India, at times I almost felt like some kind of exotic deity. ("Cows are sacred in India. You are indeed a deity for them", my brother Mauro has generously remarked on more than one occasion). I remember one day I was stopped by 63 different people who wanted a picture with me. Sixty-three. I was going out of my mind, for Selfie's sake.

The best story was last year, in Indonesia. I was travelling with my friends Emanuele and Hoang, and we had just spent 15 hours in a minivan before finally reaching our destination at 3am, completely delirious with fatigue. The destination in question was a mountain village from which we had to leave in order to see the sunrise explode in all its beauty from behind the peak of the volcano, Mount Bromo. We decided to stop there for one day and rest. We would see Mount Bromo at sunrise the day after. I was initially planning to wash my hair that evening, but my plans changed since the 'hotel' we ended up in was pretty reprehensible. We only had a barrel of cold water at our disposal, from which we were supposed to take jugs of water to pour over ourselves in order to shower. At more than 1,100 metres above sea level, the idea of throwing jugfuls of ice-cold water over my head was not exactly the happiest of visualisations, so I decided to wait and wash it the day after at our next accommodation, which was a less adventurous establishment, shall we say.

The morning after, at 4am, we set out into the cold, dark night and started our ascent of Mount Bromo. I was all wrapped up in layer upon layer of fleeces and jackets. I looked like a transgender Michelin man. I was still jet lagged, knackered after spending 52 hours of my first week in Indonesia on various means of transport. My hair was not only preposterous due to the standard 'Welcome to Asia' effect, but it also stank of sulphur: the afternoon before we had gone for a walk near Mount Bromo's crater, which continually spews out sulphurous smoke.

'Fucking hell, Roby, you really are a walking toilet with a capital T', Emanuele said, laughing.

'I know, but just wait, someone will still ask me to pose for a photo with them', I answered, quite sure of myself.

Two hours later, when we were soaking up this amazing symphony of pastel hues and light, our moment of poetry and awe was interrupted by a Chinese guy who approached and asked with a smile, 'Excuse me, could I have a photo with you?'

I smiled back, 'Sure! My friend Emanuel can take it for us', and then, turning to Emanuele, all pleased with myself, 'You see? What was I telling you?'

Emanuele took the picture, muttering under his breath, 'I cannot believe this'.

Once the photo was taken, the Chinese guy shook my hand and said, 'Thank you, sir'.

SIR.

....

He'd mistaken me for a man.

I was so upset that it took me a few seconds to join in with Emanuele, who was practically pissing himself with laughter.

To this day I think that was my lowest point in terms of my sense of femininity and my self-perception as a woman.

But let's go back to today. Right behind Dondra's lighthouse, there was a tiny beach, the kind I like, where a group of local guys were confabulating near a small boat. There you go, a typical situation where, had I been alone, I would probably not have stopped. I'm not saying that anything dangerous could have happened. I have personally never felt unsafe or threatened on any of my trips in Asia. But lying alone on a beach in your bikini with a group of five or six guys nearby might lead to uncomfortable or bothersome situations.

On the contrary, with this mega muscular, big guy Andre by my side, they left us in peace. Who knows what these young guys had met at the beach to talk about. Who knows if they all share Chamath's pure soul.

At some point, the most fearless of the group approached us and asked, 'Would you like to buy some weed?'

Ah, ecco.

We then got back on our gaudy scooter and headed to the Hummanaya Blow Hole – pretty much a marine geyser, which my Lonely Planet informs us is the second largest in the world and the only one in Sri Lanka. Basically, the sea water flows underneath the shore and bursts out of a hole due to a build-up of pressure. The water fountain created by the geological feature shoots up every couple of minutes to various heights depending on the state of the sea during the monsoon season, delighting children in the process.

Children.

In the monsoon season.

Key words. To Andre and me, it looked like a bit of a tourist trap, which cost us an entry fee of 250 rupees (corresponding to the insane sum of one pound!). A cute attraction, if I'm being generous, but nothing to write home about.

We then went in search of adventure, looking for this magnificent temple that the Lonely Planet waxes lyrical about. We got lost among the narrow country roads, which seemed to take us further and further away from the main road. We were laughing because every single local person we met pointed out the way, as if the fact we were there at all meant we had to be looking for that specific temple. In fact, they may have been showing us the way to their auntie's place, because in the end we never did find it. So we decided to go and collapse on Hiriketiya beach instead, which I enjoyed a lot. A small, secluded beach in a horseshoe-shaped cove, surrounded by luxurious forest that almost kissed the blue water with the tips of its palm leaves. It also offered us the often amusing spectacle of beginner surfers. Being so sheltered but with quite nice waves at the same time, it is the ideal spot for anyone wanting to learn to ride the sea.

There are really very few things to which I say, 'never in my whole life'. But I think that surfing is one of them, given that I don't have a great relationship with water ('Not even shower water', my little brother Mauro would specify).

Lying in the sun, Andre and I talk. About so many things. About his favourite cuisine (Indian), about Latin America, where he travelled for several months, and about his life in Leipzig, a precarious balance between restaurant kitchens and his art studio where he gives vent to all his creativity. About woods, where he loves to walk in search of pinecones, acorns and branches that he then makes into the centrepieces he sells at Christmas markets.

About the fact that once back to Germany, he'll have to find a flat and live on his own, given that staying with his parents was not suiting him that well.

We talk and talk, but he shows incredible skill in avoiding mentioning anything remotely connected to his emotional or private life. The idea starts dawning on me that he might be gay, but I silence it because I have no experience with artists. What slightly confuses me could simply be a peculiar and very delicate sensitivity. And remember, we're talking about German artists, here. This is a completely new world for me, so I suspend any judgement and wait for other jigsaw pieces to emerge.

'So you spend every November and December weekend exhibiting your works at Christmas markets? Don't you freeze to death?' I ask him, feeling the chill in my bones at the mere thought of it.

'I bring a little heater with me, but yes, it's not a barrel of laughs. Once, this woman was checking out my centrepieces, and we were actually joking about how cold it was. She asked if I wanted anything hot to drink, as she was going to get a coffee for herself, so I asked for a tea. When she came back to give it to me, I saw that she had written her name and phone number on the paper cup. 'Enjoy your tea, and call me if you fancy it', she said. I think that has to be the nicest way anyone has ever tried to pick me up. Very elegant and subtle.'

'And did you call her in the end? Did you go out with her?' I pressed, hoping that my doubt would somehow be dispelled.

'Yes, we went out two or three times, but it finished there.'

Okay, here's one more jigsaw piece.

After relaxing on the beach, Andre asked me, 'Are you finally ready for the moment you've been waiting for all these years? Shall I teach you how to ride a scooter?'

To be fair, I have to admit that someone else has tried in the past. I remember a Vietnamese man renting scooters and mopeds out, whose hair turned platinum blond out of sheer terror when he saw me pressing the accelerator instead of the brakes.

Okay, let's give it a go. And I even managed to go back and forth along this little seafront track, while a local gentleman eyed my progress with some amusement (or was it pity?), given that I was barely reaching 15km/hour but had this huge smile on my face all the same.

'Great. First lesson done', says Andre, snatching the scooter back, pretending to run away with it and leave me there… and ending up on the ground like the smart-arse that he is.

Shhhhhit! He didn't get hurt, but A) the scooter did, and I really want to see Andre's ethical and moral standards tonight when we take the scooter back to the rental place, and B) I don't think he's the best driving instructor I could have found myself.

The ride home unfolds in silence, each of us with our own earphones in under our helmets. An exclusively German practice, or exclusively Andre's, since I have never seen anybody else doing it. Each of us with our own chosen music, so as to better relax and enjoy the show of the advancing dusk stretching out its finger-like shadows.

And also to drown out our asses screaming in pain and imploring us to get off, since we had been sitting on that saddle for most of the day.

When we brought the scooter back, the shopkeeper immediately noticed the scratches. Andre decided to play a card, beloved by many, that can be described as 'being a shameless chancer' and which in some Italian regions is referred to instead as 'avere la faccia come il culo', 'having a face like one's ass'.

'Scratches? No way. Maybe they were already there. We didn't do anything.' He tried his luck, basically, but in the end he paid 2,000 rupees for the damage, without even hinting that I contribute. I then gave him 1,000. It's true that he caused it, but it's also true that he's shared so much with me, and I know that when you are travelling with a limited budget even the simplest things like bananas, beer and tea acquire a whole new value.

We then went home and, while taking my shower, Sandula

invited me on Messenger (I didn't have her down as so digitally savvy!) to have dinner with them, since she had cooked too much food. How sweet! I go to their place feeling a bit uncomfortable though, because it doesn't seem fair that Andre has to pay for a meal that they are sharing with me for free. Oh, well, do you see the benefits of helping people improve their English?

After dinner Andre and I walked to the beach for an encore of the previous night's display, but this time we were unable to find a comfortable position. My bum is hurting (and for the wrong reasons–this is the problem!). Again, the starry sky above us, the lazy waves, the distant music, his German accent and the funny bullshit he comes out with once in a while have me thinking that a kiss is all that is missing from this moment. It would round off this lovely day so perfectly. But Andre is probably thinking about the next bookmark he's going to paint.

'So, what are you doing tomorrow?' he asks me unexpectedly.

'Well, I could go to Tangalle, as I have planned. Or...'

'Or you can stay, and we see some other beaches together', he suggests.

Fab! So I don't bother him that much, after all!

Since we were both quite tired, no beach party for tonight, and we have also decided not to rent a scooter tomorrow. Neither of us would be able to sit for all those hours again. We will take a bus and go to some beaches nearby.

Another day with Andre, then. Another little surprise from the Universe. He's difficult to read, though. We find it very easy to talk about everything. He is even gifted with a sense of humour, although it's a bit too German, and I don't always understand it. We are well at ease with each other anyway. Yet, I don't sense any stronger... vibrations from his side. He is not sending any signals that he's sexually interested. Up until now, he hadn't even shown any sign of wanting to spend more time with me.

I'm having fun, anyway. And let's see if his emotional block is a circumstantial thing, specifically related to me, or a tendential one, directed towards the whole of humankind generally. Which is possible, given his nationality. Posterity the arduous verdict will declare.

And, in any case, I also have to stop filling my head with these thousand conjectures on what something could mean or what could happen. These are expectations and hopes and attachments that I build up and create, and as I should know well by now, they generally yield disappointment. So, Roby, thank God for this beautiful day, and that's that.

Height at which the Blow Hole can spurt out sea water: up to 23 metres
Italians I've met so far: 4
Russians I've met so far: 2,375
Surfers practising at Hiriketiya: 9
Surfers able to stand on the board: 5
Cups of tea drunk so far: 18
Dinner prepared by Sandula: rice and curry with aubergines
Sandula's age: around 30, maybe?
Jokes Andre made in one day: 13
Jokes that I understood: 7
Jokes that made me laugh: 4
What that woman wrote on the paper cup at the Christmas market: Klara, 0171 3211775
Kms covered today by scooter: 70

DAY 13
'Shall we have a tour of the house?'
-Weligama and Mirissa, Saturday 24th February 2018-

'Life is a beach 2.' Another glorious day of sunshine and blue sky, complete with hermit crabs and reflections on Love. Oh, yes, Andre is not as hermetically sealed as one (me) might expect a German to be! I might possibly have to review my opinion on them (possibly– let's not jump to any hasty conclusions).

In the morning we went by bus to another new beach, Weligama, where we settled in a corner. I immediately liked Weligama beach, with its long stretch of white sand and, above all, a small, luxuriant palm-fringed island ten metres from the shoreline. There were very few people, and we picked a spot to settle, away from any huts, sunbeds, etc, where you could literally breathe in relaxation and tranquillity.

I spent my time dozing off and reading this book I brought with me, *All in the Mind*, one of those self-help manuals that I never saw myself bothering with, but which have in fact constituted a substantial component of my reading material over the last two years. A book to help me understand, once again, how important it is not to create expectations or develop attachments to anything; how vital it is to stay in the present, visualise what you want to attract in your life and be grateful for what you have and what will come to you. In short, all the things that I've promised myself to put into practice on this trip.

Andre, instead, took out a sketchbook, a set of brushes and watercolours and he started painting in silence, drawing the little island in front of us. To each their own. It was nice to see him so productive and relaxed, and it was even nicer to see the awe and admiration on the faces of the local guys who gathered around us. They were gobsmacked by how much the island he was painting resembled the one before their eyes.

For my part, I was gobsmacked by all those families who come to the beach and go into the sea fully dressed. Question of the day: 'Who needs a bathing suit when you can bathe in the sea wearing your jeans and a T-shirt?' I could understand if the women didn't want to (or couldn't) display too much, but wouldn't they at least bring a spare outfit? Because that is the point: I never see anyone then changing into dry clothes. Aren't they uncomfortable wearing wet clothes for hours? *Mah*, Secret of Fátima Number Nine.

In the afternoon I took him to the Secret Beach where I had been with Chamath. A few hermit crab encounters and a swim later, we started talking about our (non-existent) love lives.

'For the last three years I have been focused solely on my art. I haven't dedicated much energy to love and dating. It's not at all easy to find someone I find interesting. Truth be told, there was a girl I would have liked to know better, but she never showed any signs of being interested, so in the end I let it go (yes, Andre, I know how it feels not to receive such signs).'

Well, this is actually a good sign in itself. Yesterday's doubt was still there, though in a milder form, both because of the lack of any sexual energy between us, and because, both yesterday and today, he has talked a lot about this Jacob friend of his, the Canadian who taught him so much in terms of art. Okay, I get it that you have just spent a few days together, and okay, I get it that you must be good friends, but it seemed to me he was talking way too much about this guy.

By the way, Andre has just offered me the opening I needed. Because I have this thing, and always have had. To some extent it's beautiful, and I like it. But equally, even as I feel it building up, I know it would be better to hold my tongue, whilst at the same time being fully aware that I won't be able to.

There's nothing to be done. Sooner or later (generally sooner), I always have to say what I think. Or do what I thought of doing. If a question comes to mind, even a strange one, even concerning a stranger who, on that day, for example, is wearing odd socks (my life was turned upside down when I started noticing how many people wear odd socks!), I know I have to ask it. Especially when it relates to things I don't understand. I have to know. I need to have the whole picture, and it must be a clear one. I want transparency inside and around me. The very thing I definitely don't demand of my windows at home, which have not been cleaned since 2010, is a fundamental pillar of my relationships. Actually, not only in my relationships; in the way I relate to others generally.

In other words, Andre has just thrown me the very thing I was writing about last night.

'How funny that you should say that. That's exactly what I was thinking about you. You're not one to give many signs. For example, I haven't figured out yet if you like my company, or if you're ambivalent about it… or if you are looking forward to me fucking off and continuing my journey.'

'No, I like your company, despite your mediocre sense of humour (smart-arse) (and moron). I'm happy that you stayed here, I wasn't expecting to meet anybody else in Sri Lanka, since this is the end of my trip.'

Oooooooookay, even though it's not clear yet what he thinks of me. But while I was trying to swim in those blue but slightly rough waves, I told myself aloud, 'Let go of the need to know how things are. You don't always need to know everything, Roby. Do you enjoy spending time with him? Yes. Has he told you he enjoys your company? Yes. If something comes out of this, fab. If nothing happens, fine. It's been good anyway. Enjoy the moment as it is. Wanting something else to happen, just because you think the set-up is perfect is a lack of respect towards the present moment's perfection. And give up your need to always label situations, sensations, thoughts, people. It's so limiting'.

I sometimes make unbelievably beautiful speeches to myself. While people around me are whispering in alarm, 'Have you noticed that woman talking to herself?', I am giving myself fantastic advice.

'What's more, assuming that something has to happen between a man and a woman is so reductive', I continue, attempting a few metres of breaststroke.

A huge theme in my life: friendship between men and women. I haven't had friendships with the opposite sex that were pure and devoid of other interests, apart from with Lucio. And even there, my mum's belief that 'Lucio is in love with you, and you with him, but neither of you has the courage to admit it' had planted the odd thought and question.

Since then, I've had many male friends, sure, but there's always been some sort of interest, maybe unrequited, or reciprocal for only a short time. Yes, it would then develop into a friendship free from ulterior motives, but most of the time it had all started with some sort of attraction.

Okay, but I am in Mirissa now, and I want to let go of all the preset ideas I have about relations between a man and a woman. Let them all go, Roby. Maybe this is one more lesson that I have to learn on this trip.

And, talking of this trip, I am also ready to explore the island's hinterland. I've reasoned that if I were to see Tangalle, which has been on my itinerary since Thursday morning, I would lose too much time, so I'm not going to. But there is great beauty and vitality to be found in a plan that... doesn't go according to plan. Besides, I have already seen a good number of beaches, more than I had initially thought. I think it's high time to start my ascent towards the centre of the country, and Andre has laid out a long list of places that he suggests I see, like Ella, Kandy, Sigiriya... An absolute must is the journey on the blue train through landscapes covered in Sri Lankan 'green gold': the tea plantations. So, a train ride it will be. Tomorrow, for a start, I am going to see my beloved elephants on a safari in the Udawalawe park, and from there I'd like to go to Ella, in the very heart of Sri Lanka. Andre flies to India on Monday morning, so it is high time to say goodbye.

Or, at least, so I thought.

On our way back from the beach we stopped at one of those stalls selling day trips of all kinds. When I asked for the safari price, they told me that it costs 120 dollars if I go on my own, and 132 dollars for two. So much for the joys of travelling alone!

'Oh, come on, sir, what a price difference', I said to the guy, who explained that, for the drivers, understandably so, the expense is all about driving to the safari park, not the entrance fee.

'I see, I do. And listen, my imaginary friend here', and I point to the empty space to my right, 'my faithful friend of a lifetime, always by my side… couldn't he count as a second person?'

Strangely, he couldn't. But the gentleman at least laughed warmly.

At that point, I turned full of hope to Andre to my left. 'Do you have any idea how beautiful elephants are?'

'We clearly have a different concept of beauty', he answered drily.

'Come on, Andre, you cannot leave Sri Lanka without having done a safari!'

He kept quiet for a few seconds, during which I looked at him like a Labrador puppy waiting for his owner to return and play with him, my eyelashes fluttering faster than a hummingbird on coke.

'Oh, Scheisse', he finally surrendered. 'You are not entirely wrong, for once (smart-arse/moron). Actually, it would be a shame to fly to India on Monday without having had this experience', he conceded.

And so, ta-da! Problem solved, 54 dollars saved, and another experience shared with Andre. I'm so happy.

'But please promise that, once the safari is over, our paths will separate', he implored me.

A smart-arse to the very end. And a moron, too. 'I promise. I've nearly had enough of you, too.'

We went back home, took a shower and then Andre came to my

184

guesthouse, given that I am practically staying next door. He arrived with a beer and several bookmarks. 'Choose the one you like so that you'll remember me.'

Ooooooooooooh, how sweet of him! And they are all really pretty.

'I thought it would be a nice thing to have a few of them with me and give them to people I meet along the way.'

Indeed it is.

We then settle down on the cute porch and start sipping our beers, while he explains the technique he uses to create his bookmarks, and I listen carefully. I really don't know anything about art.

'Listen, I don't feel like going to the beach tonight, given that tomorrow we have to wake up at 5am for the safari', he tells me. 'But Sandula and her family have gone to see some relatives, so if you want, we can go there to be more at peace and relaxed.'

Being more at peace and relaxed? What does he mean? Or what does he have in mind? I am super at peace and relaxed in my homestay, even though the lady managing it is continually popping in and out of the garden.

Okay, then. Let's move to Sandula's garden in the house next door. The Universe is winking at us through a multitude of stars, we can hear distant music from the beach carried on the night breeze, while all around us is muffled silence.

Andre goes into the house and comes out with some *Arak*, the local liqueur, which is similar to Italian grappa, and a Sprite. And I am perfectly aware that a few hours before I told myself to let go of any expectations and preset ideas about how things should go in my opinion, but how hard it is to free yourself from such a deep-rooted habit! Noticing my thoughts is the first step towards change, sure. However, from being aware of our constant mental mechanisms to being able to change them is neither an easy nor immediate step. It almost seems like a waste, to me. Such a perfect concurrence of details should unequivocally lead to the one and only conclusion of a beautiful night of cuddles. A way of celebrating life and experiencing the moment even more fully. There's alcohol, there are stars, there are even flowers in the garden releasing their sweet perfume; there's an empty house, there's us, young, healthy, attractive and even single, in a beautiful, new place, looking for adventure...

I am fully immersed in these silent thoughts of mine, and I smile because I see myself split in two, with the new Roby slapping the old Roby's hand with a ruler for entertaining the same old thoughts. Andre interrupts my reflection with an unexpected suggestion. 'Shall we take a tour of the house to see how they live?'

Just like that, out of the blue (whale). Oh là là. Wow, could he be about to make his move? Does he perhaps feel more at ease within four walls?

There's only one way to find out.

'Sure, let's go in.'

And so we go in. The light doesn't even come on for a while. We are facing each other, in the dark, very close. It's the perfect moment.

....

E non succede un cazzo. And bugger all happens.

But really nothing, *niente di niente, nada, nicevo, rien de rien, nichts.* Bloody fuck all. Andre really meant us to take a tour of the house.

Thank God he cannot read my mind. Or, why on earth, God, can he not read my mind? Points of view.

And so let's have this tour. Let's go and see what lies behind that curtain which has always separated us from Sandula's house. We discover that the four of them sleep all together in a modest bedroom. What worries Andre and his Teutonic chef's soul more, however, is the absence of a fridge. 'For example, where do they keep the butter?'

Secret of Fátima Number Ten.

After a while we go out, talk a bit more, and then he tells me, 'I'll let you go. We have to wake up soon'.

'Yes, it's better to call it a night. Thanks for the lovely evening, and see you in a few hours.'

I cover those ten metres separating me from my homestay, and although my eyes are reduced to tiny slits out of tiredness, I still wear my trademark smile, because thank God I am able to laugh about the gap between what happens in my mind, and what happens (or doesn't) in reality.

And also because I have had my answer. At least this way it will be easier to drop all those bloody expectations.

Okay then. Now I'm off to bed for a few hours, and then elephants!

Mosquito bites so far: 3
Bouts of diarrhoea: 0
Sleeping and dozing dogs spotted in various locations: 71
Pages of the book I'm currently reading: 187
Jokes I've told today: 42
Jokes that Andre has understood: 31
Jokes that made him laugh: 22
Time it took Andre to finish his watercolour: 1 hour and 15 minutes
Minutes it took me to convince Andre to come on the safari with me: 2
Times I've thought that Andre and I might kiss: 7
Times Andre has thought that he and I might kiss: -16
Bookmarks that Andre carries around to give to the people he meets: 20
How distant my London life feels at the moment: 1.7 light years

DAY 14
'It's forbidden to walk along the railways'
-Udawalawe National Park and Ella,
Sunday 25th February 2018-

I've finally arrived in hippy-magnet Ella, a real jewel. I loved it instantly, the moment I got off the train. Immersed in greenery, surrounded by plantations, with a town centre that is as small as it is lovely, with strong hippy influences that are visible in the elegant little shops or in the cosy bars with a super relaxed vibe. Basically, there are only two roads, along which you can find a multitude of bijou restaurants, cafés, bars, spas and hotels. From these two perpendicular roads branch off a labyrinth of narrow roads and tracks stretching up the mountain, making Ella the base camp for several interesting trekking itineraries.

I've just finished having dinner with a Polish girl who has a degree in Criminology and is currently living in China, where she teaches English (typical encounters you make whilst travelling). Talking with her reinforced my total lack of interest in visiting that country. She told me how people there are not at all encouraged to be free thinkers, and how they show very little compassion for animals. The government dictates the number of children they are allowed to have, and while so many people in China love European culture and want to learn English, they don't seem to have any intention of actually venturing out of their own world. It seems to me that China is another planet, but in a negative sense. India, too, is out of this world, but in such a magnificent and spectacular way.

Aaaaanyway, let's talk about my day. At 5am the driver from the travel agency that sold us the safari tickets came to pick Andre and me up. Back home, I'm not exactly a morning person, or at least waking up this early takes a huge effort, but while travelling I know that it's always for a great cause. Getting up at an ungodly hour means anticipating adventure, or a majestic sunrise to admire, so it doesn't make me grumpy. In fact, I woke up at 4am because I had to pack my backpack. One way or another, while Andre would be coming back to Mirissa, I had to get to Ella. I'd promised him that our paths would separate today, and I always keep my word.

Still cloaked in darkness, we headed off towards my favourite animals, stopping along the way for the traditional tea and roti. Roti is a type of round, soft unleavened flatbread made from stoneground wholewheat flour, and it is consumed in many Southern Asian countries, including India, Pakistan, Bangladesh, Nepal and, of course, Sri Lanka. Tea is obviously drunk by the hectolitre in this country, which is covered in tea plantations. There are many kinds of tea, and no doubt Andre would be able to tell me a lot about the three main varieties: black, white and green. As for me, I can only say that my favourite tea is either the milky one, chai, which is super sweet, or the ginger one, which leaves you with a lively and slightly spicy taste in your mouth.

When we got to the Udawalawe national park, we switched to a jeep, all to ourselves, and started our safari. This national park covers an area of around 300 square kilometres, and my Bible, the Lonely Planet guide, informs us that it is home to dozens of cheetahs, though seeing them on the safari is quite rare.

We encountered other jeeps while driving around the park, especially when there were big wild animals peacefully standing in the middle of the road or near to it. In general, however, the atmosphere was very relaxed. Our driver stopped in front of a river, and so did many other jeep drivers, as the safari guides knew that elephants would come to drink and play in the water here. And, when they finally arrived, I felt an immense tenderness towards them. A whole family turned up, with a baby elephant who was not even two weeks old, according to our guide. He wasn't yet able to stand properly, *piccolino*, and in fact he fell over repeatedly. Every time he did, his mother would use her trunk to help him stand up again. Infinite sweetness. I had facial paresis afterwards, I was smiling that much. Andre, instead, had paresis of the hands from all the photos he took, given that I had asked him to take pictures for me, too, since my camera is quite crappy. We stopped by the river for about twenty minutes, observing how the elephants would interact with each other. I felt as if I was in one of the many documentaries I've watched in my life. And I felt so at peace. This was one of the few things that I had set my mind on doing when I read on the plane that Sri Lanka is the country with the highest concentration of elephants in the world. I looked at the baby elephant, so endearing in all his vulnerability, dumbfounded by his own trunk, as he was yet to grasp its meaning and function and would even stumble over it. He would hide a little behind his mum's feet, only emerging once in a while, while other elephants were happily playing in the river, spraying each other with water.

While we go to work, do our housework, quarrel with our neighbours, write emails, send invoices, spend boring hours on public transport, cry watching movies and engage in all the other activities that make up our lives… animals carry on peacefully with theirs. Our small incumbencies or daily vicissitudes, which absorb us so entirely, are totally insignificant to the rest of the universe, which lives in full harmony with nature. Nature provides animals and plants with everything and lacks nothing. It is abundant by definition: there is an abundance of water, plants, light, fish and minerals in the soil. And so far, Sri Lanka has been a daily reminder of this. Everywhere, nature is so luxuriant. You are surrounded by bright emerald greens and plants overloaded with fruit: you have mangoes, coconuts, papayas, pineapples, bananas and so many other delicious fruits at your fingertips that you can't imagine how anyone could go hungry here. What I would never have expected, though, is to see so many animals. I've been here for less than two weeks, and I've marvelled at huge and tiny turtles, hermit crabs, dolphins, chameleons… And

I've seen two of the biggest mammals in the world, the blue whale and the elephant! Everywhere is life, energy, strength, abundance. And this gets me thinking... If we exist in such a universe, if there is a God who provides so much for animals, how much more would He provide us humans if only we were able to trust Him? How much more could the Universe give us if only we could go against all the fears that keep us anchored to the small grey reality we nevertheless complain about continuously? If we could escape our fear-induced scarcity mentality, and find our way towards an abundance mindset, how much more could we receive from the Universe?

The safari went on for a while longer and we managed to see some buffaloes, eagles, owls, foxes, peacocks, crocodiles and storks. Our jeep driver almost made me laugh when he stopped the car and pointed at a tree branch some 15 metres high, saying, 'Look over there, can you spot the chameleon?'

I mean, a chameleon spotted at that distance. While driving, by the way. That's expert eyes for you.

So beautiful! I wished the safari could have lasted a bit longer, to be honest, as I've never seen so many elephants, and so close. Now that I am writing it down, I realise that this is another attachment. Man, how sneaky and treacherous these attachments can be! They are really everywhere, so deeply rooted in our way of being. Getting rid of them won't be an easy fight, but being able to spot them and being aware of them is in itself a huge first step.

On the way back, the driver stopped at a restaurant where we fell into our first tourist trap, which inevitably happens sooner or later. Every dish cost five times what we would pay in one of those local restaurants that Andre and I like to go to. The places that local people go to are where you get an authentic experience. The food is dirt-cheap and generally good, you can interact with local people, and you don't even get charged for the salmonella, which is on the house. What's more, without anyone telling us in advance, Andre and I had to pay for the driver's meal, too. We would probably have been happy to invite him to join us as our guest, but I'd have preferred it to have been our idea, not something imposed on us. Andre had very few Sri Lankan rupees left, given that he is leaving tomorrow for India, so he tried to discuss the matter with the restaurant owner, who quite strangely stopped understanding our English at that point.

Oh well, let go of this whole thing, too.

Then, the Universe came to my rescue. As luck would have it, our jeep driver knew a taxi driver who could take me to Ella for 1,500 rupees, which is around five pounds eighty, thus saving me the hassle of taking several buses with my backpack.

And so, the moment to say goodbye to Andre, so long awaited by him, had finally arrived.

'How happy are you to get rid of me?' I asked, smiling.

'Who's getting rid of you? Let's meet up in India, too. What do you think?'

I've never made an appointment like that in all my life. 'Let's meet up at the cinema. Let's meet up outside the shop. Let's meet up outside the station. Let's meet up at the Southbank Centre…'. I've heard and said sentences like these countless times, but I have to admit I was missing 'Let's meet up in India'. He flies tomorrow to the south of India, where I am heading on March 12th.

'Let's keep in contact, come on. Also because I have to send you today's pictures. I travel quite slowly, so even if you arrive in India two weeks after me, we can surely meet up somewhere', continues Andre.

'That's perfect, then. Thanks for everything, I'm so happy to have met you. It's been the best change of plans ever', I said, hugging him.

And it was indeed. I felt a sense of melancholy rising up through my body that lingered for about a minute, but I know that other days and experiences together await us in India. And how cool to think that I'll be reuniting with someone I've met while travelling. Much as I enjoy continually meeting new people, there comes a time when you kind of need some reassuring familiarity. When Andre was telling me about seeing his friend Jacob again, that morning we met at Sandula's, I would never have thought that *he*, Andre, would sort of become my personal Jacob.

Anyway, there are almost three weeks between now and seeing him again, and who knows what could happen to either of us during such a period (quick pause in writing to touch wood and *fare le corna*–a very Italian gesture to avert anything bad coming your way).

And so, with my backpack on my shoulders, here I go to 'Ella-Ella-Ella-Eh-Eh-Eh', obviously sung à la Rihanna.

When I arrived around 3pm, I once again adopted the 'Mary and Joseph' technique, knocking at the door of several little hotels and hostels, which however all turned out to be quite expensive. In the end, I went down a small lane which seemed to disappear into the greenery, following a wooden arrow pointing to some 'Freedom Camp'. The name says it all. In essence, it's a campsite, and I haven't tried this type of accommodation so far, so why not? There is basically a small house, with some rooms available there, plus a big garden with a few tents dotted around. I could see 'Roby's' written in magic ink on one of those.

'Is breakfast included in the price?' I asked the guy with dreads and kind eyes who manages the garden, and whose mum takes care of the rooms in the house.

'No, breakfast is not included, but spliffs tonight are.'

Ah, ecco.

I settled into my tent, unpacking all my heavier clothes because Ella is 1,041 metres above sea level. It is indeed part of the luxuriant Hill Country, where the green is brighter and more intense and the landscape is dominated by tea plantations. From my tent, I have a breath-taking view over gorgeous hills and beautiful mountains. This is my luxury. It's also finally time to take out my trekking shoes, given that the main reasons for visiting 'Ella-Ella-Ella-Eh-Eh-Eh' are two beautiful uphill treks: one to Little Adam's Peak and the other to Ella Rock (of course, Ella-Ella-Eh-Eh-Eh Rock).

I've read that from the train station you can walk to the Nine Arch Bridge, which is one of the main attractions in Ella, so I set off towards the station. While walking, the realisation dawned that strangely I felt sorrier to say goodbye to Andre than to Shanaka. In both cases, I am quite sure I will see them again, but with Andre I have obviously talked more and more in depth, given that there was no language barrier, apart from his German accent. I remember one of Oscar Wilde's aphorisms, which I've always liked, and which inevitably comes to my mind every time I have to say goodbye to someone new:

> *'It is always painful to part from people whom one has known for a brief space of time. The absence of old friends one can endure with equanimity. But even a momentary separation from anyone to whom one has just been introduced is almost unbearable.'*

This is so true. I am not thinking about my friends in London or Italy at all, now that I am in such a distant and different reality. I won't see them for months, and the idea has no effect on me. Instead I spent only three and a half days with Andre and the idea of going back to being on my own feels so weird now.

'Being on my own' so to speak, that is: while crossing the road in front of the station I heard a girl call out, 'Hey, hello! I know you'.

Ehm… Maybe, but I don't know you.

'The hostel in Colombo?' she prompted. And then I actually remembered her. We had literally talked for five minutes because her backpack had broken and she was going around with a proper suitcase, which looked completely out of context in that setting, with the type of travellers staying there.

'Did you manage to sort out your backpack?' I inquire, and she tells me that yes, she bought a new one in Colombo.

Her name is Xenia, she is Polish and she is travelling with a slightly weird girl (and for me to say that, it takes a lot, trust me!). This other girl is Slovakian and has the most nasal voice I've ever heard in my whole life but, what's even stranger, has an inexplicable Indian accent. In fact, not only does she have this super strong Indian accent, but she has also adopted some of the characteristic traits I've noticed in the English of Indians I've met, such as repeating words two or three times and finishing her sentences with 'No?'

As if this wasn't enough, she's also adopted the head wobble, moving her head from left to right, almost tracing a horizontal eight (or infinity sign). The point is that when I'm talking with Indians I find it interesting and charming, even though after years of travelling around their magical land I still don't fully understand it or know how to interpret it. However, that same trait in a European woman speaking in English has a completely different effect. I don't even know how to explain it.

I've known for ages that the language we use is a mirror of our reality, and by listening to the words we choose, the tone of voice, the intonation, we can understand and infer so much about someone. Language is power, whether you like it or not. And I am sorry to say that this Slovakian girl talking English as if she was born and raised in Mumbai gives the impression that... she is not completely okay. Such a weird and displacing effect. What's the story here? How come she speaks Indian English? Moreover, her English spoken by an Indian with just a little education, maybe somewhere in rural India, would have been very good. That same English, however, spoken by a woman from Europe, and who therefore has better access to education, makes her sound like some unfortunate person who has not been able to study at all. Honestly, it was such a confusing and weird effect, an incredible contrast between what you'd expect, based on her appearance, and the ideas that arise in the mind when you listen to her. A contrast which sadly does her no favours, though I am pretty sure it will make her unforgettable to me at the same time.

Like me, they are also heading to the Nine Arch Bridge, which is indeed one of the main reasons for coming to see this lovely little town. So we started walking together, following the railway track. Ella's train station is a real gem and was even recognised as 'the best kept station in Sri Lanka'. In my opinion, it should also win another award because it's the first place I've found where you can recycle. Hallelujah! Finally some respect shown to this beautiful environment that gives us so much beauty!

A poster at the train station warns us that 'It is forbidden to walk along the railway tracks'. Never has a poster been more pointless, since everybody knows that you have to walk along the tracks to reach this truly unique and picturesque bridge that rises out of the greenery, supported by its nine arches.

Once we got there, the Universe made it so that a train arrived shortly afterwards, emerging from the tunnel dug through the mountain. The train was so evocative, puffing noisily like I've seen in old movies, and a lovely faded blue, which stood out beautifully against the green of the trees framing the landscape. How different from the images of beaches and sea that my eyes have been soaking up these last few days. It was a proper picture-postcard scene. Indeed, it's one of those iconic photos they use to represent Sri Lanka in travel guides. Gorgeous. I really liked it.

I then had dinner with Xenia and the other girl, and I finally made my way back to the Freedom Camp. In the garden, not far from my tent, the guy with dreads and kind eyes and one of his friends were lighting a small fire, and two white girls were sitting with them.

'Can I join you?' I asked, and I was warmly invited to do so. The girls turned out to be two Italians from Trieste, two friends travelling together for a few months, doing some volunteering here and there. While the two guys were rolling silently, limiting their presence there to just listening, the girls told me a bit about their trip, and guess what? One of them has done the silent Vipassana meditation retreat I've signed up to do in Nepal in April.

'It will totally blow your mind. You'll see. The first few days, I wasn't able to sleep as I was too hungry since they give you a snack at 5pm, and that's it until the morning. Just get ready. It's huge.'

Wow, I honestly don't know whether to feel more excited or more scared at the thought of it. Anyway, Nepal is over two months away, so for now let's worry about how cold it will be tonight in my tent. Goodnight, Ella-Ella-Ella-Eh-Eh-Eh.

Elephants I saw in Udawalawe park: more than 30
Smiles that seeing them has brought me: 839
Pictures I made Andre take for me: 83
Head oscillations per minute by the strange girl: 26
Cost of a night in a tent at the Freedom Camp: 1,250 rupees (around 6 pounds)
Hippies I stumbled upon during my walk in town: 211
Number of arches supporting the Nine Arch Bridge: 9
Months the Slovakian girl spent living with an Indian family in Chennai: 3 (mystery unveiled!) (Well, partially… Would I also start speaking with an Indian accent if I were to spend some time with an Indian family at this point? Or is my accent already set in stone?)
Meals I've eaten that have included rice so far: 19
Messages Shanaka has sent me today: 2
Messages Chamath has sent me today: 5
Temperature forecast tonight in Ella: 6°C (for Elevation's sake)

DAY 15

'Let's sculpt this bum, come on, Roby'
-Ella, Monday 26th February 2018-

For Ella-Ella-Ella-Eh-Eh-Eh's sake, last night it was fuuuuuuucking freezing! The only reason I'm not leaving is because I can't be bothered to pack everything again and go looking for somewhere else to stay. Oh, man, this is part of the adventure, too. The crazy humidity, as well. Anyway, I'll stay one more night, tops (but that's what I thought about Mirissa, too…).

I spent a peaceful morning reading and enjoying a beautiful breakfast with a coffee (finally!) and a chocolate and coconut roti, thanks to which I made peace with the world after the cooooold night. It was raining slightly, so I was not sure about venturing towards Little Adam's Peak. Xenia and her friend were leaving today to go to Adam's Peak itself, where unforeseen encounters and signs from destiny permitting, I was planning to go tomorrow.

As soon as the weather stabilised a bit, I focused my energies big time into my other project, parallel to the 'letting it go' one and somewhat less spiritual. I'm talking about the toning of my booty. After all, people come to Ella to do trekking, and as I already mentioned there are two main places to walk to.

I set out towards the first one, Little Adam's Peak, which, as the name itself suggests, is not at all difficult. I almost immediately met a Dutch couple, both of them really nice, with whom I initially got lost in the tea plantations, exactly when it started raining again. The Universe however came to our rescue and sent a local man our way, who showed us with lots of gestures how to go back on the right track and who, Universe my ass, wanted to be paid for his help.

198

I reached Little Adam's Peak still feeling relatively fresh, I have to say, even if the path gets quite steep at the very end. The ascent and descent must be a total of 5km, but the last 20 minutes tested us a bit. Once at the top we enjoyed the view, which was really beautiful, each of us drinking from our own bottle and sharing some biscuits. Long live the solidarity between travellers, always.

Once we'd climbed down, I bought myself a nice refreshing coconut from a toothless lady who was selling them along the road. To be honest, I am not crazy about coconut water, but at least it's thirst quenching, natural and good for your skin, or that's what they say anyway. It's certainly healthier than Diet Coke, which is what I would rather have drunk, but which they didn't have.

We hiked down from Little Adam's Peak to then ascend Ella Rock, which was definitely more tiring, for Trekking's sake. You pass through a mixture of different landscapes, from a little bridge to fields of various crops, passing beyond a small mountain village and finally climbing up a narrow path which ends with a very iconic and spectacular spur of rocks. And guess what there is up there? A small temple dug in the stone, what else?

The statue of the Buddha stands there, serene and imperturbable, contemplating that peaceful landscape every day. It took us a total of three and a half hours to go and come back, but it was definitely worth it because the view from up there was indeed spectacular. Everywhere you looked were bright green hills, gentle undulations of the Earth which almost seemed to lull your eyes in a silent and grandiose lullaby. A feast for the eyes indeed.

What was absolutely not a feast for the eyes was me. I even disgusted myself, to a level of 9/10, all sweaty, dirty and not a little bit smelly, too.

Apart from a long and very much needed shower, I've spent the rest of the day writing and reading a bit, posting an update on Facebook, WhatsApping my brothers and friends. Chamath is undeterred and continues to send me an average of three to four messages a day, to which I answer mostly out of courtesy, given that the conversation has never actually become particularly interesting. Besides, I don't even think I'll see him again in the next five years, so the only thing prompting me to write back is the manners my parents raised me with.

Shanaka, too, is another constant presence on my WhatsApp, and every message of his is a hymn to creative spelling and an almost teenager-like sweetness and cheesiness. He reaffirms every day that he misses me and that he thinks of me a lot. These things he says on one hand make me smile, because they seem like the universal sentences that you almost feel obliged to say at this stage, and on the other, make me sigh over this indiscriminate use they are subjected to. Anyway, I respond to him with more pleasure, and I do think that yes, I'll definitely see him again before leaving. I certainly don't miss him, because I'm too busy enjoying every minute of my days here, which are brimming with potential surprises, but I think of him, and when I do, I smile. With his dark eyes, his perfect smile and his imaginative English, Shanaka puts me in a good mood, and long live all the men who are able to make us smile and laugh.

Finally, I treated myself to a nice massage. Man, if I don't deserve one today, I have no idea when! I went to the massage parlour after dinner, so as to be well relaxed and ready to jump into bed afterwards.

Unfortunately, in the establishment I chose, one of the few still open at that late time, there was only a man working. In Western countries I have no problem at all being massaged by a male masseur. In fact, I generally ask for it ('Good morning, do you have a tall, muscular masseur with big strong hands working there? Fantastic, can I book a deep-tissue massage with him? A very deep one, two hours long. Thanks.'). (For the record, I've never made such a phone call. Not yet at least.) In the Asian countries I've visited, however, I always prefer a woman. Knowing how limited contact between men and women generally is here, and in truth still shocked by Chamath's revelations in this respect, I am afraid that a male masseur might take liberties I would never concede him.

Anyway, fears aside, it was a really good massage. The *coup de grâce* to make me sleep like a log, freezing or not. Tonight I'm going to bed in my jacket, too, so I should be okay (hopefully).

Coconuts I've drunk so far: 7
Kms I've walked today, according to my iPhone: 21.1
Ella's elevation: 1,041 metres
Elevation of Little Adam's Peak: 1,141 metres
My height: 1.75 metres
The masseur's height: around 1.70 metres
Small restaurants and places you can do a cooking course in Ella-Ella-Ella-Eh-Eh-Eh: 63
Varieties of curry in Sri Lanka: 85?
Cms of grey roots hidden under my bandana: 1
From 1 to 10, level of peace with the world I attained today: 10

DAY 16

'... Andre?'

-Dalhousie, Tuesday 27th February 2018-

I. CANNOT. BELIEVE. IT.

Or in Italian: NON. CI. CREDO.

This is it. This is one of those marvellous coincidences, an overlapping of events so perfect not even the best writer could conjure it up. An example of the kind of synchronicities that happen to me often nowadays and seem to intensify and become even more frequent when I'm travelling. Or maybe I just have more mental space to notice them. I stopped believing in coincidences many years ago, as I see them as a sort of message, like a wink from God almost to reassure me, 'Yes, Roby, you are doing well. Don't you see how everything dovetails perfectly?'

I might sometimes force their interpretation, but this awareness makes each day a fresh and interesting page to read in a totally new light.

Basically, this morning I emerge from my hibernation in the Freedom Camp tent, and the lady who owns the little building kindly offers me a cup of tea. Such a simple gesture, and yet so beautiful. I really appreciate these small acts of kindness and, at the same time, I'm developing a sort of reverence and extreme sense of gratitude towards food. Back home in London, or in Italy, food doesn't require much effort, that is apart from taking some means of transport, spending two hours touring the whole supermarket and finally making your way home overloaded with bags, panting up and down the London Underground escalators. Food is ready, available, abundant, prepared, colourful, enticing, lazy friendly, practical, functional and quite often not a little removed from its original form.

When I'm in Asia, however, I can always see the hard work behind food. When I buy rice, which I usually select without a second thought from an aisle overflowing with brightly coloured packages, I now see the Vietnamese women standing in the rice fields with water up to their knees. I think about the backache, the leg problems, the humidity and the scorching sun which torment them every day. And all this work for maybe one or two dollars a day.

When people far worse off than me financially kindly offer me a cup of tea, I now see the old women trekking up the hills with their already heavy baskets, filling them further with tea leaves that they tear from the tea plants while walking.

I saw the fishermen pulling their fishing nets onto the beach in Mount Lavinia. As the death dance came to an end and the men finally opened their nets, I could see in their eyes the hope for a good catch, since that would mean a good profit and therefore a good meal for their family, or maybe even some new clothes for their children. When I published those photos on Facebook, a vegetarian and promoter of animal rights among my contacts commented, 'How disgusting! Shame on them for fishing such small fish!', a view which perfectly proves my point. Food here takes on a totally different meaning, strong, genuine, direct and pure. Food is life and truth. It is effort, and a lot of it. There's no space for all the fuss we Westerners make, quite often just to keep up with the latest trend. We live in a society where specific dietary requirements now seem to be the norm and might even qualify us as people who take care of our health or worry about the environment. This desire to 'take care of one's health and wellbeing' is the driving force behind each new theory which a few years later will be exposed, refuted, debunked, proved to be scientifically unfounded and replaced by another new diet. It seems to me that in all this nutritional mayhem, we have lost respect for food. By demonising certain foods, I feel we have moved away from that sense of community and communion that eating together has always created. And so we have also moved away from other cultures, where food is precious and vital, and not something to be used or rejected as we see fit. And this cup of tea I'm being offered now speaks of the hard work of many people, and of the generosity of this lady who is wishing me a safe trip.

Oh yes, because I went to bed thinking that I would be leaving Ella-Ella-Ella-Eh-Eh-Eh to go to Niyura-Elya, but last night I chatted a bit with Andre who told me that he found it a bit of a tourist trap and did not recommend it. So, while sipping that good, sweet, revitalising tea, soaking up the vivid green of the plantations it came from, carpeting the hills in front of me, I decided to change my plans once again. I trust Andre's advice, so it's better if I go straight to Adam's Peak.

So I went to the train station to see whether they could change my ticket, which they did with no problem. What was not granted, despite my requesting it at least four times, was a window seat. I therefore found myself sitting in an aisle seat. However, as nobody came to claim the seat next to mine at Ella-Ella-Ella-Eh-Eh-Eh, I decided to sit there myself for the time being. 'Then, when the seat owner arrives, I'll move back to my aisle seat', I told myself, guided by my strong moral principles regarding seat bookings.

At Haputale, this tall and thin man gets on. He has a wrinkly and rough face. The overall first impression is that he is a bit gaunt, but there's something handsome about him. He has brown hair and definitely needs a haircut. Ten kilos more, and he would qualify as hhhhhhot, ten kilos which by the way I could happily pass on to him, if I had the superpower to remove flab from various spots, as if emptying my pockets. He's definitely the kind of guy that intrigues me, whose face seems to be silently telling a long story. And, based on a quick 3.5-second appraisal, I'd say this story includes a fair degree of excess, some discomfort and a good amount of adventure. When he enters my compartment, our eyes meet with a mutual hint of a smile. Then, just as I am silently praying to the Universe, 'Make him sit here. Make him sit here', the stranger with that seasoned aura tells me in perfect English, 'I'm sorry. That's supposed to be my seat'.

'Oh, sure', I answer, and I move aside. I don't mind losing the window seat to Mr Hhhhhhot But Malnourished. And by that same magic that happens to me every day now, several times and with anyone, we start talking as if it were the only logical thing to do. If I tried to experience this magic on the London Underground, I would probably be reported to the police after two stops.

'Hello, how are you?' I begin.

'All good. Life is beautiful', he answers in a native accent that I am not quite able to place.

'How was Haputale? Did I miss something pretty?' I inquire, given that I won't visit this little town.

'In fact, I hardly saw it. I was in a Zen monastery on a retreat. I've been there for ten days', he explains, and I manage to look interested even while my attention is drawn to an incredible discovery I've just made: my neighbour's eyes are two slightly different colours, a detail I've only ever seen in two other people and which contributes to the overall non-conventional handsomeness of that tired and emaciated face.

'Oh, what a coincidence! I've recently enrolled on a Vipassana meditation retreat I will do in Nepal at the end of my trip', I tell him. 'And the best part is that I've basically never meditated before, so I'm really curious to see how it will go. How does the Zen monastery work?'

'Oh, it's way more relaxed than what you will be doing. We would meditate in the mornings only, mostly in groups or, if you preferred, alone in your little bedroom. In the afternoon we were free to do whatever we wanted.'

'And what did you do?'

'Well, I read, I walked in the monastery garden, and I also drew a lot. I am an artist. I do several kinds of illustration, and with the meditation, the Zen stories and the spliffs I smoked (*ah, ecco*), I always felt very inspired. I filled two sketchbooks with drawings of all sorts.'

'Oh, wow, what a coincidence! You are the second artist I've met this week. The other guy does watercolours and bookmarks', I tell him.

He looks at me a bit perplexed. He frowns, pauses in silence for two seconds, and then asks me, '... Andre?'

....

I. CANNOT. BELIEVE. IT.

I look at him even more perplexed, and then a question hits me like a thunder. 'Wait... are you Jacob?'

Noooooooooooooooooooooooooo! Come on! I mean, of all the days I spent in Sri Lanka, of all the trains crossing this country, and departing from Ella-Ella-Ella-Eh-Eh-Eh every day, and then of all the seats on a train, Andre's friend booked the seat next to mine! In fact, I booked the seat next to his, given that if I hadn't changed my mind at breakfast, I would have been on another train, headed elsewhere.

Oh, my God. I adore life. I adore the world. And don't anyone dare tell me that this is a simple coincidence, because the Universe had to pull so many strings for it to happen that all I can do is visualise myself jumping up and down clapping enthusiastically, stopping only to whistle with two fingers. Congratulations, God. Wow, Universe. Hats off, really.

After hearing so much about him, here I am with Jacob, this Canadian actor and artist whom Andre met in Mexico and with whom he had stayed in contact on Facebook for years.

'Oh my God, you have no idea how much Andre talked about you! 'Jacob taught me this, Jacob taught me that, Jacob's here...' I cannot believe it! We have to send him a selfie now!'

We took a picture that I sent straight to Andre, and while waiting for his outpouring of utter surprise (but, being German, he might just say, '*Oh. Wunderbar'*), Jacob started telling me about his journey thus far. 'I left Canada in December and I will basically be travelling until I run out of money, or until they call me back for the shoot', he explains. By an incredible stroke of luck, he was chosen to basically play himself in a Canadian TV series, *Trailer Park Boys*, and this opportunity kind of solved his life, granting him the peace of mind and security to devote himself to his two passions, travelling and art. 'To be honest, I am at the end of my trip in Sri Lanka, too. In three days I fly to India.'

He's going to India, too? Another little breadcrumb left by cosmic Hansel to mark out a path which is already quite well defined.

I wonder what can be behind such absurd (non) coincidences. Is someone telling me that I am on the right path? On the right path for what? For believing that there is always someone taking care of me? That if I listen to my inner voice, my wishes, my intuition, and I align my actions to my thoughts, I am rewarded and my life is simplified? And, more importantly... if the Universe put this man on my path, what can I expect to happen when I see him again?

Because I will definitely see him again. Such synchronicity cannot be ignored.

Yes, but I also cannot ignore the fact that I've done it again. Here I am immediately projecting myself into the future, thinking about what could happen. You have to stay in the present, in this moment, in the *hic et nunc*, Roby. Okay, I caught myself earlyish. Just seeing the mental mechanisms lurch into life almost automatically is a big step forward. Being aware of one's mental patterns is no mean feat, not at all. Of course you then hope that this will lead to changes in behaviour, but it takes time. We are talking about mind muscles that require long-term training. What matters is that once again I became aware of what I was thinking, and that I shouldn't judge myself negatively for this. We must have compassion for all the old versions of ourselves that we are trying to improve, and which are not so easy to change.

'I'm getting off at the next stop, Dalhousie, but Andre, you and I absolutely have to meet up again in India', I tell him, not with the tone of someone suggesting an option, but rather stating an irrefutable truth.

There are people who arrange to meet in a café, and those who arrange to meet somewhere in India. But yes, no worries, it's a small country, see you there!

'Sure, it would be cool, meeting up there. I don't have any plans, so for me any place goes, as long as it is in a hilly area, since the heat kills me. I know that Andre will focus on Southern India.'

'Exactly, and so will I. So, see you somewhere in the south of India', I conclude, taking a handful of the peanuts he's been sharing with me, and planting two kisses on his scrawny and unshaven cheeks. 'See you in India, then. Take care, Jacob, it's been such an amazing pleasure meeting you!', I say to him, while I grab my backpack and prepare to get off the train.

Unbelievable. It still hasn't sunk in.

In Dalhousie, I go into one of the first little hotels I find near the station, and here I practice the old script I'll be repeating for the next two months.

'How much is a single room?'

'2,500 rupees' (which is around ten pounds).

'No, I'm sorry, I only have 1,200', I answer with a contrite smile while stepping away.

'Okay, madam, I show you two rooms. One costs 2,000 rupees', he counter strikes, trying his luck again, not acknowledging my declared budget.

'No, I'm sorry, it's too much, sir.'

'The other one is 1,500 rupees.' The hotel owner is trying it on again. He doesn't let up. On one hand, I'm a bit annoyed by this, but on the other, I like it. I find bargaining so much fun! It's a part of me I was unaware of before I worked in Morocco for a few months. There I learnt the subtle art of haggling, developing an appreciation for the (ample) time it requires, its particular turns of phrase, its settings... This part of me, generally repressed in London (but not entirely), leaps and somersaults at the chance to come out and play when I travel in Asia.

I follow him to check the room, which the gentleman shows me with some indifference.

'But it has no windows! No, thank you, sir.' And, as per the script in such cases, I shoulder my backpack to indicate that he really is losing me this time. It's his turn to make a move now, or I will have to surrender.

'Okay, take the other room for 1,500 rupees', he gives in.

Yes! And–wait for this–sometimes I really go for it, so I add, '1,500 with breakfast included, sir, please'.

A conspiratorial smile, hands theatrically clasped together to accompany my 'please', and that single room with a private bathroom is mine for five pounds fifty.

It's only when I see the room key that I notice its number, 23: Andre's favourite number–the one that comes up over and over again in his life. Another super clear sign. Yes. Andre, Jacob and I will see each other again in India.

As for the rest of the day, it rained all afternoon, which didn't stop me from visiting a tea plantation nearby. Tea plants decorate the surrounding hills, cloaking them in bright green. Even though I have already seen it, it's always interesting to hear about the harvesting, withering, crushing, drying, filtering and packaging. In fact, Dalhousie takes its name from a tea plantation, which seems to be the only nice thing to see around here, at the end of the day. Besides Adam's Peak, of course, which is the main reason people stop here.

It's 8.49pm, and it's still raining. I think I'm going to go to bed soon to get ready for my mega trek tomorrow morning. Or rather, tonight. I came here to trek up to Adam's Peak, and it would be disappointing to leave Dalhousie without having been on top of Adam's Peak because the weather was not on my side.

Let's see how the weather is at 1.30am.

Good night, world. Old Roby goes to bed.

Jacob's age: around 42?
Colour of his eyes: one is green and the other one is brownish
Character he reminds me of: the animal obsessed with the acorn in *Ice Age*
TV series he's been acting in for years: *Trailer Park Boys*, as Jacob Collins

State of Jacob's hair: in need of tender loving care
State of my hair: severely challenged
Cost of the ticket to visit the tea plantation with a guide: 500 rupees (£1.70)
Kg of tea leaves that each woman on the plantation has to pick in order to get paid: 20
Amount she is paid for this job: 800 rupees (not even 3 pounds)
Average no. of pictures I send my brothers daily: 9
Messages from Lucio so far: 0
Messages sent to Lucio so far: 0

DAY 17

'Then I bring beers and give you a foot massage'
-Adam's Peak and Kitulgala,
Wednesday 28th February 2018-ep

A short and troubled night, what with the mosquitoes, which ended their lives splattered against the wall, deservedly, and my iPhone which froze. I couldn't even set the alarm clock, so I was afraid to fall asleep and then not wake up for the mega early start. I do want to learn to be less attached to things, but I'd be majorly pissed off if my mobile died before the end of this trip.

At 1.45am I went outside, using my trusty little torch. The streets were initially deserted, apart from a few dogs who clearly didn't think me interesting enough to acknowledge my presence in any way. Nothing around me but darkness, silence and a chill in the air, despite my nice fleece sweater and my windbreaker. It was a bit of a walk to reach the start of the ascent to Adam's Peak, and at 2.10am I started my trek.

Fuck.

Adam's Peak has been a pilgrimage destination for more than 1,000 years, and it's considered a holy mountain for Buddhists, Hindus, Muslims and Catholics because of a 1.8m rock formation near the summit, shaped like a footprint. According to legend, it is the first place on Earth where Adam set foot after he was cast out of Paradise, hence the name. For those who don't like this explanation, Adam's Peak is also known as Sri Pada, meaning Sacred Footprint. Anything in life can be looked at from several points of view. I am the queen of this, always analysing every situation from 360 degrees and ending up super confused because then I can never work out what is right and what is wrong. What or who, for that matter. Anyway, as I was saying, a second legend associated with the name Sri Pada claims that this footprint in fact represents the Buddha's last step before leaving the Earth and rising up to Paradise. Alternatively, if we are not that religious or spiritual and prefer natural explanations, the peak is also known as Samanalakande, meaning the Mountain of Butterflies. Right at the top of Adam's Peak these gorgeous little creatures, which nature employs to teach us the art of lightness, to spur us into harmoniously flying over all the bullshit we waste our energy on and to remind us that life is short and our duty is to live it to the full by spreading beauty and serenity... Well, up here, butterflies come to die.

Ah, ecco.

The fact that I'm not in shape at all is indisputable. The fact that after this trek my big bum is in slightly better shape, is indisputable, too.

However, seeing that the Sri Lankan elderly are fitter than me hurt a bit. While I was plodding on, my face already flushed and sweating, they were walking down those big steps. Slowly, okay, but they had already reached the top and were now coming back down, all within a few hours, while I had left only 30 minutes before and I was already wondering if I would make it to the top.

After only 30 minutes of extreme glute crunching I decided to adopt the technique of 'moving forward in blocks', stopping to catch my breath every 60–80 steps. In three and a half hours I arrived at the top, around 5.40am, so in ample time to enjoy the magnificent sunrise. Thank God I had followed Andre's advice to bring something warm and possibly a change of outfit, given that I reached the top disgustingly sweaty and was greeted there by a lively wind.

Jesus. Christ. How. Exhausting.

I've always loved walking. It helps me relax and tidy up my inner space. There comes a point when the legs just move on their own and you can fully concentrate on your thoughts. Maybe all this is even more true when you are walking uphill. No wonder many people say that trekking in the mountains is almost a spiritual as well as a physical exercise. And as exercise goes, this is serious, for Peak's sake. The broad path where I started my ascent soon turned into a stone staircase which became steeper and steeper, and more and more crowded.

While climbing slowly and with effort, whilst also keeping a cautious eye on the stone steps which were irregular and potentially dangerous, I entertained myself by observing the families coming down happily and noisily. Jokes, gags, children offering their elbow to their old parents, children carried on their fathers' shoulders, groups of teenagers and young twenty-something guys, giddy and excited in that way that is reserved for the young.

We are all so different, and yet so alike in so many things. And thank God for that.

And I've found myself thinking about my family. Partly because today is my mum's birthday. In her New Age guru speech, Piper had told me that she knew she had chosen to be born in her family because she had to heal a specific wound which she had been carrying from her previous lives.

This confession had puzzled me not once, but twice. Since when do we choose to be born in a specific family? And since when does Piper believe in reincarnation?

This same concept had also reached out and slapped me from the pages of a book by Robert Schwartz, and it had sounded crazy to me even then. Our soul chooses which family to be born in depending on which environment will allow it to better learn the lessons it needs to evolve. We all plan our existence prior to coming here, challenges included, to balance our karma and get to know ourselves better. However, since we have been given free will, once we arrive on Earth we can choose how to deal with the challenges we set ourselves when we were floating in infinity. We are free to face them with anger and bitterness, or with love and compassion. And after all, we're talking free will up to a point, given that the lesson we are meant to learn will continue to pop up in our life until we've learnt it. From this perspective, our family becomes a sort of training ground for the soul, and through its lessons we can free ourselves from the patterns which hold us prisoner.

The first time I read this concept, my initial reaction was 'Yeah, right, come on. Now it's us who choose. Please, give me a break'. When Piper reiterated it, presenting it as a truth known by many, I felt a crack opening in the shutter I had quickly pulled down on this concept.

And this is exactly the idea that accompanied me up those thousands of steps. Since my brother's wedding I've felt a strange nostalgia, and now, even though I'm on the other side of the world, I'm in contact with them daily. This has got me thinking. So let's say we do choose to be born in a specific family... why on Earth would I be so crazy as to choose mine?

Seriously, come on. What would I have come here to learn?

My parents have always taught me to be charitable (haggling in Asia aside), to save, to work hard, to help others, to be happy with little. Specifically, my mother has always taught me to live life singing, but I could learn that from Celia Cruz, too. I could draw up a list of all the things I've learnt from them, but was I born a Mussato for this? *Mah.* And now that I'm writing it, I realise I've thought about it the wrong way. I've focused on the things I've learnt because I saw them modelled by my family members, while Schwartz and Piper support the view that you learn by reaction. If your soul has decided that in this life it wants to learn and practise forgiveness, it will choose to be born in a family where it will be abused in different ways, because it's only by forgiving them that it can move forward.

Step by step, in my blocks of 60, I've explored the twists and turns of such an original and intriguing concept. And I've even been able to give myself some answers. My elder brother Alessio has forced me, from day one, to develop an incredible amount of patience. With my arrival, the amount of attention my parents could give him unavoidably diminished and, as per the script, he developed resentment and jealousy towards me. Nothing new, to be honest.

214

Countless elder siblings have experienced this trauma. The fact is that we've never been close. There's always been a gap between us that I am not able to fill, and which makes me suffer. And so, just loads of sighs, and a continuous acceptance of his closed attitude towards me, which he expresses in several ways. So could Alessio be my personal trainer for building up the patience muscle? Well, he certainly has the body for it, being the fitness freak that he is. Plus, no one knows more than I do how much patience the Universe has required of me over the years. In my work, my relationships and my friendships, it is as though the Universe was constantly sending me lessons on the importance of Being Able To Wait. Or maybe Alessio is in my life to teach me unconditional love: the ability to love someone just as they are, whatever they say or do to us, without making our affection for them depend on 'if': 'I love you IF you behave like that, IF you stop doing that, IF you start to…'

I almost have to laugh. I am basically thinking that I should be grateful to Alessio for all the emotional detachment he has shown me my whole life. For Staircase's sake, this is what you wind up thinking about while trekking up a mountain in the middle of the night.

In those three and a half hours of general oxygen depletion, I saw lots of elderly people coming and going, several people with deformed feet and fathers carrying their disabled children on their backs. All of them apparently trying to earn some karmic points and godly protection through this physical sacrifice.

The power of religion. I sometimes wish I had the same strong faith, with no shadows or doubts. It must be of great help in many circumstances. But probably, in others, it can be an obstacle.

After much pondering and reflection, an awful lot of people watching and God knows how many of my 60-step "blocks", I finally reached the top. Just before the very last section are some stalls selling the ever-present and never-failing chai. I had brought some biscuits with me, which I happily shared with all the people sitting at my table, and I started my first conversations of the day, since there were still 20 minutes to go before sunrise. There was a Sri Lankan family which seemed to have come out straight of a magazine, since they were all so beautiful. Yet, the mother brought her fingertips together to her mouth while looking at me and tilting her head. A gesture I've already seen countless times in India.

A gesture which in Italy could mean 'What the fuck do you want?' or equally its more delicate version, 'What are you talking about?' or, in the best-case scenario, 'I'm hungry! When do we eat?', in Sri Lanka and India is a compliment. By bringing their fingers to their mouth, with the fingertips all touching one another, they mean that you are pretty and deserve a kiss.

Even drenched in sweat. Even dressed like a colour-blind tramp. Even feeling like an apocalyptic toilet on legs, I always meet someone who makes me feel beautiful here. Thank you, Sri Lanka!

There was also a newlywed couple from New York on their honeymoon. 'What? You are travelling for three months? Wow! Even with such a beautiful occasion to celebrate, we couldn't take more than two weeks off, and that was already a lot by American standards.'

Yes, I know that your country is NUTS. 'You must have made a nice, focused selection of places to see then, having such a short time here. What would you recommend?' I asked.

'Ah, don't miss Sigiriya and Kandy, we both loved them a lot (yes, I won't miss them for sure). Another place that we strongly recommend is Kitulgala. We were there yesterday. Apart from the fact that it's really gorgeous in terms of scenery and landscapes, we went rafting and had so much fun.'

Actually, why not? I don't have any specific plans for the next few days, and I've never tried rafting. Besides, it's one of those things that make me feel good, because it makes me feel like I'm doing some exercise, that I'm a big fan of sports and the outdoors, while in fact I just have to sit in a rubber dinghy and at most row a bit. Ehm, it could actually be a good idea.

I didn't have time to ask the American newlyweds what their

216

view was on the death penalty and gun permits, because the sunrise was practically knocking on the clouds to be let in. And so, one final effort to climb the last few steps separating me from the actual peak, and I was finally at the top of the highest mountain in Sri Lanka. And what could there be, at the top of Adam's Peak, if not a temple?

Here, every morning at sunrise, they hold a religious ceremony to coincide with the sunlight spreading across the valley below. For Sri Lankans, it's almost compulsory to do this trek at least once in their lifetime and to see the big sacred footprint (whoever it belongs to) guarded in the little temple at the top. A bit like going on a pilgrimage to Mecca for Muslims.

It's very crowded, with all of us crammed in trying to see as much as possible. Squeezed and pressed from all sides, I admire the first rays of sunshine resiliently breaking through the clouds. I look away from that superb natural display to observe with curiosity the procession of several gifts, accompanied by musicians. It's such a special moment that, just for a change, I am moved. The sunrise takes on a completely new meaning, even more magic than usual, while we await the sun on the eastern side of the peak. When the most fervent pilgrims scream in delight, 'Sadhu!', an exclamation of good wishes, it's time to move to the western side to admire the perfectly triangular shadow made by the peak on the landscape beneath. Nature's perfection rendered by the interplay of light and shade, framed by clouds and greenery. It is a breath-taking view, even if it lacks the silence that could make this moment even more powerful. We are such a large crowd, up there, and it's hard to think that all this will repeat itself every morning for months on end.

My heart brimming, I look at all the people around me who have undertaken such a trek in the name of a religious fervour which I unfortunately lack. I look at the praying men, almost all of them barefoot because the temple is a sacred space. I observe their faces, their eyes closed in prayer, their clasped hands, their aura of serenity, and I almost start laughing at the memory that pops up of a question which so many people asked when they heard about my upcoming trip, 'But do you feel safe, as a woman, travelling on your own in those countries?'

Every time I am asked this question, I react with a smile that hovers between amused and a little sad, and I'm not sure why but I get the image of Jesus on the cross invoking, 'Father, forgive them, for they know not what they do'. Sure, I say it to myself with less gravity, and swap the 'do' with 'say', but I always associate this question with people who haven't travelled much. Maybe they've been on holiday, sure, and I hope so for them. But travelling is so different. And even if they've travelled, they maybe went to countries similar to theirs, which they know a lot about and where therefore they can feel safer. What's different and far away, what you don't know, always becomes this dark, shadowy place on the world map, to be swiftly labelled as dangerous or impossible to visit except as part of an organised tour.

Maybe, in some ways I have my father and his vision of the world to thank. Defining it as 'Manichean' would be an understatement. For him, there are only two types of countries: '*i paesi normai*', the normal ones, and '*quei mati coa guera*', the war-ridden ones. What I've never really been able to understand is what he bases this distinction on, given that my father definitely does not keep abreast of current affairs. He can't actually know whether in that precise moment a war is going on, for example, in Sierra Leone. He probably based this distinction on memories of past conflicts which stuck in his mind, and then proceeds by making sweeping associations. In this way, Albania is '*un paese mato coa guera*', as would be Syria, Ethiopia, Rwanda, Egypt and, naturally, Sri Lanka.

The more my father talked in that way, the bigger my desire to see the world grew, as per the standard rebellious mechanism that all teenagers know quite well. In Europe, we are so incredibly lucky as to have so many countries, which are all so different from each other, and yet so close. A long (to varying degrees) train, plane or even coach ride, and you find yourself in a different linguistic, historical, architectural and gastronomical world.

Growing up, I was obsessed with the USA. My bedroom

was covered with American flags, posters of Rocky Balboa (who embodied the American Dream better than him?), pictures of the Grand Canyon and Marlboro Country advertisements, with those vast, breath-taking landscapes.

As often happens in life, after a few visits to the USA, I realised that I didn't in fact find much there that was so different and spectacular, or at least nothing that actually took me to a different world. Instead, countries like Morocco or Egypt, with their many differences from my reality, fascinated me.

The turning point, the trip which literally opened up a new portion of the world to me, was India. Going to India is like entering another time-space dimension, where sounds, smells and colours are all more intense than usual. Every five minutes you try to make sense of what you see but realise you don't have the tools or knowledge to find an explanation. Indeed, it was my trip to India, and then to the other Asian countries I've visited, that opened my eyes to what the English poet Samuel Coleridge meant when he talked about the 'willing suspension of disbelief'. When travelling in these countries you are required every day, and several times a day, to willingly suspend any judgement or belief in order to surrender to the surreal around you. Because it seems impossible to you that to this day whole populations are still living in that way. Or thinking in that way. Or conceive love and marriage in that way. Or relate to death in that way. Or can eat rice *at every single meal.*

India paved the way for my many trips to South-East Asia, which must be one of the easiest areas to travel. Thailand, Laos, Cambodia, Vietnam and Malaysia followed one another in a succession of enchanting beaches, centuries-old temples with intricate decorations, vibrant green landscapes the like of which I had never seen before, almost orgasmic combinations of tastes, and people as smiling and peaceful as they are generous and curious.

And now it's the turn of Sri Lanka, the country of serendipity, which has little in common with its Indian cousin, contrary to what I had expected.

How much lighter I become when I am travelling. Not only because I get away, physically and mentally, from the problems and complications of my London life, but also because I shed fears and prejudices. I have time to indulge in inspiring and uplifting reflections, so different from the much more practical ones that occupy my mind most of the time back at home. By travelling, I uproot myself from my tiny little world which sometimes feels so important and filled to the brim, and with no expectations I step lightly towards each new day and its surprises.

Shit, what if we could live each day of our lives with this attitude! Wouldn't it be amazing? For Travelling's sake.

These thoughts and many more kept me company as I made my return journey down Adam's Peak, which proved to be another nice test for my kneecaps, for Wear and Tear's sake.

When I arrived back at the Blue Sky Hotel, around 9.30am, the owner smiled at me broadly with the two teeth he had left and addressed me with a peremptory, 'Sit down'. I've noticed this is quite a common order in Sri Lanka. I had my breakfast while talking to him about my night trek, and at check-out I gave him the bracelet I was wearing, the one with all the Madonnas, since he had told me he was a devout Catholic. I've always liked bringing things with me which I can then give as presents along the way to the people I meet, even if 98% of the time they are children. But with no teeth and a wrinkled face, he somehow reminded me of a cheeky little boy.

'And how are you going to manage now, without Mary?' he asked, almost worried.

'Oh, don't worry. Mary is my mum's name, and she's always with me. Actually, today it's her birthday. Let's send her our best wishes together, shall we?' And so, with a 'Happy Birthday' sung to the sky together with a wizened old man, my super short stay in Dalhousie came to an end.

So, next stop: Kitulgala. Let's go with the flow. Literally, too, now that I think about it, since I am going there to do some rafting. I took a bus which was supposed to be direct, but turned out to be very indirect, stopping for a long time in Maskalya and at Gingepewhatwasthat, a town with an unpronounceable name.

The bus journey was brightened up by the presence of a poor man's Denzel Washington, who smiled to me as soon as he got on. A beautiful, warm-brown skin tone, intense, sweet eyes, a baseball cap, a red T-shirt setting off his complexion nicely with the sleeves slightly tight over nicely shaped biceps.

How hhhhhhot. Big time. He is one big hhhhhhhottie. I mean, really big, and tall. Looking at him on the sly while pretending to admire the landscape constantly changing outside the bus windows, I noticed that he was even hhhhhhotter in profile. I gazed at him a few times, hoping to catch his eye. I had already prepared an icebreaker: 'There's something very American about you'. His size and his baseball cap made me think he might be American, probably the son of migrant Sri Lankan parents. Definitely the tallest local man I've seen so far. And also the most muscular.

So this is when they wake up, my bastard hormones. And they pump into my bloodstream, filling my head with all kinds of ideas and scenarios. I see the conversation flowing well, with interesting questions and successful jokes, I visualise the smiles (oh, his teeth are so white! And he even has all of them!), I can hear him asking me, 'Where are you going? Why don't you change your plans and come with me to...?' (I wonder where he's heading.) I answer, 'Yes, why not? I love changing my plans last minute'. And yet, while writing this, I realise that nothing could be further from the truth for the London Roby who plans every day down to the millisecond with a degree of precision that only a Tetris champion could hope to better.

While my heartbeat accelerates a bit, just imagining the possible consequences of a simple, 'Hello, how is your trip going?' the unthinkable happens. The bus driver honks at another bus coming from the opposite direction and, to my dismay, an inexplicable sorting of passengers occurs which takes my Denzel away from me.

Nooooooooooo!

Okay, another lesson on letting it go. Farewell, a poor man's

Denzel Washington. May life smile on you. And, if it is in our destiny, may our paths cross again.

For Libido's sake, though. Now it's my bloody problem. Before my departure, I had even debated bringing along a little help to overcome moments like these when the 'pitcher plant', as my friend Ale calls it, wakes up in a rage of primordial hunger. At the time I had opted not to, for a series of valid reasons. One, I could already picture myself in some embarrassing situations, with my little helper rolling out of my backpack across the floor of some hostel dorm, for example. Two, the idea of taking care of my libido spikes by myself was based on an assumption of male scarcity, which in itself would actually have attracted such scarcity. I know the Law of Attraction and I've been practising it for a while, so I refrained from making this mistake. The Universe, in all Its infinite wisdom and providence, will never send me the Big Urge without also introducing me to someone who could help me handle it (yeah, but in the meantime It's removed Denzel from my life, in all Its wisdom and providence, for Universe's sake).

So, trying to put carnal desire and hormonal turbulence aside, I get off at Kitulgala, which looks like a strip of houses in varying states of disrepair, with several offices selling rafting, tubing, canyoning and abseiling trips. Tubing is basically riding inner tubes or inflated rings down a river, with your bum in the water. I've done it before in Laos and quite enjoyed it. I remember it made me feel very peaceful, flowing down the river, propelled by the water alone, with no noise around me besides natural sounds, literally immersed in nature myself. Then, of course, there were some bars along the river which would throw a rope at you so that you could grab hold and be dragged to the bank in order to buy a drink, before returning to your inflated ring and continuing your fluvial descent. Canyoning is the act of navigating down a fast-flowing mountain stream in a gorge using a variety of techniques, including hiking, climbing, abseiling, sliding and jumping. At the most, you might have some ropes to help you climb down vertical rock faces or when crossing particularly exposed areas. Apart from the fact that I've never done it, and I think it requires specific equipment, something tells me that, with my usual inimitable luck, I would quite likely twist an ankle or worse. So no, no canyoning for me. And the same goes for abseiling, or rappelling, which is the controlled descent off a vertical drop, such as a rock face, by descending a fixed rope. It sounds too technical and too dangerous, and it doesn't spell fun for me, but concentration, attention and effort. No, it doesn't suit me. So rafting it is, then. But first I need to find accommodation, and this takes me some time.

One gentleman selling these sporting excursions tells me that his son can take me to this marvellous and cheap resort, immersed in greenery near the river.

I waste an hour waiting for this son, who finally takes me by tuk-tuk to the resort which is indeed quite marvellous, but also very far away and very empty. So empty that the owner doesn't turn up for over 20 minutes. The dorm would be all for me, but the bathroom is like 50 metres away, in a totally different section. They don't have a towel to give me and the two waiters, the only other two visible people besides me, are not able to give me the wi-fi password.

You know what? I'm leaving. I'm tired, sweaty and pissed off. I've wasted an hour. I don't have any accommodation yet because I am not staying here under these conditions, and now I'm even stuck a few miles from the town. I initially decide to go back 'downtown', and I pick up a tuk-tuk on the fly, but I then ask the driver to stop 200 metres later because I actually don't know if there's anything to see in town, and decide that maybe it's better to stay here, near the river. I give him 50 rupees, which I feel are a good payment for the 200 metres done, and I witness what can probably be identified as 'an outpouring of Sri Lankan cursing'.

Oh, well. Travelling is also about these moments when things don't seem to be going right and you are quite pissed off. So I set off like Mary and Joseph once more, looking for an establishment with a room for me (that fits my requirements), and the second hotel I visit tells me that they have a bed in a dorm for 2,500 rupees, which I manage to lower to 2,000 with breakfast using my usual technique: 'Oh, but I'm travelling alone, sir, and you know everything is always more expensive when you are alone. Please…'

I think that Lady Luck is on my side again: when they show me the room, it's actually a huge single room with A/C and elegant wooden decorations around the ceiling. When I look more closely, I realise that they represent scenes from the Kama Sutra. *Ah, ecco.* The perfect room for Denzel and me. Man! Cruel and mocking destiny!

At reception, I ask about their rafting trips, and the waiter, who doubles up as a receptionist, too, calls a friend, a certain Sanjaya, who is in charge of these trips. After 15 minutes this guy arrives. He is cute, albeit a little short, and he has a nice presence, albeit a slightly compressed one. Short brown hair, brown eyes, a cheeky expression. Ten centimetres more and I would forgive him for the small brown stains on his molars. Shall we say that oral hygiene in Sri Lanka is probably not in the top ten of priorities?

'Hi, nice to meet you. I'm Sanjaya. I show you video of trips I organise, so you decide if you want to do or not. Today we do a nice rafting, with four people. The river is full with so much water, they have a lot of fun. If there is a lot of water, we can do big jumps. The trip change based on how much water there is. It can be dangerous, but I know the river well, I have many years of experience'.

He must have started working when he was 12, then, because I don't think he can be older than 30. Anyway, the video convinces me. After all, this is exactly what I came here to do.

'Great, then tomorrow morning I'm coming to try this rafting experience. How many of us will there be? Do you know yet?'

'Zero, for now. Only you.'

Ah, ecco. There you go. Of course.

'But maybe other people buy ticket tonight. But no problem, we do trip even if only you. You are special. I take you rafting anyway', he reassures me, while I smile at his marketing technique masquerading as a compliment thrown in nonchalantly.

He may not be able to conjugate verbs in the third person singular, but this Sanjaya immediately comes across as switched on. He is from Shanaka's planet, rather than Chamath's.

'Perfect, then. What time do we leave? And where do we meet up? And do I have to bring anything special?'

'Fantastic. We leave around 9am. I come take you with tuk-tuk. Wear clothes for swimming if you want. Maybe surely you get wet a bit. You can change clothes later.'

'Okay, marvellous. Then see you tomorrow morning', and I say goodbye, pondering over what new worlds of possibilities are opened up by the pairing 'maybe surely'.

'Or you want come to a party with me tonight?'

....

I feel like laughing. Shit, man, I'd really love to see a party in Kitulgala. Who knows how they party here, in this isolated place, and out of season, too, given that the hotel is basically empty. But the old Roby prevails: I'm knackered, having woken up so many hours before sunrise to trek Adam's Peak.

'No, thanks. You are very kind, but I am really tired.'

'No problem. Then I bring beers and give you a foot massage.'

....

(Please picture in your mind as many emojis as you wish with eyes wide open in disbelief and confusion.)

But… I mean… Is the shortie trying it on? Or such is the loneliness and boredom in this little town that any chats with a foreigner are infinitely welcome? My inner Pollyanna doesn't know how to reply to my inner Samantha Jones who drily remarks, 'Sure, and all passing white men get a complimentary welcome foot massage as well'.

The suspension of disbelief. I'm always struck by how some guys don't see a difference in height as a deterrent to trying it on. Anyway, I laugh to myself, because the evening seems to be going in a very unexpected way, and if the conversation is nice and funny, I wouldn't really say no to a foot massage… By the way, I have no memories of when and by whom my feet were last massaged. Maybe it was in Bangkok. On Khao San Road. Someone I paid at a massage parlour.

'Okay for the beers. For the foot massage, we'll see', I put a brake on his fantasies.

In the evening, while I'm reading on my veranda, along comes Sanjaya with two huge beers. So huge in fact they almost fill me with performance anxiety: I know perfectly well I won't be able to finish mine.

'Hi. All okay? You want a glass for beer, or okay like this?' Oh, how thoughtful. 'Don't worry, drinking from the bottle is fine', I reassure him, working hard to decode each utterance because his English, like Shanaka's, requires a lot of patience and focus.

'So, where are you from, Roby? What job you do?' Sanjaya asks me, carefully listening to my answers. He then starts telling me about his family, with whom he lives not far from here. His father has a shop (I didn't ask what kind of shop), his mother is a teacher, his younger sister works as a hairdresser. They are doing pretty well, I'd say.

'Can we go drink beers inside your room?' he then asks me, out of the blue (whale, of course). Can you believe our shortie? He doesn't waste time, for Initiative's sake.

'No, it's a beautiful evening. I prefer to sit outside', I wriggle away.

'Tell me about your job. Do you like it? How many years have you been doing it?'

'Yes, I like it a lot, but not always tourists to do trips. Season job, you know. If zero clients, I help my dad in the shop. Not very much money, but it's okay.'

The conversation flows, at a slow pace, making me smile at his mistakes one minute, and inspiring tenderness the next, as he tells me about his world that is so different from mine.

At some point, around 40 minutes later, his friend, the one working both as waiter and receptionist, comes over and starts talking to him in Sinhalese. Of course I don't understand a word, but from the tone I get the impression that he is telling Sanjaya off. Sanjaya seems defensive. He sounds like someone who is justifying himself. His friend says something in reply, quite sharply, I'd say. Unbelievable how much you can understand of a conversation without knowing its content, just by watching and listening carefully.

Anyway, this was clearly a simple order of the no-ifs-or-buts variety, because the friend goes away immediately, and Sanjaya looks at me, sighing.

'What happened? Is there a problem?' I inquire.

'Not nice that you and me drink and smoke together if people can see.'

Ah, ecco. There you go, the cultural difference has kicked in.

Okay. But which part exactly is not good? Is drinking alcohol openly not accepted? Or does it look bad because it's a woman drinking in this case? Or is it the combination of beer and cigarettes which is morally frowned upon? Or the fact that we are doing it openly, and that 'people can see'? Or the fact that a young guy is with a woman?

This last thought immediately gives way to two more, which are:

1. 'A young guy and a woman together'... Shit, it hadn't occurred to me! Not only how many centimetres shorter, but how many years younger than me is he? Age has always been quite an important factor for me, and one I often end up fixating on. When I first arrived in London, one of the most shocking things for me was that I wasn't able to guess people's age any longer. On the one hand, the faces were so different from the Italian ones I was used to, whose lives I could easily imagine and whose ages I could try to estimate. In London there are so many nationalities and ethnic backgrounds that the game becomes much more complicated. How can I evaluate the ageing process of a Vietnamese face? And at what age, exactly, do Black people start having wrinkles? Culture and lifestyle play their part in making this whole age-guessing game

harder. In Italy people start living on their own on average...
shall we say around 26–28 years? If we are optimistic. In
England many people go to live on their own when they are
very young, and in any case, they've often graduated by 21.
Imagine meeting a man with a good, well-paid job who lives
on his own. In Italy such man would probably be around 32–
35 years old; in London maybe just 26. And let's not forget
a further truth. There are many people who, every single
weekend, or sometimes even on weekdays, artificially alter
their moods and energy levels for recreation or work, to the
point that they completely wreck their looks. In conclusion, I
find it really hard to guess people's age in London.

2. Fundamentally, I'm a shit, immediately ready to judge. I am
    aware of this, and I've been trying to work on it for years. It's
    not even that I *convey* a judgement. I am quite good at not
    expressing it verbally, for example. I even believe I can hide
    it well, to some extent. Yet, Judgement pops up suddenly
    and starts jumping all over the place in my mind. I swear
    that I don't initiate any mental activity to conjure it up. Just
    like that, it appears and starts dancing around so vigorously
    that I cannot ignore it. Poor Sanjaya had asked me to go and
    drink the beers in my room to avoid being told off like that,
    not because he wanted to try it on. Roby, not all men want to
    try it on. Especially when your roots are growing out!

Of course, voicing all these questions to Sanjaya would require an
immense linguistic effort on his part, both to understand and answer
them, so I don't even try.

'Ah, I had no idea. I'm sorry that your friend told you off.
Well, then we can go into my bedroom', I suggest. The alternative
would be to say good night and send him away, but it doesn't seem
nice. Besides, it's not even what I want, because in any case he is
showing me a cross section of a reality I don't know anything about,
and which interests me. And also because Sanjaya is cute, with

his flowery violet T-shirt and jean shorts. He looks self-confident, he's got a sort of masculine aura that I cannot quite define, which nevertheless unravels with every language mistake he makes. The two images, the confident man who knows what he's doing and the childlike struggle of someone grappling with a language they don't speak well, create a mix which I like a lot.

So I invite him in to sit in my huge bedroom with the Kama Sutra decorations. I even consider pointing them out. I decide not to. I don't think I am the one who has to make a move. To be fair, by inviting him into my bedroom I have already taken a big step. Sure, circumstances kind of forced my hand, but I know perfectly well that I could have chosen differently.

'How did your friend manage to see us from the restaurant?' I ask him, to understand whether he had instead been sent by the manager.

In response, Sanjaya looks around, takes my hand cream from my bedside table, and announces, 'Okay, now I give foot massage'.

....

So no, Roby, you are not an ill-disposed shit, immediately ready to judge. Or, at least, this time you had guessed right. What is up with these Sri Lankan men?

This discovery of mine must be shared with the world. Calling all women looking to forget their troubles! Come to Sri Lanka! The only effort you have to make is maybe managing the generous male attention you'll receive.

'Okay, let's see how you massage', I give in.

....

And fuuuuuuuuuuck, his massage was a-ma-zing! But he wasn't just good at massaging. What I admired most was probably how he kept looking straight into my eyes without saying anything. To be honest I actually wanted to laugh a lot, because it felt like a scene from a Bollywood movie, such was the intensity of his gaze. I have to say, however, that in all the Bollywood movies I've watched, I've never seen so much suggestive physical contact.

Actually, it was more than just suggestive. The certainty of how it was going to finish lingered between Sanjaya's solemn silence and my smile, which I just about managed to hold back from bursting into outright laughter.

'I massage leg, too. Can I? You are very tired, walk Adam's Peak today.'

Who would have thought, when this morning I was admiring that huge sacred footprint, that my day would have ended in a bedroom with Kama Sutra-inspired decor images and a guy giving his all to remove the fatigue from every inch of my feet and legs?

'Oh, yes, very tired', I agree. 'But not too tired.'

And, exactly like in a perfect Bollywood movie, I can jump directly to a few hours later when Sanjaya left, with a simple 'See you tomorrow'. After all, what else could he say? I have indeed bought a rafting trip with him.

'Yes, see you tomorrow morning. Good night', I said, closing the door and almost crumbling with tiredness, but also floating a little in a warm fuzzy cloud of afterglow and yes, let's admit it, happiness.

While in bed still smiling, my last thought was for the Universe, apologising for having been a doubting Roby that afternoon on the bus.

I smile even more and shake my head when the jingle from an old Italian Duplo advert blasts in my mind: '*Togliti la voglia, resta sempre in forma!*' 'Get rid of that longing, always stay in shape'. With this jingle still playing, I wished Kitulgala goodnight, and I repeated to myself that it's really interesting when things don't go according to plan. I should have been in Kandy now, instead I ended up with Sanjaya in Kitulgala.

Universe, I trust You. Continue doing Your thing, because You do it mega well.

Steps to the top of Adam's Peak: 5,200
Altitude of Adam's Peak: 2,243m
Times I stopped while climbing up: 27
Guns the American groom kept at home: I didn't ask him

Feet I've seen so far with six toes: 0, and thank God

Length of the Buddha's (or Adam's) sacred footprint: 1.8m

Sanjaya's actual height: 167cm

Teeth he has missing: 2

Score he deserves as a masseur: 8.5

Age my mum turned today: 73

Frittelle alla crema **(cream donuts) she gulped down to celebrate:** at least 10 (by her own confession via text)

What Sanjaya and his receptionist friend actually said: Namut maṅgula, oba dannē nædda obaṭa mehi matpæn pānaya kaḷa nohæki bavat, sǣma kenekma obava dakina bavat?

Original positions in the Kama Sutra: 64

DAY 18
'I come, I come, I come in 30 minutes'
-Kitulgala, Thursday 1st March 2018-

It's 3pm and I feel so sleepy. Rightly so, and happily so, may I add. I'm more than happy to miss out on a few hours' sleep if it means investing them in such pleasant activities;-)

So, in Kitulgala there's really not much to see, but it is gaining in popularity among young, sporty adrenaline seekers thanks to the white-water rafting you can do here, the hiking expeditions in the jungle and the cave explorations. I've already seen plenty of caves in my life. I go hiking often and really enjoy it, but the word 'jungle' immediately conjures up the image of thousands of insects throwing themselves at me and managing to sting even through layers and layers of protection, both cloth and chemical. For these reasons, the only activity I'm actually interested in is the white-water rafting. Incidentally, it seems that the river here, the Kelanya Ganga, is the very best place in Sri Lanka to do it.

Sanjaya arrived at 9am on the dot. Once again, he found me reading on the veranda.

'Good morning. You sleep well?' he asked, with a smile that told a long story.

'Yes, very. I was knackered, I fell asleep the moment you left. So, are we ready? Has anybody else joined us last minute?'

'No, nobody (*ah, ecco*). Now water level is too low to do rafting. We wait a bit, maybe later they open the dam nearby.'

And that's exactly what happened. We killed time chatting a bit more about what his job is like in high season and about his social life. I've discovered that the best fun these guys have is driving by moped to hang out somewhere on the roadside and chat the time away. Seems pretty different from what I'm used to.

'But what plans do you have? When do you go away?' Sanjaya inquired.

I hadn't thought about it. It must be so hard, for him and all the others working in the tourist sector like him, making all these acquaintances that end before they really get started. Ehm, now that I think about it, I'm sure plenty of men would actually see this as a blessing.

'Maybe this afternoon. I have a hostel booked in Kandy, but I haven't decided 100% yet', I explained.

'No, stay here. It's beautiful here.'

With a few words, he has said everything that he had to say. Yes, it's beautiful, but let's see how the day goes.

By 10.30am the water level had increased before our very eyes, so Sanjaya and I took off towards the rafting place.

We arrived at a small wooden hut by tuk-tuk where they kept the kayak and the dinghies, and literally with the dinghy on his head, my mini instructor led the way towards the river.

Before getting on the dinghy Sanjaya helped me put on the life jacket and safety helmet, all the while staring intently into my eyes, serious and focused. For Bollywood's sake, his intensity is borderline comical.

After all the safety checks, we set off along the river. In itself, it was no great adrenaline ride, partly because the water level wasn't that high, I imagine. We only met two rapids, and they were not that exceptional. However, what literally enchanted me was floating and then swimming in the river surrounded by butterflies. Wherever I turned, there were butterflies flitting about around me. Some of them were almost touching the water, others would come near the dinghy and others still were fluttering among the greenery on the bank.

Those who know me are aware of my love for elephants and of my more recent love for butterflies. Life has taught me that we need more lightness, that mentally flying above our problems makes them look so small and less important. Lightness doesn't mean superficiality, nor is it about adopting a couldn't-care-less attitude. Lightness to me is being aware that the grand scheme of things is indeed so very grand, that it is crazy and entirely pointless to get all hot and bothered over minor details, when there are just so many flowers to land on.

Here I am, floating along the Kelanya Ganga, with these small wings beating around me. Such a magical and poetic moment! Then I thought that maybe they were on their way to die at the top of Adam's Peak, and I'm not even sure if this killed the magic or actually enhanced it. But it was certainly a special, unique moment, the like of which I had never experienced before. One of those moments of pure bliss, when there is nothing around you but birds singing and water gurgling, when you are so immersed in the peace and serenity of nature that you become peace and serenity yourself. Having these white butterflies flying around me while letting the water transport me really felt as if Mother Nature, the Universe, God, whichever term you prefer, was telling me to let it go and trust. Trust that they won't ever let anything bad happen to me and will always be there with me, in this beauty to which I will always, always, have access.

Go on, Roby, let it go...

And all of a sudden, I'm laughing. Out of the blue (whale), the translator in me started wondering how to translate this famous 'let it go' into Italian. For the first time, it occurred to me that, technically, 'dalla via', 'give it up', is also a valid translation. Well, I may not be someone who gives up in life, but if last night is anything to go by, I wouldn't mind giving it up (again) today.

In this regard, Sanjaya has asked five or six times already what my plans are for today. As I wrote earlier, the idea was to leave today for Kandy, where I had already booked a hostel, but this would mean a longer journey and missing out on the chance to clear the gathering hormonal clouds with another steamy monsoon storm. Staying here, on the other hand, means spending one more day immersed in nature and having time to write and read peacefully. Plus my hormones would be super grateful, and tomorrow morning I could catch the train at Hattan and get to Kandy quicker than if I were to take the bus today.

Speaking of hormones... I'm almost bewildered by this surprising (at least by my standards) number of encounters. Maybe it's true that the less you look for something, the more you find it. How many evenings have I wasted meeting up with people I had met through a dating app, forcing things because I WANTED to find someone, because I WANTED to be in a relationship, because I DIDN'T WANT to feel lonely anymore, because I DESERVED to have someone in my life? And the harder I worked at organising and going out, always in the hope that it would be the last first date, the more I met men who were not worthy of my efforts, or who would end up disappointing me, if not hurting me. I was coming from a forceful, controlling, scarcity mindset. Now that I am concentrating on just feeling good, and where every choice I make is based on answering this simple question, 'What do you want to eat, do, see, experience today to feel good? What do YOU want to do, Roby?' opportunities are flowing through my life and I am choosing whether to seize them or not. From working hard to make things happen, I'm now in a position where I decide what to seize and experience. What a change! Earlier on I was living with clenched fists, ready to fight. They were also clenched in the attempt not to lose what little I had managed to catch. Today I live with my palms open beautifully wide. More surface for the sun to warm, more space for butterflies to land on, more skin to caress.

Same day, 00.10am

Ehm... Not really. Famous last words.

Go figure, for Rafting's sake. Even a guy 1.67m short with stained teeth has stood me up. Instead of picking me up and taking me somewhere (possibly up against a wall), he has stood me up. And I don't have a fucking clue what has happened and why. This whole thing sadly reminds me of Potato Masher: all his careful planning to secure our date and then, when the time came, he would vanish, only to reappear a few days later without much of an explanation or even as if nothing had happened.

Sanjaya asked me five or six times to stay and change my plans. 'You stay, okay? I have a barbecue with friends, but then I come see you.'

Cool, staying here one more day and relaxing can only do me good. He came to my hotel twice in the afternoon for no apparent reason. And just as he popped up out of nowhere, so he disappeared after five minutes, asking on both occasions, 'It is all okay?', as if my life had undergone who knows what cataclysmic change during those few hours, here in the middle of nowhere. When he didn't find me on my veranda he even came to the river looking for me and found me sitting on a rock in the middle, meditating. By the way, on that rock I reached new levels of harmony with nature. I've been hugging trees for a few years now, but yesterday I started caressing the big rocks in the river, sending them my love and thinking they have probably never been touched before. I'm reaching scary levels of hippiness.

Anyway, Sanjaya came around 8pm with a bottle of beer and a small transparent plastic bag containing a considerable amount of weed.

Ah, ecco.

He put the sachet on the bedside table, passed me the beer and said, 'I have to go to barbecue now, I'm sorry. You relax now. I buy beer for you. I come back around 9.30pm, okay?'

Sure, no problem, for once you are not sitting on your mopeds parked under a tree by the roadside and actually have something nice to do! Go and enjoy yourself. I have my journal, my book, my texts to answer…

At 10pm, however, I still hadn't heard from him, so I called him.

'Hi Sanjaya, I just wanted to understand if your plans had changed.'

'I come. I come in 30 minutes', he answered, blabbering on

however with a whole string of 'he' and 'my friend' which I didn't understand a word of.

At 11pm, still no trace of Sanjaya. I called him again, halfway between incredulous and pissed off, at him but even more at myself for having fallen back into the same habits and disappointments, a thousand miles from home. But this time I am not going to repeat the pattern I dragged on for months with Mr Potato Masher.

'Sanjaya, you just had to say that you wanted to stay there', I went straight to the point.

Again, a machine-gun round of 'he' and 'my friend', which failed to provide any explanation, especially given that in Sanjaya's vocabulary 'he' is not necessarily a 'he'; it could also be 'she' or even 'you'.

'No, sorry. I come in 20 minutes.'

'No, no, I don't wanna see you anymore, I'm tired. Stay there with your friends. Bye.'

Thankyoubye.

On the bright side, it hurt me less than it would have a few months ago. Who knows what happened, and honestly, I don't particularly give a shit. It's pointless to insist on finding an explanation where, according to my behavioural code, nothing would justify behaving like this. So, to some extent, thank you, Mr Potato Masher, for having continually presented me with this lesson until I learnt it. Now I quickly remove myself from situations which look bad right from the beginning, without wasting too much energy trying to understand why someone would behave like that in the first place.

There is a nice starry sky, and I can hear the river flowing in the distance, undeterred. Carry away this little disappointment, waters of the Kelanya Ganga. It's time to go to bed because tomorrow I have to catch an early train to Kandy. And while I look at the Kama Sutra inspired decorations, trying to commit some of them to memory, I happen to glance at the bedside table.

Oh, fuck, Sanjaya's weed… What shall I do now?

Well, I'll think about it tomorrow. Even if I already have a few ideas.

Elephants I have at home and in my garden (statues, pictures, ornaments etc.): 63

Butterflies I have at home and in my garden (statues, pictures, ornaments etc.): 31

Price Sanjaya asked for the rafting trip alone: 2,000 rupees

Price I will pay him after his nice no-show: 1,500

Beer I've drunk: ¼ of the bottle

Barbecues I went to in the summer of 2017: 13

Times Sanjaya mentioned 'my friend' on the phone the first time: 7

Times Sanjaya mentioned 'my friend' on the phone the second time: 9

Times I've washed my hair since my arrival: 14

Times it looked nice: 0 (Maybe this is why he has stood me up?)

DAY 19
'Oh, and this is for him, too'
-Kandy, Friday 2nd March 2018-

I've behaved like a real lady. I went to the receptionist, Sanjaya's friend, and I left him the money for the rafting trip. For sure some women would have taken revenge for the no-show by leaving without paying. Instead I contented myself with paying the price I initially wanted to pay, and not the one he gave me. 'Oh, and this is for him, too', I added, nonchalantly giving him the weed Sanjaya had left in my room, sealed in its sachet.

There you go, elegantly and with no pointless grudges, I brought my super short Sanjaya chapter to a close. Closed for me, anyway, given that today he has sent me at least five messages. His written English is so mangled that I can't understand what he was trying to tell me. His spoken English is definitely better, and indeed he also tried to call me twice, but I didn't answer. What do we have to say to each other?

Next stop, Kandy! Many people have strongly recommended it, and I don't want it to become my next Tangalle, which I never reached in the end, despite planning to for days and days.

The train journey from Hatton to Kandy was marvellous, one of those experiences that really make you feel, 'I am in another world'. The train in itself, all blue, looked like a giant, self-confident pencil drawing bright, sweeping lines through a gorgeous sheet of green. We passed through tea plantations and lush vegetation, and throughout the whole journey the train doors were open, so that we passengers could sit on the floor with our legs dangling out, enjoying the beautiful landscape passing before our eyes. One of those moments

239

when you feel so utterly and beautifully free. I sat there, in one of the door ways, with the wind caressing my arms, face and legs, and I felt so free. At peace. Content. Serene. London seems so far away. The people I was giving so much of my mental space to, like Lucio, first of all, or the friends who were repeatedly absent when I needed someone to let off steam with, or the numerous 'meteor men', flashes in the pan of my love life... They have now been replaced by this mixed bag of new characters, all so different, who are populating my imagination with their original stories. In London, I couldn't get through a day without questioning myself continuously. And the questions would grip my soul in a purple-blue choke hold: 'Will Lucio be able to recover? Was talking to his family a good move? What is really tying me to that friend, if I don't feel appreciated or understood by her? Why do I keep attracting men who don't want to stay in my life? Will I ever have a child?'

All questions I am unable to answer, and crashing up against all these uncertainties was making me feel more and more powerless, directionless and confused. The questions I ask myself here are of a completely different nature: 'What do you want to do today, Roby, to feel good? What would you like to eat? Do you fancy spending time with that person? Do you want to rest, or would you rather go out and explore? What do you really crave in this moment?'

Freedom is also this. The possibility to think only and exclusively of yourself. I am aware it's an immense privilege, denied to so many people. Giving myself all the attention and care that I know I have given so freely and quickly to too many people, who, in the end, did not deserve it. It may look like selfishness, but it's only when you really feel good within yourself that you can feel good with others. It's only when I've given myself what I need that I will stop seeking it from others, thereby cutting out co-dependency, expectation and need. It's only when I can create deep inner wellbeing that I will be able to formulate new plans and positive thoughts. I'm not in any hurry, but I am so curious to see which new ideas I will fly back to London with in May, after my three months' travelling. Because I already feel it deep down that this journey will be a big watershed for me, a bridge between Roby in a crisis and Roby who is aware that she has a thousand and more resources and is always supported by the Universe.

I spent the whole journey talking with Hannes, a 27-year-old German guy who, just for a change, couldn't believe my age. The fact that everybody thinks I am younger than my age is starting to make me wonder. Up until now I have explained it to myself in various ways, some of which are quite superficial, like 'Maybe it's because I have a nice skin' ('Well, let's say it's because you still have spots', my brother Mauro's voice corrects me). But honestly... Could there be a sort of immaturity in me, which I like to call 'playfulness', but which in fact is a not so developed sense of responsibility, of consequences, of danger? Or am I simply a victim of prejudice? Hearing '40', many people conjure up in their mind images of a completely different lifestyle: married with kids, or at least with a partner, for example. Certainly not someone who is still sleeping in hostels, dressed in cheap travelling clothes and unable to drive a moped. Well, 40 is actually the new 30, and I feel sorry for you if you have such rigid ideas about what is right or appropriate for a specific age.

A few years ago a Spanish guy, Abraham, defined me as a 'girl woman'. He said that my age defines me as a woman, but my personality and attitude made him see me as a 'girl'. Who knows, maybe this is just one more expression of the constant uncertainty that hangs over me, this feeling of hovering halfway between two worlds and dimensions: well-grounded in the Western world, but so in love with the Eastern one. Stable and practical, but with so many traits of a bloody hippy. Concrete, but spiritual. Realistic, but optimistic. Woman, but girl.

I've recently studied the difference between the left and the right hemispheres of the brain, and I wasn't able to decide which one prevails in me. In the end, why all this need to define myself? Control issues, anyone? Besides, now that I'm putting it down on paper, why do I see it as an issue? What if this was exactly my wealth and gift, this ability to combine traits so far removed from one another, which ultimately gives me a more comprehensive view of things? How much simpler would life be if we started to see all those things we have labelled as problematic under a new light? What new thoughts and behaviours would we be able to adopt, if we could change the filter through which we see our reality?

I know for sure that one day I will regret not being mistaken any longer for a possible 29 or 32 year old, or a 'girl woman', so enough with the useless worrying.

'How is your trip going?' I asked Hannes, using one of the most common icebreakers.

'No, I'm not on holiday or travelling. I work in a hospital in Galle.'

'Oh, wow! That's cool! And how come you ended up in a Sri Lankan hospital?'

'In fact it was the only one I found which allowed me to do a volunteering programme I was interested in', he explained.

'Oh, so you are here doing medical volunteering? That's twice as nice.'

'I'm not sure I would define it like that. I am at the hospital every day with the doctors there, and they allow me to watch their procedures, but I can never take part in them, despite having qualified, and despite paying 1,400 euros per month to be here.'

Ehm… No, I wouldn't define that as volunteering. You pay 1,400 euros? And you basically don't do anything, apart from watch? No. Training, maybe, but not even.

I really don't understand this thing of paying in order to do some good. Having said this, given that I am as contradictory as India, I have enrolled to spend two days volunteering with the elephants at the Millennium Elephant Foundation. I will start on Monday, and I've paid 9,000 rupees, around 45 euros. I've never had such an opportunity, the chance to spend a few days in close contact with elephants, and I'm not letting it pass me by. But, I mean, I would never pay the other 1,355 euros, whatever the activity. At least, this is where I stand in March 2018.

Once I arrived in Kandy, I dashed to the hostel I had booked on Booking.com, where I have a nice bed in a female-only dorm, but the girls there didn't seem particularly sociable. This is both unusual and understandable. After you've been travelling for some time you get to the point when you just want to be on your bloody own, without getting into the same conversations about your itinerary and experiences and travelling tips.

The Lonely Planet guide describes Kandy with an abundance of compliments, but to be honest this town hasn't impressed me much. Yes, it is clustered around a pretty lake which promises plenty of beautiful walks. And yes, it is surrounded by hills crowned with little colourful houses which are a joy to behold. Still, nothing to leave me awestruck. Kandy offers multiple colonial-era buildings in the typical architectural style of the city, but since I am as ignorant as a dry chestnut in terms of architecture, I wouldn't know how to explain or identify it. According to my Bible, the Lonely Planet guide, the most impressive example of this style is the Temple of the Sacred Tooth Relic, located within the Royal Palace complex.

The tooth in question belonged to the Buddha, no less. Whenever I encounter relics, I always experience a certain mental rejection and physical disgust at the idea of body parts which have been preserved for centuries. This initial reaction then gives way to a sceptical, 'Who can guarantee that it actually belonged to whoever they say it did?'

What really fascinates me, however, are the stories surrounding the relic, how it made its way to the present day.

So the sacred tooth of the Buddha is said to have been snatched from the flames of his funeral pyre in 483 BC, and was smuggled into Sri Lanka eight centuries later, around 400 AD, hidden in the hair of a princess.

Let me repeat that: hidden in the hair of a princess. A detail which maybe only Steven Spielberg would have been able to invent. Of course the sacred tooth moved around a few times before reaching Kandy. From here, however, it was then taken back to India when Sri Lanka was invaded, but King Parakramabahu III finally managed to retrieve it. The tooth, which is an incisor, to be precise, has become a symbol of sovereignty, and the belief was born that whoever had it in their possession had the right to rule the island. Of course.

Without the briefest of moments to consider the irony whereby the tooth of the Buddha, one of the world's most famous pacifists, had come to represent the right to dominate others and impose all sorts of violence, the relic's vicissitudes continued. In the 16th century the Portuguese managed to seize it and, just to change the pattern, they decided to burn it in Goa in the name of their fervent Christian ardour. After all, this was the tooth of a nonbeliever. So imagine their disappointment when, with an incredible plot twist in perfect Agatha Christie style, the Sinhalese revealed that the Portuguese had in fact stolen a replica tooth. The real incisor of the Buddha was still safe and hidden away.

In truth, an air of mystery still envelops the Temple of the Sacred Tooth Relic, with rumours claiming that the tooth kept here is in fact the replica. And I say 'kept' because the tooth is not visible to visitors, but kept inside a stupa-shaped gold shrine.

I have to admit that in all the times I've suspiciously eyed a relic wondering if it did really belong to that saint or person, I never considered the possibility that I was looking at a replica. Maybe Stephen King was referring to events like this one when he said (something like), 'life has so much more imagination than we do'.

To be honest, this whole story about the Buddha's incisor is what I liked most about this sacred temple. After a while palaces and temples all end up looking the same to me. Art and architecture don't speak to me clearly, they don't touch me as deeply as nature, for example, manages to. Nature goes straight to my heart. It speaks a language I understand intuitively, with no need to stop and decipher it.

I was there walking from one building to another in this big Royal Palace complex, when I heard, 'Hey, Roby!' It was Hannes again, this time with his girlfriend, Clara, who spoke very little. Maybe she was still pondering the tooth's adventures.

'Tell me, do you like the palace?' I inquired. By the way, it's actually more like a complex of palaces, because it includes the King's Palace, the Royal Audience Hall, the Queen's Palace, the King's Harem Quarters, the Queen's Bathing Pavilion and, finally, the Temple of the Sacred Tooth Relic. Which, to be fair, is the most beautiful part.

'Yes, it's pretty, but I was expecting something different. But I loved the columns inside the Temple of the Sacred Tooth Relic. Maybe if it wasn't so hot, I would enjoy the visit more.'

'Yeah, I agree.'

'We were thinking of taking a tuk-tuk up to Helga's Folly, which by the way is at the top of a hill, and so maybe it's cooler up there. Would you like to join us?'

'Sure', I answered, having read something about this extravagant hotel.

'So we can share the tuk-tuk fare', his girlfriend, Miss Pragmatism, pointed out.

Helga's Folly is the other big attraction in Kandy. The name says it all. It's an eccentric, absurd, incredible hotel. A folly, indeed. Just imagine a collaboration between Gaudí and Dalí. It is often described as something between a hotel, an art gallery and a surrealist dream, and is without a doubt one of the most extraordinary boutique hotels in Sri Lanka. And probably the one with the best view, taking in the whole of Kandy from its location at the top of a verdant hill.

Once inside, I had the very weird feeling of being visually assaulted. We took a seat in the tearoom area, where Hannes and I ordered a cocktail. Despite looking around all the areas open to visitors, Clara refused to get anything to drink, thus showing quite a remarkable degree of stinginess.

What an unappealing trait, being stingy, and how unsexy, too. I myself had to struggle a lot with this part of my personality, which seemed to have such deep roots. I come from a Venetian family where the watchwords are '*Lavora e risparmia*, work and save money, because you will always need money, so set is aside'. It took me a few good years of my adult life to develop a more relaxed relationship with money. And, ironically, as soon as I learnt to let go of holding that famous 'fistful of dollars' so tightly, money started to flow in my life with ease and regularity. Exactly as the 'letting it go' philosophy maintains.

If only I'd found it as easy to apply to the rest of my life.

I later discovered that Clara is only 19, which might explain why she was so reluctant to part with every cent.

Wherever I looked, there were strange objects piled up on top of each other, objects you would never expect to see in a hotel hall and which looked even stranger because they were juxtaposed with others which were completely unrelated. Skeletons, newspaper clippings, teacups, candelabras covered in melted wax, chairs, tapestries, paintings, statues, dice, portraits, mosaics… There was so much information coming at me on a visual level that I couldn't verbalise my sense of wonder. A curious person like me could really spend a whole day in a place like Helga's Folly. I could pore over every detail and pontificate endlessly, admiring how an artist's mind works. *The Telegraph* wrote:

> *'It's difficult for a hotel to be more original than Helga's Folly. Every inch of the walls, floors and ceilings is covered with paintings, frescoes, murals, photographs, mirrors, sculptures, giant candles and antiques. Some visitors find the experience creepy, others liberating. There is a clear obsession with death, and all the furnishings exude extravagance.'*

Helga da Silva Blow Perera, who designed and manages the hotel, grew up surrounded by Hollywood celebrities of the '50s, together with writers and politicians, in an atmosphere of general intrigue. A sophisticated and eccentric lady, she is a former Dior model and was born into one of the most prestigious political dynasties of Sri Lanka. The Stereophonics, who stayed here during their tour of the island, even dedicated a song, 'Madame Helga', to her. She is probably one of the very few hotel owners who prefer to have their hotel half empty, and who offers a 50% discount to writers and artists. She lives here, surrounded by pictures of herself and of her guests, but we weren't lucky enough to see her.

Anyway, a truly outstanding boutique hotel. Pure folly in its most artistic expression. A totally spellbinding and incredible place. I wonder what kind of people book a room here.

We then came back to the lake (sharing the tuk-tuk fare once again, to Clara's delight), and there our roads parted. Unless I bump into them again tomorrow. Anything is possible.

Goodnight, my dear Diary. I have to prepare my backpack for Dambulla.

Pilgrimages that Sri Lankan Buddhists have to complete in their life to the Temple of the Sacred Tooth Relic: at least one (it boosts their karmic score immeasurably)
Cost of a visit to Helga's Folly: 3 dollars
Madame Helga's age: 73
Husbands Helga has had: 3 (currently married to Desmond)
Skeletons I counted in the room downstairs: 12
Messages Sanjaya has sent me: 5
Messages from Sanjaya which made sense: 0
Messages from Sanjaya which I answered: 3
Rats or mice sighted so far: 0
Bouts of diarrhoea and other nice stomach problems so far: 0
Chances that in my lifetime I'll ever hide a tooth in my hair: oh, man, never say never, but I'd say… probably 0.1%?

DAY 20
'If you take pictures, you can look at them at home'
-Dambulla, Saturday 3rd March 2018-

One of the best decisions I've made in terms of organisation has been to empty out half the stuff from my backpack and leave it at the hostel in Kandy and travel light to Dambulla. I am only counting on staying there one night, and I will have to pass through Kandy again anyway. The people at the hostel were super kind, as people here often are, so I locked my humble belongings in the safe there, and off I went to catch the bus, with only half the baggage.

I might have already mentioned it, but the bus and train fares here are shockingly low, especially for someone living in London and used to spending ten pounds a day to get around.

As soon as I got off the bus, which was beautified as standard with plastic flower garlands and psychedelic stickers depicting gods and Bollywood actors, I went straight to see the Golden Temple, otherwise known as the Royal Cave Temple, one of Dambulla's main attractions. Seeing a museum just next to the temple, I came up with another great organisational tip. I went inside and put on my best smile, 'Good morning, how are you? Look, unfortunately I don't have much time available, so sadly I won't manage to see your museum. I was wondering however if I could leave my backpack here with you while I visit the Golden Temple?'

The gentleman there seemed quite happy to round up his daily salary with my 50 rupees' tip.

My legs are still killing me after Adam's Peak. I should have probably stretched a bit afterwards. ('Probably'... Come on, Roby. You are about as fit as a crippled snail. You clock up 5,200 steps in

248

one go and don't even stretch, for Hindsight and Hamstrings' sake). Yet, the effort of climbing more steps to reach the Royal Cave Temple was diminished by the sheer breath-taking beauty of the place.

Astonishing.

The Royal Cave Temple is an archaeological site as well as a UNESCO World Heritage Site and the best preserved cave temple in all of Sri Lanka. It takes its name from the caves that house the temple's main attractions, which mostly relate to the Buddha and his life. You arrive there after a short trek which ends in a largish square where street food vendors sell their snacks and monkeys gather in large quantities, taking a varying degree of interest in the human activities going on around them. From there you can access the external courtyard of sorts, which today was flooded with sunlight and crowded with people. They were all busy lighting candles and incense sticks in front of several statues, before falling into prayer. In stark contrast with this explosion of light, colours and noises, the caves are dark, lit by candles, and permeated with reverential silence. Each cave contains statues and murals of the Buddha in different positions and with different facial expressions, gazing back at you with the chuffed smile of someone who knows a lot and is almost laughing at the way we complicate our lives. Some of the paintings and statues are poorly lit, despite the many candles, which contributed to the sense of awe I felt.

As a matter of fact, these paintings decorating the cave walls with scenes from Siddhartha's life and teachings inspired so much admiration in me. And respect. Peace, but also a strange kind of envy. A sense of my smallness. Calm. Strength. A sense of union.

A smile comes to my face when I realise that basically the Buddha was one of the first celebrities in history, given that his influence is still so strong after thousands of years.

Around eight or nine years ago I read a book lent to me by my New Zealander tenant, Caroline, the cat-loving vegetarian who wouldn't take a single step if it had not already been analysed, approved or championed by her spiritual guru. The book was called *Cave in the Snow*. It was the biography of Tenzin Palmo, the first Western woman to become a Buddhist nun, who spent 13 years alone in a cave in the Himalayas. I remember not liking it at all, maybe because it had been warmly recommended by a woman I didn't admire or even respect much.

Actually, let me rephrase that. It wasn't the book I didn't like, but the life and the ideals of this Tenzin woman. The Roby of eight years ago wondered what the benefits were of living so detached from the rest of the world to the point that you missed your own mother's last years.

I remember reaching the end of the book with a whole series of biting and bitter questions I would have loved to put to the Buddhist nun. What good do you bring to the world spending your life in such solitude? If the ultimate goal in one's life, in my opinion, is to love and be loved, and if you give and show love mostly through actions, what is the point of a life spent like this? Who benefits from it? What good do you do to the world by removing yourself from it?

Besides, this Buddhist teaching of detachment from everything… Back then, I was pretty sneery about it. Who knows, maybe if I had been born in Sweden or Iceland (let me go with stereotypes here), part of me, even back then, might have agreed. Instead, one of the effects of reading this book was to reinforce my sense of Italianness, which I'd only really felt strongly on a few occasions. Maybe it's because I'm Italian, and so in touch with my emotions, that I have always let them carry me away big time. Up and down, down and up, from peaks of pure joy over really stupid things, to waves of sorrow over dramatic movies. Detachment, my ass. Almost 20 years ago I even got a tattoo of the comedy and tragedy symbol, the two masks laughing and crying respectively. That's how much I saw myself as swinging between those two emotional states. This was the only way I knew how to feel like I was behind the wheel of my life, like I was living it fully. I used to dive headlong into any and every emotion, voluntarily putting aside my knowledge of how similar situations had ended up in the past because I wanted to experience the emotion life was offering me in that moment.

Tenzin Palmo's life choice seemed so extreme, and so impossible for me to understand, that I dismissed it with a profound and categorical, 'This woman is as crazy as a bag of rats'.

Yet, the more I travel in Asia, the more I notice the serenity and calmness its people exude. The West's neuroses, our stress, our constant chasing after something or other... All this is light years away from how people live in this part of the world. Initially I told myself that we worship false gods, like materialism and ambition, and that removing these monsters from the equation frees people up to deal with what really matters. Hence their omnipresent smiles, their ability to accept whatever life throws at them. And it's somehow different from the Christian faith, with its drinking from the bitter cup. Buddhism is a philosophy, not an actual religion. But I now know that there is so much more.

In these caves lit by flickering candles that reveal different angles of statues and glimpses of paintings with each trembling of the flames, I feel immensely small. I think about the people who carved those statues or painted those images... What were they wearing? What language did they speak? What food was waiting for them at home in the evening? What were they thinking while working on this sacred art? And then, for a split second, I feel as if a hand is gently squeezing my heart, like the way you would hold a robin, so delicately because you know how scared it must feel. I think of all the millions of people who have been in these caves throughout the centuries. All the prayers, all the requests, some similar and some completely different. All the styles of clothing and footwear, all the moods, all the languages. All the trips by all the different means of transports. All to get to the peace of these caves. And the fact that I am here now, so far from home, asking myself all these questions, makes me wonder how many other women like me have come to this temple and observed its comings and goings. How many other inquisitive and reflective souls like mine have been here?

And out of the blue another question pops up, and as quickly as it arrives, it disappears: was one of those souls mine? Have I been in this place before?

What. A. Mindfuck.

I think this was the first time I properly considered reincarnation. But why assume that anyone who once shared my attitude must be a former version of me? That just because someone thought like me, they actually *were* me? Is my need to feel unique so strong that I can't imagine anyone else seeing the world like I do, when at the end of the day I know that we are all on the same boat? How many times have the stories of people so different from myself resonated with me? Why not rather embrace the concept that we are really just one, transcending not only race, religion and social status, but also time, stretching back countless centuries? That we are linked to those who came before and those who will come in future because we are made of the same stardust?

Wow, if spending one hour in these caves has me soaring this far beyond the realms of time and space, imagine where Tenzin's thoughts might have taken her during those 13 cave-dwelling years! Who knows what heights she reached, in her mind and soul...

I went out into the sun, filling my lungs with fresh air and coming back to the present. Spending time in those caves has had a strange effect on me. A beautiful, strange effect.

I went to get my backpack from the museum, picked up the bus from the same stop I had got off at a few hours earlier, and continued on to the Dambulla Budget Hostel, a place which clearly takes pride in its cheapness. This hostel comes with the tiniest kittens I've ever seen, while my double room comes with two of the longest, skinniest worms I've ever seen. Fabulous.

A quick shower, some mini tickles for the kittens, and then off I head to Sigiriya, probably the place I've been most excited about seeing in the whole of Sri Lanka. A dramatic and enigmatic sight, the iconic rocky outcrop rising up out of the forest in the middle of nowhere is visible from kilometres away. To be more precise, Sigiriya is technically the complex at the top of the rock, but the two things are as one. Another archaeological complex and another UNESCO World Heritage Site which some even consider the eighth wonder of the world.

I got there by bus, arriving in the early afternoon, and immediately got down to the business of traipsing up this enormous rock, a brown mass in a sea of green. First you walk through a series of trenches and gardens to reach the foot of the ascent. Once again, there were many, many steps to climb, and as I got started I wondered in awe and admiration how they managed to build a city at the top, where most of the archaeological remains are. Or, even more incredible, how they managed to form those humongous lion's paws, at the base of a narrow stairway carved in the rock, which is the only way to reach the top. In fact, these two paws, which were found in 1898 by the British archaeologist HCP Bell, are all that remains of a gigantic lion, complete with body, head and four paws. The stairway leading to the top went from the front paws straight into the lion's mouth, which was the entrance to the Royal Palace.

Before making the final ascent via a series of modern steel staircases, you pass in front of a long wall decorated with wall paintings. The Lonely Planet guide informs me that they could have covered a good part of the rock face, which is 140 metres long and 40 metres high. The images mostly depict women, around 500 of them, most of whom are naked from the waist up. Unfortunately most of the paintings are now lost forever, having been scratched away when the palace became a monastery so as not to disturb the monks' quiet meditation. What a shame, though I can see their point.

I am not often moved by buildings. Yet here, thinking about all the hard work required to create that statue, so high up, I felt really emotional. Besides, Sigiriya is a truly magnificent place, probably the most incredible archaeological site in the whole country. The ruins occupy a single rocky column which dominates a vast plain, a natural fortress even before it was a military one.

The modern steel stairway for the final ascent was overcrowded with tourists, so we were all moving quite slowly, step after step, and to kill time I started talking with an Indian gentleman of around 50 years old.

'Good afternoon. Are you here on a school trip?' I asked, given that he was surrounded by teenagers, all with the same rucksack and uniform.

'Yes, we come from India, and we stay for five days. Have you ever been to India?'

'Oh yes, several times actually. To be honest, I was expecting Sri Lanka to be quite similar to India, but it's not at all.'

'Oh, no, no. India and Sri Lanka are very different. India is better.'

Of course. And I add, internally, the world is the same wherever you go: we will always think ourselves better than our neighbouring countries.

'So are you a teacher?' I inquire, to steer the conversation away from nationalism.

'Yes, I teach maths. Do you like maths?'

'Well, let's say I prefer literary subjects', I answer him, with perhaps the biggest understatement of 2018.

Then, with a touch of solemnity, he adds, 'Make sure you take many pictures. If you take many pictures, you can look at them when you go home'.

....

Ehm... I kind of already know that? I'm continually baffled by the apparently simplistic views I encounter so frequently in Asia.

Once I arrived at the top, I became fixated on getting two photos of me, one facing away (my favourite pose–I must have at least 100 photos of my back in front of landscapes of varying degrees of beauty) and one where I am jumping. By asking a few people to please take these photos for me, I ended up being photographed with a class of school boys, all smiles and giggles. They all seemed a bit embarrassed about this unusual thing which they didn't know how to manage, such was the distance between their world as Sri Lankan teenagers and mine as a white woman of an unspecified age.

Anyway, at the top of Sigiriya, surrounded by an expanse of
eye-popping green, I understood another great truth. Unexpectedly,
I had my Third Great Epiphany: Jesus Christ, people who can take
a decent photo are few and far between! In the end, however, I
managed to get exactly the picture I wanted, of me jumping in the
air with my knees bent and feet thrown up behind me, bursting with
energy and vitality despite the hundreds of steps I'd climbed.

And once again, gazing from this magical vantage point across
that green canopy, so resplendent it almost hurt, I had one of
those moments which occur so often while travelling. I call them
'moments of bliss': when you are fully immersed in what you are
experiencing. When you admire a landscape, and you really take
the time to see it. When you hear nature's sounds and you really
listen to them. When you don't have any thoughts to take you out
of the moment you are living, leaving you to enjoy it fully. From
this complete immersion in the present, which Eckhart Tolle talks
so much about, we derive an incredible sense of peace and serenity.
And from this unique peace and serenity we can start feeling a sense
of communion with everything around us. And from there we can
start thinking about all those who throughout the centuries have
followed one another on this isolated rock, living here, fighting
here, visiting here. Thoughts flow freely, one after the other. 'È tutto
un attimo', as our great and beloved Anna Oxa would sing: it's truly
just a moment.

I wandered around the ruins for a while, and then slowly made
my way down.

On my bus journey home, Sanjaya sent me two texts, both of
which were practically incomprehensible. WhatsApp would even
meet him halfway with its audio message option, if only someone
would show him how to use it. But it certainly won't be me. Anyway,
they go something like, 'Hello, how are yuu? Yuu com back one ohter
day? I sorry not possible I come that night'.

Give me a break, come on. Besides voice notes, could someone
also teach him about letting it go? I told you two days ago that you

wasted my time, so let's end it there. With this in mind, I don't even answer him.

And, quite rightly, he calls me.

And, quite rightly, I don't answer him.

I take back control of my moods. This trip is showing me day after day how good I can feel on my own, that I am able to entertain myself, enjoy the small and big things and interact with whomever I want. The moment I put my happiness, albeit temporarily, into someone else's hands (literally, thinking back to the massage he gave me that started the whole thing), I am setting a trap for myself, and I can be sure that sooner or later I'll be disappointed.

Much sooner, in this case.

I'm starting to recognise the pattern, though. The mist shrouding my many 'misadventures' is finally clearing. How many times have I met up with my friends and started the conversation with, 'Why do I get them all, for fuck's sake?', before filling them in on yet another romance gone wrong? I actually started to doubt that I really do 'get all the crazy ones', as if I were a magnet for men who are emotionally immature/commitment phobic/'free spirits'/continually running away/unsure of what they really want/Peter Pan my arse. Maybe the answer was different. Namely that, since I was the only constant in all these encounters and micro relationships, maybe *I* was the problem. And I've given it a lot of thought, trying to figure out what separates me from all the others who might be in life-long relationships, or able to move nonchalantly from one relationship to another, or married with kids. I mean, I know women who are so incredibly obnoxious, or boring, or angry with the world, and yet for years they have been with a man who might even adore them and put them on a pedestal. What is so wrong with me that I cannot find anyone?

The sentence in itself says it all. 'I cannot find anyone.'

As if the purpose of my life were to find someone.

As if it were a timed race, where I have to run around looking everywhere, even in the most unthinkable places, to see whether maybe there was someone there who could like me. And I also dislike the verb 'find', because it implies 'to look for'.

I remember how much I hated my friend Elisa when she would tell me, 'Roby, your man will arrive when you least expect him'. I thought, well, if that's the case, then I will never meet My Man, bearing in mind that even when going for a quick pee in a pub I make a curious and hopeful sweep of the room, just in case…

It pains me greatly to admit it, but nowadays I actually do think it will happen like Elisa said. Which doesn't mean I have to voluntarily stop my search. No. I will stop without even realising it, without perceiving it as a defeat or giving up, because I will be busy with so many other amazing things which will fill my days, leaving me brimming with light and colour.

So yes, the problem was partly me. I don't want to say entirely, because I really have met some poor specimens, and it wouldn't be fair to overlook their immaturity and baseness. Maybe by becoming more careful with my time and attention and giving myself more space and time to really see what the other person is showing me, rather than what I want to see in him, my love life will take a qualitative leap.

Anyway, I am travelling, and I want 'to be light', enjoy myself and with no strings attached. So, Sanjaya, thanks for that night, but as I said, thankyoubye. Chapter closed.

When I got back to my room I found a tree frog in the bathroom, and I'm not even joking. I didn't have the courage to face it. Anything that jumps scares me a bit: too unpredictable and quick. I've closed the bathroom door and put a towel underneath, hoping that it will stay there all night and not creep out and jump on me or into my mouth while I'm sleeping. Oh my God, a scene straight out of a horror movie, for Amphibian's sake.

Just for a change, for dinner there was *kottu*. There's not much for it: if it's not curry, it's a *kottu*. Sri Lankan cuisine has not won me over as I'd hoped it would. I really don't see myself, once back in London, going to a Sri Lankan restaurant to relive these incredible gustatory experiences.

I dined by myself, peaceful and serene. And I've been by myself a lot today. Peaceful and serene. What a great gift, the ability to spend time alone. Maybe it's more of a conquest than a gift, or maybe it's something different for different people. What I do know is that even if I didn't have any proper conversations with anyone today, besides a few lines and jokes, I feel satisfied. More than that, actually. Today I've had such deep and elevated thoughts that all I want is to be on my own.

I am enough. And there is so much freedom in this.

Today more than ever I feel as if I had thousands and thousands of small lights inside and around me. And I'm not talking about the marvellous stars I see above me, but about the souls which have walked this Earth so far.

We are all one. We always have been, and we always will be.

I just hope that the tree frog doesn't become one with my face tonight.

Number of caves making up the Royal Cave Temple complex: 5
Year UNESCO declared it a World Heritage Site: 1991
Places in Sri Lanka nominated as World Heritage Sites: 8
Statues and images of the Buddha in the Cave Temple: 153
Age of the oldest among them: 2,000 years
Year the Buddha was born: 563 BC
Year the Buddha died: 483 BC
Times the Buddha was stood up by a girl: who knows?
What my father would say if I were to talk to him about reincarnation: '*È qualcosa che si mangia?*' (Is it something you eat?)
Original height of the Lion statue in Sigiriya, of which only the paws remain: 14 metres
Times I was moved to prayer: 6
Kottu **dishes I've eaten so far:** 8
Length of the kittens: 9 centimetres
Kg I've lost so far: 2

DAY 21
'How ar you? I miss you'
-Polonnaruwa, Sunday 4th March 2018-

A bit of culture today, let's say. A two hour bus ride takes me to Polonnaruwa, Sri Lanka's medieval capital back in the 11th century, another UNESCO World Heritage Site and home for a time to the famous tooth of the Buddha. From here, kings ruled the central plains of the country 800 years ago. At that time Polonnaruwa was a commercial and religious centre of great importance, and the glories of that age are hinted at by various archaeological treasures, which give us a good idea of what the city was like back then. These archaeological remains from around 1,000 years ago are what tourists come here to see, and indeed the whole town is brimming with temples, tombs, stupas and statues. Polonnaruwa seems to be organised into two distinct areas: on one side is the town with the king's palace and the royal court, and on the other is a vast more natural area, dotted with holy buildings, nestled in the greenery.

The first thing I liked about Polonnaruwa is its name, which sounds just too cute. For some reason, it seems perfect for a little dog: 'Polonnaruwa? Come here, sweetie, let me give you a cuddle. Come on, Polonnaruwa!' The second-best thing about this huge archaeological site is that you can visit it by bike. This is new to me. To some extent, it reminds me of the grand and magnificent Angkor Wat in Cambodia, albeit tiny in comparison. I'm probably making the link because you can explore the site freely and with a means of transport, not on foot, as I've done so far in all the other archaeological sites I've visited, like the Roman Forum, Ephesus in Turkey, the Acropolis in Athens, etc.

Knowing this, the moment I got off the bus I rented a bike, which was quite heavy and antediluvian, so I could dart happily among the ruins. And I was really flying joyfully and light-heartedly down those pathways and dirt tracks until I stopped at the first temple. I got off the bike to see it properly, and though it was just a faded memory of its original glory, I saw that it is still a holy place today. What does this imply? It implies that as a sign of respect you have to walk barefoot on its floor.

Now, it's one thing walking barefoot in a holy place with a roof and, therefore, protected from the elements, and quite another taking off your flip-flops and walking on the scorching ground because, for Heatstroke's sake, it's 40 degrees today. For a moment I even tried to be stoic about it, but then I saw myself in that marvellous Coca Cola advert from the '90s. A woman arrives at the beach, and the moment she sets foot on the sand she gets burnt. So she starts throwing things onto the sand and stepping on them. First her book, then her bag, then her hat, advancing by just one step each time. When she runs out of objects, she starts taking off her clothes, stepping on them to avoid the scorching sand. Off goes her T-shirt, off go her shorts, arousing the attention of all the men on the beach.

Well, since we are in a holy place, it's probably not a good idea to adopt this rather peculiar solution. Why take off your clothes when you can go and buy a fantastic pair of socks to wear with your flip-flops? So, my bicycle and I headed back to town to buy a pair of socks, and with them on, I instantly transformed myself into Miss Germany.

Out of all the ruins, the one which probably moved me the most was the Rankoth Vihara stupa, which is 54 metres high and the largest in Polonnaruwa. Faded by time, it exudes solemnity and calm, and walking slowly around it while admiring the surrounding vegetation, I felt a deep serenity within. The same serenity, peace and calm we see in every detail of the three big Buddha statues in the Gal Vihara group, all carved into a large granite rock. This is another sculpted marvel I'll be taking home with me from this dive into the past. Going back to the 12th century and located in the northern part of Polonnaruwa, these statues represent the Buddha in three different positions: standing and with his arms crossed, representing Enlightenment; sat in a meditative position; and reclining, about to reach Nirvana. The statues are all majestic and imposing, and you feel compelled to admire them in silence. What is most striking though is not even their dimensions, but the calm emanating from every feature, the refinement of the details, the harmony of the lines.

I really enjoyed the sense of tranquillity and freedom that riding around as you please from one temple to another gives you. The whole area is really pretty, with the contrast between the lush forest, the dirt tracks and dusty lanes and the ancient ruins, which still inspire silent reverence. Yet, Polonnaruwa didn't thrill me. Maybe it's because, once again, I prefer nature and animals by far to art and archaeology, or perhaps it's that the ferocious, fetid heat just diminishes my enjoyment, depriving me of the will to live. Or maybe it's because in Rome we have more ancient ruins. Anyway, I've decided to remove Anuradhapura from my itinerary. It's another former capital and archaeological site strongly recommended in general, but I guess it can't be very different from Polonnaruwa. Or maybe they are two worlds apart, but something's gotta give. There comes a point when you have to accept that you will always miss out on something. Every choice we make always comes with some regret for what we are not choosing, so I prefer to think that Polonnaruwa and Anuradhapura are very alike, to make my life easier.

Another solo dinner, though this time it was served by a really cute waiter. A young face, nice eyes, but grey hair. I would have guessed he was around 55, instead he explained, in a mathematically exemplary way, 'I'm 41 years old. I was born in 1978'. Maths is therefore up for debate in Sri Lanka.

To be fair, it was in my hometown Treviso, too, back when I was at the secondary school. I will always remember my maths teacher, Mrs Bettiol, who one day gave us our classwork back after correcting it. Both my classmate Elisa–close friend and try-hard–and I were given eight as a mark. Even though in Elisa's equation the final result was $x = 3b$, whilst in mine it was $x = 27/5c$ (or something). 'What matters is not the result, but the working. The way you worked it out was correct, Mussato. You got lost because you made a mistake in the calculations, but the working was correct', Mrs Bettiol later explained.

It's a bit like saying that at the end of the day it's the intention that matters, and I strongly believe in this. Sometimes, we make huge cock-ups, or we end up hurting someone or making a situation much worse, convinced that we were acting for the good. 'The road to hell is paved with good intentions', they say. The intentions were good. The execution, maybe, not so great. The result, possibly, a total shitshow. But it's the intentions that matter.

I'm sure Mrs Bettiol never dreamt for a millisecond that she was giving me an extraordinary life lesson at the time.

Talking of intentions, Sanjaya's remain a mystery. He's written me three more messages today, each less understandable than the other, and all of them particularly deep and emotional, indeed peaking in the incipit: 'How ar you? I miss you'.

Oh, God, please. When I hear sentences like 'I love you' or 'I miss you' abused in such a way, I feel immediately and profoundly irritated. I am someone who savours each word. Because of my studies as an interpreter and translator, I've been paying attention to the semantic value of every single word for decades. The fact that they get used so cheaply, maybe by people who think this is exactly what we women want to hear, irritates the hell out of me. Both Sanjaya and Chamath seem to be sure that ten minutes are enough to lay the foundations for deep and everlasting love. I'm sure a lot of the blame for this belief lies with Bollywood movies, where love blossoms from a quick glance and where, without knowing anything at all about each other, the two protagonists are ready to overcome any obstacle to be together. He sees her, she looks at him, pudically lowering her eyes. Next thing, you are bombarded with songs in falsetto all about how sweet it will be to be together forever, and how beautiful it will be for him to fall asleep with his fingers running through her (generally long, black and straight) hair. All the songs are accompanied without fail by choreographed dance routines which basically involve the entire neighbourhood and include moves that allow the woman to express not just her sweet and naïve side but her more sensual one as well.

For sure, Western women have been totally conned by all the fairy tales and the Disney movies of our childhoods. They have instilled in us the idea of a Prince Charming who solves everything. Making us believe, incidentally, in a very subtle way, that marrying Prince Charming is our goal. However, in Asia they are doing equally badly, albeit in a different way.

I also believe that, since they both work in the tourist sector, and therefore have transient relations with female clients, Sanjaya and Chamath try to immediately play their best cards. In their (mad) concept of love, these cheesy declarations must really seem to them like the words All Women Have Always Wanted To Hear.

Instead, go figure. They only annoy me.

Shanaka's intentions are much clearer, and his approach is way better. After asking him I think four times, I managed to make him stop addressing me as 'Madame Roby'.

'Roby, I want see you again. Come to Mount Lavinia before you fly to India. Now you see a lot of Sri Lanka. Come see me again. I am very beautiful, too.'

He puts me in a good mood, Shanaka. He makes me smile. For me, this is a weapon bound for success if you are trying to win a lady's heart. A sense of humour, not cheesy lines. Shanaka raises some good points here, which deserve careful consideration. I have nine more days here in Sri Lanka, and if I ask myself what it is that I want to do, the answer which arises is 'volunteering with elephants and seeing Shanaka again'. But this thought is quite peaceful, it doesn't have the force of, 'Okay, let's do everything I can in order to see him again, because I must see him one more time before leaving'.

Let's see what other surprises these next days bring and, when the right moment arrives, I will make my decision. Which, obviously, will be the perfect choice for that moment, the only one I could make at that time, in the situation I'll be in.

First capital of Sri Lanka: Anuradhapura (250 BC–1017 AD)
Second capital of Sri Lanka: Polonnaruwa (11th–13th century AD)
Area of the archaeological site in Polonnaruwa: 122 hectares
Average temperature the last few days: 34 °C
Cost of my single room with a private bathroom: 3 pounds per night (tree frog included)
Cost of the pair of socks: 1.50 pound (basically a rip-off, but the shop owner reassured me, 'Good quality, madam')
Germans who stopped to talk with me while I was wearing my socks-and-flip-flops combo: 3
Other nationalities who brave this combination, so unforgivable for us Italians: the Japanese
Centimetres of dust I removed from my face in the evening: 2
Length of the reclining Buddha statue: 15 metres

DAY 22
'You work in a cemetery, too?'
-Kandy and Kegalle, Monday 5th March 2018-

Today has been quite a beautiful day! I said goodbye to the hostel's tiny kittens, which haven't even grown a millimetre over the last few days, and I went back to Kandy, where the other half of my backpack awaited me. Since the bus was going as far as the Royal Palace, I took the opportunity to visit the British Garrison Cemetery, the only thing I really wanted to see before leaving Kandy, and heading towards my next adventure.

I've always loved cemeteries, and in London I've seen so many. The English weather, with its wet days and grey skies, is just so appropriate for pondering the futility of this human life while wandering among the tombstones. I love looking at the photos, calculating how old people were when they died, admiring the statues, especially the dramatic ones, like angels bent double in grief, crying inconsolably over a grave. I like reading the inscriptions, always hoping for something original. On that note, I was once in a Malaysian cemetery where the tombstone of one poor lady, who died around 1820, reported solemnly that she 'died a spinster at 21 years of age'. I mean, for Premature Death's sake, as if dying so young wasn't enough, she also had to suffer the humiliation of being remembered as a spinster for generations to come.

Needless to say that in my worst moments of depression over my romantic life, I've thought a lot about that grave.

Equally sad, though in a very different way, was an inscription on a tombstone in London's famous Highgate Cemetery. The grave belonged to another woman, half smiling in the photo, who had also died quite young; she hadn't even turned 40. Her loved ones thought it a good idea to remember her with these words: 'She was a lawyer. She wanted to be a marine biologist'. Not only did you die young, but you didn't even manage to do what you actually wanted, for Unfulfilled Dreams' sake.

Anyway, it's one thing to visit an English cemetery with squirrels scampering here and there, occasional flowers left by those who still remember the dead, moss growing on the various statues and cold and damp penetrating your bones–the weather itself is conducive to melancholic reflection. But it's quite another to visit a cemetery under the merciless sun, guided by its young caretaker, who clearly couldn't think of anything he'd rather be doing. The Lonely Planet itself recommends you have a chat with this caretaker, who will share the place's many curiosities with you.

'Hello, are you the caretaker?' I ask this guy who is weeding a grave and has a remarkably composed manner. He's more or less as tall as me, thin, with brown hair, brown eyes and a dark complexion.

'Yes, I am the caretaker, madam. How can I help you?' His English seems quite good, if a bit... mechanical.

'If you have some time, could you give me a guided tour of your cemetery? Do you know that the Lonely Planet guidebook praises you and warmly recommends you as a guide?'

'Thank you, madam. Yes, I know I am in that guidebook, and I am very happy for this. Do you want to put your luggage in a safe place while I tell you the history of this cemetery?'

I would have replied that a cemetery must be one of the safest and most tranquil places ever, but something told me that he probably wouldn't have understood my joke.

And so my guided tour of this small and well-kept British colonial cemetery begins. Over 150 English people who died between 1800 and 1951 are buried here. In this land of Buddhism, surrounded by architectural styles so different from what I'm used to, this place seems so familiar and kind of comforting. And the caretaker even familiarises me with the deceased, telling me about their deaths and a few details about their lives. This walk among the graves becomes a collection of interesting stories rich in humanity.

In fact, the best part of the Garrison Cemetery is probably the caretaker himself. Imperturbable, he would shower me with dates and anecdotes, keen to share all his knowledge with me, but all the while remaining somehow distant. He inspired a fondness in me. He is one of those people who trigger a soft pain in my heart because there is something in them which seems not to add up, something you can't quite define but somehow grasp intuitively. Or, at least, I can't define it. In some ways he reminded me of Dustin Hoffman in *Rain Man*, so maybe this strange aura I perceived has something to do with slight autistic traits on his part. I don't have much experience in this respect, and recognising such characteristics in people from a culture so different to mine, who therefore have a different mentality and behavioural code, is even more difficult. But it would explain how he can remember all the inscriptions on the 163 tombstones of the cemetery by heart.

By heart. 163 inscriptions!

'I'm sorry, but I don't believe you. You are telling me that you know every single tombstone by heart?'

'Yes, madam, I don't tell lies. I can show you if you want.'

'Yes, please! I read somewhere that there is the grave of a man trampled to death by an elephant in this cemetery.'

'Sure, Mr John. Follow me', he says, sounding very professional. On the way to that tomb he picks a flower which he immediately gives to me. 'This is for you. You can put it behind your ear'.

When we arrived at the tomb in question, he made sure I was ready for the show. 'Are you ready? Can I start?'

'Wait, can I film you? I have a feeling this is going to be something great', I told him.

'Sure, it's a pleasure for me.'

I get ready with my phone camera focused on his serious, composed face, and he begins. 'Okay. I start, then. One, two, three. This monument is erected by...', and he started reciting the inscription without any hesitation whatsoever. Besides, at a speed which made it quite difficult for me to follow him reading it from the tombstone.

The fact that his recital lacked any theatricality, delivered in an almost robotic monotone which hardly suited the tragic nature of its content, made the whole scene even funnier for me. I was standing in front of a tomb, with a flower behind my ear, filming the cemetery caretaker who, standing rigid and serious, was reciting its long inscription by heart, looking straight into my camera, almost with a little performance anxiety, as if I were interviewing him. Infinite sweetness.

'Wow, you really did know it!'

'Yes, madam, I don't tell lies. Do you want more proof?'

'Oh, if you would be so kind!'

Even if he didn't let much emotion shine through, I am sure that showing off his memory gave him a certain joy and pleasure. I personally found the whole thing so funny and endearing, original as it was. So I asked him to recite three more inscriptions for me, which he delivered all in the same tone, devoid of any narrative enthusiasm.

'Wow, you know them all by heart! It means that you like your job a lot', I complimented him.

'Yes, I do what I like, in the open air, and nobody checks on me', he confirmed, in the same inexpressive, almost flat tone.

'Oh, like me! I became a freelancer so that nobody can check on me while I work', I explained.

'Oh, do you work in a cemetery, too?' he asked me, a bit surprised.

....

The. Infinite. Sweetness. And The Third Big Misunderstanding, after the one with Shanaka in the sea and with Chamath at the beach.

I stayed with him a bit longer to hear him recite a few more inscriptions, from the graves of women who died from diarrhoea (what a shitty way to go!), soldiers killed on the battlefield (occupational hazard), ladies scorched by sunstroke (they clearly didn't use sun cream) and men who fell prey to tropical fevers, cholera and malaria. If you managed to live past 40 at that time you could count yourself very lucky, for Not So Long-evity's sake. And if none of these hazards killed you, then a cricket ball might, as was the case for a very lucky cemetery resident, who died after one struck him in the head.

This must have been the weirdest and funniest visit I've ever made to a cemetery. Saying goodbye with an almost pompous handshake, the Sri Lankan Rain Man felt the need to tell me, 'My grandfather was a caretaker here and he gave Prince Charles a guided tour when he came here on his official visit,' adding, 'Please tell your friends'.

The SWEETNESS. What a pure soul.

Wondering what I would have died of if I had lived in those times (probably sunburn or tropical fever, given my pale skin and the fact I'm a delicacy for all kinds of insects), I went back to the hostel where I had left the rest of my backpack. I quickly repacked and set off on my next adventure 50 kilometres from Kandy, which I have been so excited about... The elephants!

In fact, in my pre-arrival ignorance, I had no idea there were elephants in Sri Lanka. I feel strangely emotional thinking that so far, without having remotely planned it, I've seen the blue whale and elephants, the two biggest mammals in the world. How beautiful. How blissful.

I began my trip with the idea of volunteering for a time in each of the countries I visit. However, I realise that to really do something useful I would need more time, like for example the chance to stop somewhere for a few weeks... And it's a luxury I can't afford. To be honest, I was planning to volunteer with children, but when looking through my Lonely Planet Bible the Millennium Elephant Foundation jumped out at me. It's an NGO where, for 9,000 rupees, around 40 pounds, you can spend a day in close contact with elephants. This goes against my principle of NOT paying to do voluntary work, but it's also true that I wouldn't categorise spending a day with elephants, washing and feeding them, as work. It's an experience like many others (well, better), and it's also well-known that elephants consume significant quantities of food each day, which means that keeping them requires significant funds.

So here I am at the Millennium Elephant Foundation, a family-run NGO aimed at improving the living conditions of elephants in Sri Lanka, funded entirely by voluntary work, donations and the experiences sold to tourists visiting the centre.

I arrived in the afternoon, in time to get to know some of the other volunteers. I met Jade, one of those gorgeous girls who always make me wonder if they have the vaguest idea of how beautiful they are. In this specific case, my second thought was, 'What is she doing here, surrounded by elephants, when she could be in a city working as a model or generally making every man she meets fall in love with her?'

Now that I am putting this in writing, I see how much judgement there is–albeit positive–in what I've just said. And what lines of reasoning arise as a ripple effect, where someone's beauty seems to predestine them for specific careers and situations. And where, therefore, someone's ugliness would limit their options. Apart from the fact that animals are only interested in our souls, and not our physical appearance, I take my second thought back.

Jade's role seems to be managing the centre, the bookings and us volunteers. Over dinner she told me that she often has to go to Colombo for photoshoots or to film advertisements, as she works for a model and extras agency which regularly gives her work because of her fair complexion. *Mah*, they probably give her work simply because she is stunningly hot!

She is helped by Richard, a blond Canadian with blue eyes who's been working at the centre for the last seven months. 'I don't know how long I want to stay. The management has been asking both Jade and me to stay here for another year, as they like how we're running the centre. To be honest, I didn't know anything about elephants, but I couldn't bear my office job anymore, so when I stumbled upon this foundation online I thought it could be an interesting change', he explained.

....

Who doesn't feel fed up with their office job and decide to go and take care of elephants?

Richard took me on an introductory tour of the centre, showing me where we volunteers sleep (in a little house), where the elephants sleep (in an open space in the forest), and explaining more or less what to expect from tomorrow.

My 'working' day, if we want to call it that, starts at 7.30am. I am as thrilled as a little girl! I've counted eight elephants so far, whom Jade has introduced to me: Lakshmi, Rani, Ranmenika and Pooja are the four females, and Raja, Kandula, Kavari Raja and Bandara are the males. Lakshmi is kind of the superstar of the centre, having featured in several international movies, while her daughter Pooja is the first elephant born in captivity in Sri Lanka. Jade has also explained that each of them has their own personality. There's one elephant who loves cuddles, one who acts the spoiled princess, another who takes no notice of you, a jealous one etc.

Thinking about it, hearing that animals have a personality is no short of astonishing. I mean, I know that it's true, for example all the dogs I've had were different from each other, but now that I'm taking some time to ponder this, it has a strange effect on me. What marvellous creatures they are, and how much better the world would be if we were able to coexist peacefully.

The elephants in this centre have been rescued from forced labour or from being tied up alone in a temple. I still remember the abysmal sadness I felt when I saw the elephant in the temple I visited with Andre by scooter. Something was very wrong. All he did was sway back and forth continually, for no apparent reason, in a disturbing, unhealthy way, clearly deeply hurt by a lifetime of loneliness.

I unpacked my stuff in the volunteers' little house, which comprises two bathrooms, two bedrooms and a sort of recreation area, with books, a cassette player as well as a few games like ping-pong and table-football. As always when there are books around, I immediately checked their titles and discovered, to my great pleasure, that one way or another they are all about elephants. I've already chosen my next book, inspired by the picture on the cover: a cowboy with a baby elephant, against a typical 'Marlboro Country' background.

At the moment there are four women, so we sleep two in each room. Guys sleep in another building, around 20 metres from ours. Among the volunteers, some are staying here one or two days, like me, while others are staying for a few weeks.

Dinner was shared on a long table on a veranda and had a lovely community feel. While we would normally be talking about our trip, what we liked doing and what we'd recommend seeing, tonight's conversation was more centred around elephants, why we like them, and what made us decide to come here for a close encounter with them. I never would have imagined it: being sat at a dinner table with other elephant lovers from all over the world talking at length about these gentle giants who touch something inside us.

After dinner we spent some time in the recreation area, some playing table tennis, some laughing and chatting, and some minding their own business, reading or writing. Being the social butterfly that I am, I dabbled in all these things. But now I wish you good night, my dear Diary. I'm off to rest these tired limbs. In the last few days I've zipped from one place to another, travelling quickly, and I could really do with a good sleep. And when I wake up a dream will come true! *Viva gli elefanti!* Long live elephants!

Kg of leaves and fruit an elephant eats on average in a day: 200
Average lifespan of an elephant: 55–70 years
Year the Millennium Elephant Foundation was founded: 1999
Thickness of the skin on an elephant's trunk, feet and butt: 4cm
Muscles in an elephant's trunk: more than 100,000
Weight an elephant can lift with his/her trunk: up to 250kg
What elephants have in common with hippos and rhinos: they are not able to jump

Messages Sanjaya sent me today: 2
Messages Shanaka has sent me so far: 19
Messages Antonio has sent me so far: 5
Messages Andre has sent me since his arrival in India: 9
Messages Chamath has sent me so far: I've stopped counting them
Messages Mr Potato Masher has sent me so far: 0
Level of importance I attribute to men at this specific point in my life: 3
Level of excitement at the idea of spending tomorrow with my beloved elephants: 10!
Clean pants I have at the moment: 4
Phone calls made to my family so far: 3

DAY 23

'Let's go to see a cricket match'
-Kegalle and Mount Lavinia, Tuesday 6th March 2018-

What an original, beautiful, intense day, during which the Universe has spoken to me loud and clear! No, not through the elephants, despite the fact I include speaking Elephantese on my Tinder profile super powers list (after seven years on dating apps you really have to come up with something new to pique people's curiosity, or at least entertain yourself...).

Let's start from the beginning. One thing I can say for certain is that the elephants are treated well here. This is clear from all the care and treatments they receive in the morning to the fact that the centre is trying to abolish elephant-back tours, replacing them with walks side by side. The structure that goes on the elephant's back, which can accommodate four to six people, can end up weighing almost 200 kilos, while the straps that keep it in place can press on their organs. Moreover, as Jade explained, the Millennium Elephant Foundation is also trying to replace chains, which are sometimes necessary, with special anklets made in Austria that are just as strong but don't hurt.

The first thing you do in the morning, between 7.30 and 9am, is prepare the breakfast for the elephants, keeping in mind that each of them has different tastes and needs in terms of supplements, vitamins and medicines. We went to the kitchen and started preparing some dough balls where we hid the vitamins or supplements' pills, as specified in each elephant's medical record. We then moved to a large open space outside bringing with us all the dough balls we had just rolled. One by one, the mahouts brought out the elephants, to whom we volunteers gave the dough balls, putting them directly in their mouths, as per the quantities and methods specified in the medical records. While one of us was feeding an elephant, another was checking her feet and brushing them clean. This was my job, cleaning the feet of one of these wonders of nature. As a matter of fact, it's not uncommon for stones, twigs, splinters and what not to get stuck in an elephant's foot. This morning, for example, one elephant arrived with a few stones wedged perfectly into a crack in his foot, and Richard spent a good amount of time trying to remove them with the aid of a little lever.

This is the point when you feed the elephants, clean their feet and check that they are in good health generally and that their sores and wounds are healing properly. One of the female elephants, for example, currently has an infection behind one of her knees, which Richard and some of the long-term volunteers had already cleaned and treated with a cream.

After breakfast and medical treatment, it's time for cleaning. So we headed into the jungle, coming to an area you might consider the elephants' bedroom. It's basically an open space where they sleep and eat dozens and dozens of kilos of branches and shrubs. We swept and raked the whole area to create a clean place where the elephants can rest without the risk of being hurt by sharp branches, and we also sifted through all the vegetation removing potentially dangerous shrubs and twigs.

The really magic moment, however, came when we started shovelling the elephants' shit. And I'm not talking about a few droppings. No. I'm talking about epic quantities of faeces, humungous heaps of excrement, kilos upon kilos of dung, wheelbarrows filled to the brim with elephant expulsions. A vast ocean of shit.

We had to shovel it into a pushcart to then wheel it over–and here comes the most marvellous part–to a small factory attached to the centre which, the only one of its kind, produces recycled paper out of elephant dung!

Paper made from elephant shit. We do live in a wonderful world.

I was there, shovelling all that poo, and yet I was feeling... Oh, my God, dare I say it? Yes! 'Happy'! But just writing it makes me laugh, because the two sentences seem entirely at odds with each other.

What if, at the end of the day, my father was right? When I was a child, whenever one of us three children would complain about something, of any kind, from a health problem to an injustice endured at school, from a fight with a friend to a prank one of us had played on another, my father would always respond with the same invitation/order, '*Vai a scavare una buca*', go and dig a hole.

A tireless worker and strong supporter of the idea that work ennobles man, my father believed that by digging holes, for no fucking reason, with no purpose in mind, we would forget that anything was amiss. The physical work, in other words, would help you get over your problems. Through the sweat and the effort, you would free yourself from tension and irritability. I've always seen this conviction of his as funny, and it's indeed one of my favourite stories to tell people about my father. And yet I have to admit that I agree with him. When I was 18, I went to a summer camp for children in Auronzo, in the Dolomites, where I worked for three weeks as a cleaning lady (or, if you prefer, skivvy). That experience taught me that cleaning bathrooms, and floors in particular, makes me feel very calm and relaxed and enables clear thinking. I don't know if this is one of those cases, or if what made me feel so good was just the whole setting: the jungle backdrop, the fact I was there volunteering with people from all over the world, cleaning an open space while elephants looked on. Or maybe I was just laughing to myself because of the absurdity of it all, or because I was imagining my friends asking, 'No, sorry, let me get this straight. You paid 40 pounds to shovel shit?'

'Yes, but it was elephant shit', I see myself answering happily.

The point is that I felt really good. At peace. From Padernello, Treviso, Italy, via London, UK, our career woman, as many people see me, has finally hit the big time: shovelling shit in Sri Lanka. But, again, this is elephant shit. And they even make paper out of it!

Many different thoughts sprung up in my mind while I was busy loading the pushcart with spadefuls of dung. I looked at this abundance of shite and pondered on the fact that nature is abundant by default. If we take a look around us, we see an abundance of water, light, mineral salts, flowers, leaves... It's we humans who have created the narrative of scarcity, which drives so much of our lives. Many of us live with the constant thought that a specific thing can finish, that there isn't any more of it, that it will not come back again. And so people stay in the same office job they hate so much for 20 years 'because jobs are hard to come by'. They stay in an unsatisfactory relationship 'because who can guarantee I'll find someone else?' They keep objects and clothes from decades before, 'because they just don't make them like this anymore, and who knows when I might need them again?' Or they drag on friendships and relationships that don't serve them anymore and add nothing to their lives 'because at least it's better than being on your own'. Scarcity, in so many forms. And every time we act from a scarcity mindset, we block the Universe's generous inventiveness. The Universe would unfold Its magic, if only we'd allow It to. Animals, plants, flowers never consider this problem. They concentrate on their simple existence, every day, and as a result we have trees yielding dozens and dozens of fruits, turtles laying hundreds of eggs, flowers blooming endlessly. And elephants shitting kilos of dung. How can we ever doubt that a Universe that takes so much care of Its animals and plants wouldn't do the same, if not more, for us?

After transporting several pushcarts full of faeces to the paper factory, we moved on to what was the most wonderful part of the morning for me. We accompanied the mahouts and their elephants to the river, around which the whole centre has been built, basically. Here, using a piece of coconut shell, we washed these marvels of nature for 40 minutes.

It's official: elephants are cleaner than me. The things travelling teaches you about yourself! Wow.

'I mean, do you get my point now?' I can almost hear my friend

Emanuele saying. He lived with me for four years and took the piss out of me for my personal hygiene on a regular basis, to the point that his nickname for me was 'stray dog'.

Yes, indeed. How often in life do we only truly learn something when we experience it first-hand? People can repeat a lesson until they lose their voice, but nothing teaches better than personal experience.

I've washed three elephants, and it filled my heart with joy to see how much they were enjoying it, laying on one side in that brown-grey water, with their trunk lazily floating, their eyes closed and even a half smile on their faces. The only flaw in this moment of bliss was standing knee high in that murky river. I was a bit grossed out and worried about leeches attacking my calves, but luckily none showed up.

This experience was a real privilege. How lucky am I? What amazing animals. What a world full of wonders, all more available and within our reach than we think.

In the afternoon I went for a stroll with a mahout, walking beside his elephant, occasionally feeding it some foliage. I wanted to ask the mahout a few questions about his life, what it was like living with such a big animal, if this was always his childhood dream, how he feels about his elephant... But unfortunately his English was worse than my mother's. So I kept silent, looking adoringly at the elephant next to me and admiring the nature surrounding us. The only interruption to the flowing of my thoughts was the occasional command that the mahout would shout at his creature.

I might have felt at peace, but not peace of the senses. In fact, amongst my many reflections, I also found myself wondering what a mahout would be like in a moment of intimacy. God, please reassure me that I'm not the only one who looks at someone and wonders what they are like in bed ('You are not, don't worry', 'Thank you, God').

By definition, a mahout is a keeper and driver of elephants. Mahouts work their whole lives alone with their elephants, so I can't imagine them being particularly open or in contact with their emotions. Their job includes barking orders at their elephant and sometimes reproaching them when they move away or don't obey. It doesn't strike me as a job with much room for kindness... But who knows, maybe mahouts have to develop extreme sensitivity to understand their elephants' moods, which might be their strong point in bed. More to the point, I wonder what it would be like to be intimate with someone you can't even really communicate with and whose life is a million light years away from yours.

....

And while I write this I start laughing. It's fair to say that over these last three weeks I've had a good go at finding out what this is like.

The walk with the mahout ended at the river for the mandatory practical joke. I climb on top of the elephant's back, he fills his trunk with river water and then empties it over his back, completely soaking me. It's a bit like when you play hide-and-seek with children. You can see them perfectly well, and yet you wonder aloud where they could possibly be hiding. Same thing here. You are sitting on the elephant knowing perfectly well what's coming. But how many times do you get to experience this in your life? So you just enjoy it.

And that is not all, my dear Diary. The experience that will make me go to bed tonight feeling very grateful, with an even bigger and more deeply felt 'Thank you, God', happened during my visit to the Eco Maximus company. As I said earlier, this is the only company in the world that makes paper out of elephant excrement. One of the managers took us volunteers around on a guided tour, explaining the different production phases. First, they dry the poo in the sun before boiling it with disinfectant for a few hours, until it becomes a sort of sludge. This greyish substance doesn't stink at all. Not surprising really, considering that elephants basically shit all day long, so the food only sits a short while in their stomachs. Basically, the vegetation they eat is barely digested. That's why their dung is optimal for paper production: it contains pure cellulose.

This disinfected mush is then mixed with water and passed through a sort of metal grill, where the material retained settles and creates a sheet of paper which will later on be dried, coloured and refined.

This is the procedure in broad terms. The tour ended at some long tables in a corner where many local women were sitting, hard at work. Each of them was making something different with these sheets of recycled paper. Some of them were making little boxes, some calendars or envelopes, while others were making bookmarks or journals.

'Shit, I actually really need a journal', I told myself, since I'm writing a lot each day and I'm about to finish you, dear Diary. Next to these tables was a shop selling dozens and dozens of different items, all made out of recycled paper, and where most of the volunteers headed once the guided tour was over, to buy souvenirs.

As for me, I stayed behind to talk with our guide. 'Hi, thank you so much for all the explanations. It's been really fascinating to learn all this. Now, I hope you don't mind me saying this, but around the factory I've noticed the posters in English explaining the different production phases. I've seen that each of them has been translated in many languages, Italian included. Well, I'm Italian and I'm a translator, and it's a professional hazard I guess, but it almost pained me to see those Italian translations. They must have been done on Google Translate, because even I had trouble understanding them and had to go back to the English sentence to get the meaning. Some of them are not only grammatically incorrect, but actually make no sense at all', for Automated Translation's sake. 'As I told you, I'm a translator. I'm a volunteer here and I have a few spare hours. If you want, I'd be happy to translate these posters, given that there are a lot of mistakes in the Italian', I offered.

'Oh, how kind. Please come with me to see the boss. Let's see what he says.'

We went into an office, the guide explained the situation, and in no time at all I was sitting in front of a computer translating a two-page document.

When I finished and was about to leave, the boss interrupted his 'Thank you. Thank you very much, madam. Thank you…' to excitedly yell something in Sinhalese to one of his employees. The girl went out of the office and came back two minutes later with…

Oh, yes.

With a journal. Exactly what I needed.

And not only that. The journal was part of a three-piece set including two smaller diaries, so a total of three notebooks in different sizes.

I was about to say, 'Oh, how kind, you really don't have to! Helping you has been a pleasure for me', when they put the notebooks in my hand and I saw that on the cover of all three of them was a yellow balloon floating up into the sky, above the words 'Let it go'.

I think that my smile must have reached my lungs. Out of dozens and dozens of items they had to choose from, they gave me a journal, which is exactly what I needed. And out of all the things that could have been written on its cover, we have 'Let it go'.

If I really stop and think about this, it gives me shivers. Marvellous shivers, though.

Thanks, generous Universe. Thanks for these synchronicities, which make me feel like I'm on the right path.

It seems to me that the Universe has been talking to me in every possible way during this trip, as never before, and I'm learning to listen and to understand. Or, more likely, the Universe has always been talking to me, and I was just too immersed in my own little world to notice.

Onwards with letting it all go, then. I'll continue working on it, I promise.

Still wondering if 'let it go' could actually also mean 'give it up', I've decided to follow Shanaka's suggestion and see him again. Having fun, yes, but without any attachment. My volunteering day finished at 4pm, so I said goodbye to Jade, Richard and all the other volunteers and took a tuk-tuk to the train station. Three hours by train and here I am back in Mount Lavinia. Oh, yes, what an emotion-packed day!

Before recounting my reunion with Shanaka in minute detail, I'd like to write a few words about this experience at the Millennium Elephant Foundation. Would I do it again? Definitely yes, for a few days, but I don't think for longer than that.

It's clear they really do love elephants and take care of them as best they can, but in the end, we volunteers don't do much work: from 7.30 to 9am, from 10 to midday and then later from 2 to 4pm. If I decide to invest my time volunteering elsewhere, I would like to feel more 'used'. I expect my time to be used up doing many activities. In other words, I don't think I'd enjoy staying there for a week, with all that spare time. It's also true that I've seen very little, in just one day at the centre, and the volunteers who stay longer are probably given other tasks. It's equally true that, knowing myself, I would probably have made the most of that spare time working shifts at Eco Maximus, learning how to make paper out of poo (you never know what might come in useful in life) or translating and reviewing every document I could get my hands on.

Anyway, from elephants I move swiftly and nonchalantly to... What animal could Shanaka be? A weasel, maybe! Brown, lean and agile. Haha!

Talking of 'letting go', besides attachments I also have some serious work to do on expectations (which are themselves a form of attachment to an idea we develop about something). I was expecting some kind of romantic reunion, or at least a passionate one, given how much he went on about my coming back and seeing him again. Instead, my life is once again more *Bridget Jones's Diary* than *Sex and the City*.

Shanaka arrived around 9pm at my hotel, where I booked a room explaining that it would probably be two of us staying there. He arrived holding a plastic bag with two beers inside (sweet, thoughtful weasel), and greeted me with, 'Hello Roby, there is a cricket match. Let's go watch it in the house of a friend'.

Ah, ecco. Oh, I see.

And there I was imagining him, if not taking me there and then up against a wall, at least coming into my room and greeting me properly as God intended. Do you see how dating works in Sri Lanka? Quite pragmatic, concise, no frills.

'Hello, Shanaka, how are you? Okay, let's go', I smiled, both because I was happy to see him again and because the scene was so different from how I had imagined it. No kiss, no pat on the cheeks, no playful slap on the bum, not even a handshake. Two beers, though.

Anyway, it's nice to see that the world is the same wherever you go. Sports come before anything else. After all, poor Shanaka, he works 13 hours a day at the Shelton Seafood Restaurant. I don't think there's much of a party scene in Mount Lavinia, at least not in this season, and he only has four days off a month... When you look at it this way, cricket matches become incredibly important.

Okay, then, I follow him into the tuk-tuk, and we go to this flat, which by the way was pretty cool. When Shanaka told me we were going to see one of his friends, I was expecting to meet another guy. Instead we were welcomed by a plump Swedish lady in her seventies, and a Sri Lankan man in his fifties with long grey hair tied back in a ponytail. He struck me as a kindly, Sri Lankan version of Bob from *Twin Peaks* (the image of him hiding behind an armchair haunted me for months when I watched that TV series as a teenager).

And so a day that started with me shovelling elephant shit ended with me sitting between two Sri Lankan men, one of whom was trying to explain the rules of cricket to me while the other one was continually undoing and redoing his ponytail. And I am just sitting there smiling and half laughing about the whole situation.

Several cries of joy for Sri Lanka's victory and two beers later, we say goodbye to the two friends who didn't seem remotely interested in finding out anything about me.

'We have to go out for dinner and celebrate, Roby. Sri Lanka win. This is very good!', Shanaka insisted. 'I know a very nice and elegant place, just right for you. You like for sure. It's near.'

Here we go again, Shanaka wants to pass himself off as a man of the world. 'Shanaka, you know that I don't care about elegant places (do I need to remind you that ten hours ago I was shovelling elephant dung?). Honestly, I prefer by far the small venues you locals go to spend the evening. I don't want to go to places for tourists. There's plenty of places like that in London', I try to make him understand. But there was nothing I could do or say. Shanaka was inflexible, so in the end he took me to the Lion Pub, definitely a posh place by local standards.

'I order a beer and chicken spring rolls for me. What do you want? You take spring rolls, too. At least two. You will like them so much that one is not enough, you want more.'

What a sweet thought. And an accurate one. The spring rolls were indeed delicious.

When the bill came, I didn't manage to get my way. Shanaka refused to listen to reason. 'You come back for me, so I pay dinner and I am happy to do it', he repeated. Yes, okay, but this dinner cost you a quarter of your monthly salary, which makes me feel uncomfortable on the one hand, and on the other leaves me wondering why Shanaka wanted to... show off in this way.

Finally, after a tuk-tuk ride (which, thankfully, he let me pay for) we were back in my room. And I'm happy to report that here Shanaka proved to be better than I remembered. I still wouldn't want to see us standing side by side in a mirror, but let's say that he's generous and pays a lot of attention to detail.

An emotion-packed day indeed! And quite a long one, too. Anyway, I'm happy at the idea of staying in the same place for the next few days. Let's enjoy the seaside and this micro love story.

Average times an elephant defecates in a day: 16
Kilos of poo ejected daily: between 180 and 200
Year Eco Maximus was founded: 1997
Website where you can learn more about it: www.ecomaximus.com
Elephants currently held in captivity in Sri Lanka: 135

Average daily cost to maintain an elephant: 50 dollars
Elephants currently at the Millennium Elephant Foundation: 9
Punishment for killing an elephant: death sentence
Monthly wage of a mahout: 200 dollars
Minutes I continued smiling after reading 'Let it go' on the diary: 2
Number of tuk-tuks in Sri Lanka: I'd really love to know
Mistakes Shanaka makes on average in a sentence: 3
Cricket rules he explained: 8
Rules I understood: 2
State of my hair: Attacked, and conquered, by a mysterious disease, as Giacomo Leopardi would put it
Cm Shanaka has grown since I last saw him: 0

DAY 24

'I must tell you one thing. I am very poor person'
-Mount Lavinia, Wednesday 7th March 2018-

I really needed a day like this, pretty much pure, pleasant idleness. Which is something I am not at all good at, even when on holiday. I've always been like that, someone who does 100 things while planning 200 more.

A friend of mine in London once described me as 'a social experimenter', in the sense that I am generally always running around, going to all sorts of events, dipping my toes in countless different situations, interested in several courses and so on. There was a time when I thought I was restless, but I've since come to the conclusion that it's simply my zest for life and desire to live to the full every minute of this Earthly experience that God has given me the chance to live. Recently, however, during a seminar on limiting beliefs, all those ideas we hold unconsciously, without being aware of them, I've learnt that doing many things is associated with thinking we are 'not good enough'. People who believe they are not good enough will do anything to prove to others that it's not the case, that on the contrary they are able to do a lot of things, all the time, and to do them well. 'Look at me, I am worthy of your love and attention, too.'

Fantastic. So basically high achievers might actually be struggling with the lowest self-esteem. It's an upside-down world. Like arrogant people, who are in fact the most insecure. Or people who are angry with the whole world, but are basically just really hurting inside, as anger is ultimately sadness in disguise. What complicated mechanisms.

If I really want an explanation for my hyperactivity, I could find a pointer in an observation made by a woman I know, the mother of one of my friends, 'Wow, you do so many things in order to not stop and think'. This thing she said really struck me. I've thought long and hard about it because I'm naturally disposed to giving space to things people tell me (and a healthy new habit for my mental and emotional balance would probably be to stop doing it. As my guru Alessandra once said, 'Not everybody says correct or interesting things that we should listen to').

Do I really work so hard at not stopping and thinking? Someone might get this idea from looking superficially at my lifestyle. However, if they stopped to take into consideration the fact I work alone from home, and therefore live in a silent world (filled with imaginary friends) for most of my day, they would probably see things differently. And anyway, in April I'll do my silent Vipassana meditation retreat in Kathmandu, towards the end of my trip, so I will have 12 hours a day to sit with myself and my thoughts.

Fuck me, 12 hours a day... It's all a bit scary. I don't know if it scares me more on a physical or mental level.

Never mind all that. For now I'm sitting by the sea, at a table in Shelton Seafood Restaurant, with my feet buried in the sand and a watermelon juice with a yellow straw in front of me. Today I'm enjoying the sea from a distance and writing, given that I am having my period, and an abundant one at that, and I prefer not to wear a bikini. The total opposite of that Tampax advert from the '80s: 'Tampax freedom. Why compromise?' By the way, that's probably the first slogan in English I learnt. Those women decided to go rollerblading, running in the fields or playing football exactly when they had their period. The lady in the Nuvenia Pocket advert, however, beat them all by far, with her brilliant idea of skydiving precisely when she was menstruating. I can still hear that jingle: 'Nuvenia Pocket, sicura e vai. Nuvenia Pocket, e vai, vai, vai...'. Nuvenia Pocket, secure and go. Go, go, go...

'Go fuck yourself', I'd say today, knowing how periods actually feel. Damn the power of advertising, which means I still remember this after 25 years, and damn these misleading representations of reality.

As for me, I wear my Lines Seta Ultra with wings, which I brought with me from London just to be sure, and *yes, I do compromise.* So I'm staying here just sitting and writing, winking at Shanaka when nobody is looking, and chatting a bit with other tourists and travellers, enjoying this beautiful day of sunshine and sea.

This morning I went to Colombo for a stroll around, but maybe because of the heat, which wears me out, or because I don't find Colombo particularly interesting, I came back here after only three hours.

Today is Wednesday and I have in front of me five more full days here in Sri Lanka, before flying to crazy, colourful, incredible, deafening, intense, brutal, surprising, sweet and bitter Mother India. I think I'll stay here until Friday. At first I contemplated going to Trincomalee where, incidentally, a friend of my brother's is staying, a psychiatrist Mauro has told me so much about and whom I'd like to meet. I mean, if we never managed to meet up in Treviso, why not get together in Sri Lanka? That's how small the world has become if you want to see it that way. Unfortunately, Trincomalee is on the other side of the island, and it would take me more than half a day to get there, so in terms of time and energy it doesn't sound ideal. It's way better to stay here and reflect on this first month, and on this country which has truly enchanted me with its natural beauty. Maybe, maybe, out of all the countries I've visited so far, it's the one which reminds me most of a tropical paradise. I would have never expected to see so many animals or have such a close encounter with many of them. From blue whales, to elephants, to sea turtles… And, talking of animals, in one month I got only a few mosquito bites, none of which turned into the hard, swollen buboes I've always suffered from in other Asian countries. Yippee! The lotion I prepared before coming here has proved brilliant! A note for Roby the businesswoman: perhaps I could think about marketing it. 'Roby's magic lotion to ward off bloody evil bastard mosquitoes. So much for Autan!'

The name might be a bit too long, but I definitely think it has something.

People here are very calm and kind, even if the men are a bit too insistent. This would not have struck me if we had been, let's say, in the south of Italy, or in Brazil, but in Asia, with all that I've seen in Vietnam, Laos, Cambodia and India, I wasn't really expecting it. In the long run they become tiring, with all their attentions and piercing stares, even if they are never dangerous.

What makes me laugh more, however, is that they are all so into us Westerners when they don't realise that the cultural difference is waaaaaaaaaaaaaaaaaay bigger than the geographical one. I think of Chamath, who had never had dinner in a restaurant before, or who had never had a 'real' conversation with a woman. I think of Shanaka who asked me if I wanted to go swimming with him, a proposal which by the way will remain one of the most original and romantic I ever received. It surprises me that adults have managed to grow up whilst staying so pure and naive inside, and in the end it's exactly one of the reasons I love Asia in such a deep and visceral way. And this is me talking, whom so many see as a Pollyanna type ready to trust everybody and believe in the good that has to be there inside each of us, as it just can't be otherwise in my fairy world.

One mistake I made initially was to expect Sri Lanka to be a sort of less intense and diluted version of India, while in fact they are two very different countries. They differ not only in terms of male behaviour towards Western women, but also religion, population density, poverty levels…

One thing which seems to be completely redundant are bathing suits, both for men and women, since basically everybody goes to the beach (and in the sea!) fully dressed.

Good, it's time to go. Shanaka will come and find me when his shift is over, and let's see what tonight will bring us.

01.20am, in my room

Eh, what did tonight bring us... ?

Mah, I'm not sure what to make of it myself.

I was in my room waiting for Shanaka when I received a very long message from him. Just like that, out of the blue (whale, of course), a profusion of grammar, syntax and spelling mistakes. I managed to make out the meaning more or less, drawing on all my skills as an interpreter. The message was: 'Hello Roby I am very proud becaus you invite me but I have to tell you one thing, I am nott rich (I'd say that's pretty clear!), very poor person, last thre days I enjoy with you. I am very hapy for everything. But today I cannot go with you (where?). Because today not very many clients. Many people have restaurant I get good tipp. And I want to enjoy all life with you. But money is still for everything. I live very difficult with my family (but didn't you tell me they live on the other side of the island?). Next month nobody is at restaurant (exactly my point, so why don't you go and work the season on the other coast, where everybody will go?). I receive smal salary and this money is for my parents. I am very poor boy but I don't like to see that I am poor, I am sorry for this, please don't mistake me. Thanks you for everything, God bless you for all your. If you can help for me and for my family for Happy New Year celebrations, if you can help me this is big merit in your life, madam. Thank you Roby. Today I am poor.'

....

I was shocked.

Where is he coming from with this message? And where is he going? All afternoon long at the restaurant we exchanged smiles and winks, and in the three hours I've been away he comes up with this stuff? And I'm such an idiot because I just confirmed two more nights with my hotel to spend more time with him.

'Shanaka, don't end it in this way. Come here and let's talk about it. You don't have to spend anything. Actually, I wanted to tell you this yesterday–why did you spend so much money at the pub and with the tuk-tuk when we could have walked to a less fancy restaurant? Come here and let's talk about it, and at least let's say goodbye properly', I write him back.

He answers, 'I don't want say goodbye to you, but today I don't have money'.

What does he think we are going to do in here? Play poker? 'Why do you keep talking about money? Come here and we'll stay in. I just want to understand what thoughts you are having.'

'Okay, I come soon', he gives in, quite easily in fact.

While I wait for him I tell myself, 'Please, please, please, I can't have fallen for it. Not the cliché.' I don't want to believe that at the end of the day they are all looking for money, one way or another, as so many people warned me they were. Or papers, so that they can leave and start a new life. Because while this may be a tropical paradise, it's a poor one with few good opportunities.

With my personality, which I define as a cross between Pollyanna running happily through a cornfield and Candy Candy playing with the squirrels, I cannot believe that Shanaka is doing exactly what I had been warned about. My reflective part comes to my aid, reminding me that the whole 'Everybody is the same, everybody is after money' idea doesn't hold water for me, because 'everybody' is a generalisation I automatically won't accept.

Shanaka arrives half an hour later, in all his sudden poverty but with one beer.

'Listen, Shanaka, that whole rambling speech about you being poor today, I haven't really understood it. Of course you know me very little, but I think you've had a chance to see that I couldn't care less about appearances. I'm not rich either (even if, of course, in his eyes I'm a millionaire... In rupees, but still a millionaire). Last night I didn't want you to take me to that pub, I told you many times. Instead you wanted to appear differently from how you normally are. I am only interested in a person's mind and heart, not in their money.'

'Roby, I would never ask you for money', he says.

'Ehm, you've just done it? '

And the Sri Lankan smart ass solves it with a 'Yes, but I cannot explain why'.

And indeed he didn't. After all, I didn't insist. I didn't like the turn our conversation was taking. Luckily, I managed to steer it onto our day together, the places I have visited in Sri Lanka and the fact that India is waiting for me.

'Do you really want to waste the little time we have talking about money?'

'No, Roby, I don't want', he returned to his senses. And cuddles there were.

Afterwards, Shanaka left me to go and sleep in his room, above the restaurant where he works. What didn't leave me, though, is the slight doubt that he wants to exploit me, or had maybe even planned to since the beginning. And when a doubt creeps in, it's difficult to go back to how things were initially. But doubts are closely connected to fears, and if there's something I've been trying to work on over the last few years it's facing my fears. And making choices out of love, not out of fear. So yes, I could feed this doubt with the fear of having been manipulated, that everything was calculated... but I would have to invest so much energy in this useless and harmful vortex. Because feeding fears requires huge levels of concentration, and I think it's way more beneficial to focus my thoughts on something nice instead. Especially considering that thoughts become things, so they have to be selected and managed carefully.

So let this fear go, too, and let's put the whole thing to bed. Let's see what happens tomorrow. Besides the fact that it will be another marvellous day of blue, green and light.

Fruit juices I've drunk so far: 26
Percentage of Buddhists in Sri Lanka: 95% of the population
Percentage of Buddhists in India: 0.8% of the population
From 1 to 10, the score I'd give Colombo as a city: 5
From 1 to 10, the score I'd give Mount Lavinia as a seaside resort: 6.8
Score I'd give myself for how I'm approaching this trip: 21!

Pollyanna's full name: Pollyanna Whittier
No. of parents she has: 0. Both parents died when she was only eight years old. The protagonists of cartoons in the '80s were all particularly lucky.
Pollyanna's trademark feature: she plays the 'happiness game' which her father taught her. Basically, she is always able to be happy, setting aside the negative aspects of a situation to focus on the good.
Words I've learnt in Sinhalese: 5

DAY 25
'I have to go to the fish market'
-Mount Lavinia, Thursday 8th March 2018-

Today has been such a laaaaaaaaazy day, spent almost entirely on the beach, where I arrived late in the morning. All those days I spent racing from one place to another like the Duracell bunny have taken their toll, and I just want to rest a bit before flying out to India, the second leg of my three-month trip. God knows I'll need plenty of mental and physical energy once there!

On the beach I met this couple who got married at 23. Every time I hear stories like theirs I wonder who makes them do it, even with all the love in the world. Why do they feel the need to tie the knot so early in life? Why the hurry? Honestly, this is one of the many things I don't understand.

It's equally true that I should mind a good sackful of my own fucking business, but I've often reflected on these couples getting married so young. Moreover, they had been together since they were 12 years old. Classic childhood sweethearts, basically. There's a small part of me that probably envies them, because I think about how much heartache and how many disappointments they have managed to avoid. If you've been with the same person all your life, you don't know how it feels to have a broken heart, pick yourself up bit by bit and rebuild your life. You have never experienced what it means to find the strength to start it all again and put yourself out there, to then have to deal with a multitude of men who are afraid, confused, 'free spirits' or wannabe Peter Pans, maybe divorced or still tied to a broken marriage by a few lingering loose ends, probably along with some nice baggage in the form of children and a few addictions, which seem to catch up with everyone by this age. She won't have the faintest idea of what the procedure is when you meet someone, exchange a few messages in a chat, then move to phone numbers so that you start having conversations, based on which you begin building up some positive views about him, and you find yourself going along to the first date all hopeful, making an effort but not looking too gorgeous because you are not sure whether you are going to like him. Instead you like him a lot, and so you start waiting for signs of life from his side, and you find yourself checking the double blue tick on your WhatsApp messages. Everything seems to be going well, maybe you even get past the big fifth-date milestone, which these days almost feels like a huge accomplishment. And then, in the thick of it, you see that one day your message doesn't get delivered, he doesn't receive it, and while you try to remember if he told you that he was going somewhere with poor reception, you notice that strangely you cannot see his WhatsApp picture anymore and you realise that, for no apparent reason, and in any case without an ounce of balls, as he couldn't say it to your face, he has changed his mind.

He's blocked you.

And you go from being incredulous, to shocked, to disgusted, to outraged, to nauseated, to depressed, to desperate, to thinking you'll remain single forever, visualising yourself in a fleece tracksuit, woollen socks pulled up over the joggers to keep out the draughts and huge dog shaped slippers, lying on the floor of your kitchen, lifeless, half eaten by your cats. And while you try to rally your strength once more and shoo away these horrible thoughts, you take some solace in thinking that at least you live in a century where none of your relatives would ever think to inscribe on your tombstone, 'She died a spinster'.

Oh, fuck, I've literally just suggested this idea to my brother Alessio.

There you go. She will never know how it feels to go through all this. I envy her this. But there is also a part of me that feels she has missed out on many beautiful things. It's the part of me that once in a while, when sitting on a plane or lying on a beach, goes browsing through her memories looking for the most romantic moments or most intense experiences of love. Some of which, incidentally, have been with men who have played no particular role in my life. Sure, maybe she's had all these moments with the same man, and yet I still believe that at the end of the day, I'd rather have all my adventures, because one way or another they have formed me, even broken me, leading me to rebuild myself in a new way every time.

Well, maybe not really all of them. I'd have happily done without some of them, let's be honest. But I strongly believe that everything always goes in the best possible way, and if my journey had to include several romantic misadventures, disappointments and frustrations, it's because it had to go this way. And I will only understand the reason they happened in the future, in hindsight, when I'll be able to look back calmly and from a distance.

Thinking about it, for example, this trip itself is born out of a concurrence of events from which the only possible solution for me was to take some time out from everything and everybody.

In this respect, talking about the trip and my dating misadventures, I wonder how things will evolve in India with Andre. I am sure we will meet up. He's been keeping me updated on his movements, and he travels very slowly. Within a week I should be able to catch up with him. I don't know myself what I hope to happen. We definitely get along so well, he is an interesting and super organised guy and we have a good laugh together, but his body is way too skinny for my tastes.

Maybe I'm being mean. ('Yours is way too humungous for his tastes, more to the point', Mauro's voice pops up in my mind. And, one second later, Alessio's chips in drily, 'Actually, if he has any taste whatsoever, he won't even look at you'). Unfortunately, the absence of any muscular definition makes him little attractive to me.

The same can be said about Jacob who is nevertheless, like Andre, quite charming and intriguing, albeit definitely harder to figure out. Or maybe I simply have to spend more time with him.

Oh well, in short I'd say that when it comes to men, the picture is already quite full, even in India. For One-Track Mind's sake.

Honestly, it's so difficult to break one's patterns and get free. What a long journey. From becoming aware that you have an issue, to observing when the thoughts in question first spark into life (because it always starts with thoughts), to changing the reaction you would normally have in that situation. Changing it, or simply not having any reaction. Catching yourself *in flagrante* and telling yourself kindly, 'Aha, Roby, I caught you right when you were harbouring expectations. I've surprised you just as you are mentally building up an idea of happiness which depends on whether certain events happen or not. But you know that happiness starts within you. And you know that expectations are a cause of sorrow. But don't worry, you have already done well to realise you were about to fall into the same pattern and stop yourself. You'll see. Practice will make everything easier'.

Talking of men and obsessions, the little man Shanaka has told me that tomorrow morning he has to go with his boss to the fish market, which happily opens at 2am. Can that even be true? At 2am? There, I'm missing a fisherman from my list of male encounters. If I wasn't, maybe I would know more about such things. Anyway, he couldn't come to see me, so I've put aside my expectations for a night, if not of passion, with some nice sparks at least. I've decided to go out in Mount Lavinia looking for a restaurant, and I think it's the first time I've felt a bit... Let's say not quite at ease. There were several groups of men in the street who would stop talking as I passed. I remember what Chamath had told me, that he indeed meets up with his friends along the roadside. Sri Lankan customs, then. In the end I've settled for a not so healthy but reassuring Burger King, because I knew I would find other Westerners there and also because after a month of rice and curry, I was really craving something greasy and fried.

In any case, I'm baffled by the prices in Burger King, for example, or even in the supermarkets. From the little I've learnt by talking with Shanaka, Chamath, Sanjaya and the others, salaries in Sri Lanka are very low, and yet you find prices around that seem so out of reach for locals. Very likely they are indeed places intended mostly for tourists.

Right, then. With these observations of mine on microeconomics I draw the curtain on this peaceful day. Goodnight, world!

Average salary of tea plantation workers: £3 a day
Average salary of hotel workers: £42 a month
Average salary of a soldier: 7,400 dollars a year (How disgusting. 150 times higher for what? Killing other people?)
Times I've been asked, 'Where are you from?' so far: 749
Times I've been asked, 'Are you married?' so far: 701
Sri Lankans I've seen so far who are taller than me: 6
Year I first ate at a Burger King: 1994
Calories in a Burger King Whopper: 660

DAY 26
'It's not nice, if you have my thing inside your belly'
-Mount Lavinia, Friday 9th March 2018-

Once again, today I've been a bit of a beached blue whale. And actually, wait a second, I can already see that I'm a smaller whale than I was when I arrived. On the one hand, the carbs I would normally eat for breakfast (cereals, biscuits, slices of cake, bread and jam etc) are nowhere to be found, and on the other, wine practically doesn't exist here, and most of my meals are boiled rice with vegetables. Add to all this the fact that I am definitely more active and on the go than I'd normally be in my London life, and you can see how I've managed to shed some fatty tissue. It will be interesting to see which is the greater figure at the end, my centimetres of regrowth or kilos of weight loss!

I started today in sporty mode, with a nice long solitary walk on the beach, entertaining myself with one of my favourite pastimes, people watching, a swim with Shanaka and finally a game of volleyball with him and the other guys from his restaurant.

I was the only woman, and a white one for that matter, in this group of brown-skinned young guys, who must all be 15 years younger than me. Looking at the scene from outside, who knows whether I would think, 'That woman must have something going on with one of the guys'? I actually don't think I would. The difference in body size and age would not make me jump to that conclusion, which makes me smile even more, acknowledging once again how much more imagination the Universe has than we do.

I then lay for a few hours on one of the sunbeds in front of the restaurant where Shanaka works, where everybody knows me now, dozing and working on my tan.

I ordered a watermelon juice – by now I can say this is my favourite drink here – and, rightly so, it was Shanaka who brought it to me. He came close with his usual perfect smile and asked me, completely out of the blue (whale), 'But don't you want to get married and have children?'

....

Boom!

Just like that, as if he had asked me, 'Would you like to eat fish today?'

It had been a while since I last wallowed in the swamplands of victimhood that bubble up in my heart when I think about these things.

Now him as well, for Sensitivity's sake...

I hadn't thought about any of that in a while, which was exactly what I hoped this journey would give me, a chance to focus instead on discovery and wonderment.

Yet, the pain is all still there, and right on cue, within five milliseconds my eyes were brimming. Of course, the biggest journey we have to make is within ourselves. You can go all the way to the other side of the world and carry your problems with you. What I hope, no, what I *know*, is that this journey will change the way I relate to this issue. If you cannot change the outside circumstances, you can change the way you approach them. The way you respond to them.

Apart from the fact that the beach didn't seem to me like the most appropriate place for such a conversation, I answered, 'Sure, I want that. I've been obsessed with all that for years. What's more, one of the reasons for this trip was actually to take a break from the emotional torture I was inflicting on myself by constantly thinking about it'.

'And if you discover in India that you have my baby?' Shanaka asked me, point-blank.

'Well, I would keep the baby, and it would be the best of miracles.'

'But I wanna touch the baby', he explained.

This sentence, so simple and concise, had a strange effect on me when he said it, but now that I am writing it, it makes me laugh a bit. It makes me think of when I was five, in my third year of kindergarten, and the nuns chose me to play the Virgin Mary in the Nativity play (Those poor nuns. How could they have known? #themoralfallofavillagegirl). I had to sit with a little Jesus made of chalk, which weighed several kilos, on my lap, and all the little shepherds came to touch it in adoration.

I also laugh because clearly nobody has explained to Shanaka that you cannot get pregnant if you have intercourse during your period, or in the days immediately after. And I certainly won't be the one to set him straight.

'Shanaka, isn't it a bit early to talk about things like this?'

He answered drily, 'Okay, I want you happy, and you can keep the baby. Maybe you can sponsor me, so I come to see him'.

....

Ah, ecco. He has finally uttered the magic words. *Sponsor me.*

Oh, God. For Cliché's sake. Did Shanaka really play his part so well that I didn't see through it at all? Can it be true that he had a plan from the beginning, a script he follows with all the foreign women who fall for it?

Thank God that whenever he said 'I love you' I always answered firmly and clearly that he shouldn't abuse these words, which are pointless in our circumstances, and that he should simply see me as a holiday friend. Yes, I've had a nice time with Shanaka, but at the same time, I was always laughing to myself about it and was well aware that it amounted to no more than a series of bright, colourful moments. And I thought he felt the same way. I really cannot bring myself to believe that he has tricked me, despite all the awareness I think I have about the Asian world.

Shanaka then went back to the counter to take various orders to their respective tables, and an afternoon of not so positive thoughts began for me. With his words, Shanaka has opened some old wounds I hadn't felt in a while. And even poured sand in them.

301

Wishing to experience my journey with a light heart, I probably didn't give this matter much thought. What if I did indeed get pregnant by a local guy? How would I handle this? Would I let him know, or would I keep it a secret? And how would I one day explain it to my child? And if I decided to tell the guy, what possible scenarios would open up? Would I really sponsor him, knowing I would be taking on a really heavy burden?

Stop it, stop it, slow down, Roby. These are all questions I cannot answer, and which weigh heavily on my soul.

All this is certainly putting me off any further flings here, though. But I also know perfectly well that all this self-torment is absolutely useless, and that things will go as they have to go, which is the only possible and perfect way.

Now I'm also wondering if I want to go to Negombo or stay here in Mount Lavinia until the day of my departure. On the one hand, Shanaka is here who, apart from what he said yesterday and earlier on, can make me feel good. However, he works all day long, so this would mean three full days of loafing around, which feels a bit like wasting time. If I were to go to Negombo, instead, I would see another place in Sri Lanka and I would also save some money, given that I am currently paying for a double room with an ensuite.

I'm sitting at a restaurant table looking out over the sea, sand between my toes and the breeze on my legs. Five minutes ago I showed Shanaka what I've written about him in my journal, and his only answer was to leaf through the subsequent blank pages, saying, 'Maybe here you write of new Indian holiday friend. It's not nice if you have my thing inside your belly. Okay, some people are for fun, but you have to stay a pure heart in love'.

....

Can you believe our little Shanaka? On the one hand he stuns me with his straightforward and pure way of thinking, on the other, I end up laughing over how he expresses himself, not to mention the huge distance between us. How can we fully explain ourselves and understand each other when we lack the tools to become immersed in the other person's life? However, with these words he confirms that he is a little puppy with a clotted-cream heart. 'You have to stay a pure heart in love.'

Come on, I can't believe he had a plan from the beginning.

Later on, in my room

Well, let me continue where I left off earlier.

His words, together with the grey, negative thoughts I'd entertained in the afternoon, had made me want to smoke. Shanaka was serving some clients, so I asked his colleague Kanishkar if he had a cigarette for me. Next to my table were two guys, whom Shanaka had earlier on defined as 'Indians. Bullshit people'. One of them took out his packet and offered me a cigarette, so we started talking. They were soldiers on leave in Colombo for a few days. The conversation actually turned out to be a very good and interesting one, touching on a completely new topic for me, namely the beauty of Pakistan, their country of origin.

Now, I don't know Pakistan, but one of them was really good-looking with very dark hair, olive skin, a dazzling smile and emerald-green eyes, which had quite an effect on me. And let's not forget the biceps peeking out of his short sleeves. It was just such a shame about the obscene quantity of black hair popping out of the neckline of his T-shirt.

We spent a good hour talking together, during which they showed me several videos of Pakistan. In my whole life I have never found myself showing videos of Rome, Venice or Florence to foreigners. However, I've noticed this phenomenon on multiple occasions: the worse a country is doing, the more its citizens are proud of it. I don't like patriotism as it is, but I understand this 'inverted patriotism' even less.

'Do you see how beautiful our homeland is? It's an underestimated country, with so many amazing places, and the people are so hospitable and generous... I am proud to serve my homeland', the other guy said when we were halfway through with the videos. In fact, I am only quoting one sentence here, but I think he must have used the word 'homeland' more than ten times. And while I love the way words like 'discombobulated' and 'bamboozle' sound, others like 'homeland', for example, instinctively bother me somehow, at an intellectual level. They trigger something deep inside me.

'Yes, from these videos, Pakistan really seems like a country worth visiting. Maybe I'll add it to my mental list of countries to visit (or maybe not). But I have to confess that hearing you talk about 'homeland'... It's a word that has always bothered me. To me, it's a wall that people put up to separate themselves from others. Above all, I can't understand why you would give so much, maybe even your life, in the name of a concept that doesn't even seem to give you much in return', I told him very honestly.

'Well, you don't have a well-developed sense of homeland because you were not born or raised in a country that might be invaded from one moment to the next.'

Okay, fair point and correct observation, but I'm not convinced yet. Homeland and nationalist pride are two values that just don't have space in my mind, and which I can only see as creating distance and separation.

Two cigarettes and five videos later the two soldiers left, and I called Shanaka over to say goodbye and arrange to meet later. He came to my table a bit upset. 'I don't like you talk for long with two Indians. Bullshit people'.

....

Jealousy can have so many faces! Including the one belonging to this serious young guy with lovely teeth and an earnest expression, so sure that he is right. Setting aside the fact that the guys were Pakistani, I've already encountered this automatic hatred between Sri Lankans and Indians several times. Why is it always the same old story? Why in every country is there such a distinction between its north and south, and resentment between neighbouring countries? Why does human nature always tend to create separateness and distance, focusing on what divides us rather than what unites us?

'How sweet! You're jealous', I say teasingly. 'Anyway, for your information, they were Pakistani, not Indian. Or are Pakistanis 'bullshit people', too?' I add, gently making fun of him with a smile.

In return, however, he gives me a small moral slap on the wrist, remarking, 'I don't like you ask for cigarettes. You are rich and can buy your packet. Or you ask me, not to bullshit Indian people. My colleagues offend me saying, 'You don't have money to buy a cigarette for your holiday friend?'

....

There it is. Talking of that huge distance between us. More like a yawning abyss. What can I say to such bullshit? Bullshit that nonetheless clearly matters to him?

Do I actually have to start apologising? But, more importantly, should I even be giving airtime to this kind of BS? He took it in a completely different way from how I meant it. I'd say that's his problem. Besides, I didn't think I was being disrespectful towards him by talking with two other men for a while, in front of everybody else.

'Yes, I have the money to buy my own packet, but I am on the beach and have no intention whatsoever of walking 700 metres to the shops to do so. Besides, I don't want a whole packet, I just wanted one cigarette. And anyway, I don't understand exactly what pisses you off, the fact that I talked for an hour with two men you don't know anything about, and had a really interesting conversation by the way, or the fact that they offered me a cigarette, and your friends said those things to you.'

I could only smile about all the parallel worlds that exist, but this whole thing has left a sour taste in my mouth. I had imagined our last night together as fun, light-hearted and carefree, with a lot of laughter and cuddles. Instead he is angry, I feel judged and misunderstood, and now it's started raining.

For Last Night in Mount Lavinia's sake.

Am I really considering feeling guilty because I accepted a cigarette someone offered me? Roby, are we joking? You don't owe

Shanaka anything. I have been easy-going and kind. If he saw it as a sign of disrespect that, in front of everyone, I talked with two men who were sitting next to me and against whom, out of his own ignorance, Shanaka holds a preconceived grudge... Well, this is entirely his issue. Have I really come to the other side of the world to have someone telling me what to do? Someone I've only spent a few nights with and who knows so little about me?

Shanaka, I believe that in this specific circumstance you deserve a little *vaffanculo*, or a 'go fuck yourself'. And I say it with shiny eyes because this scene of yours has made me feel guilty.

And I also think this conversation has helped me decide what to do.

Still Friday, Saturday morning actually, 01.20am
In the end he came to see me in my room, but to be honest the magic was spoilt, and I wasn't in the best of moods to welcome him. I avoided explaining how he'd made me feel. I didn't see the point, especially since I had already decided to leave tomorrow, so I thought it better to skip any unnecessary dramas.

Setting aside this afternoon's events, we spent our last night together remembering how we met instead, what we said to each other.

'Do you remember how it all started?'

'When I ask you to swim with me.'

'Haha. And I told you that I was afraid if I didn't touch, and you understood that I thought you would touch me! Hahaha. But no, everything started with, 'Hello madam, do you want a coffee a cappuccino a fruit juice a smoothie a sandwich a local boy?'

'I don't say that, Roby.'

'But maybe you thought so', I wink at him, embarrassing him a bit.

It's pleasant to relive the bonfire on the beach, the evening on the terrace with the red lanterns soaring above the sea into the blue night... Nice memories.

After a while, and with a certain nonchalance, Shanaka reminds me, 'You know, Roby, Buddhist New Year is April 13, more or less in a month. My birthday is some days before...'

He didn't say the words openly, but it was quite clear what he meant. In the end I gave him 50 dollars, for which he thanked me profusely. But I didn't do it with an open heart. Maybe in my mind I had imagined saying goodbye to him and leaving him some money anyway. After all, rather than donating money to perfect strangers, it's better to give it to someone who definitely needs it, and with whom you've had some sort of connection. But it should have happened off my own bat, not because he pushed for it repeatedly and openly, to varying degrees.

So, yes, my hand was stretched towards him with a banknote in it, but my heart was a bit on the defensive. Its placid waters had been stirred up by the murky underground current of doubt. Has Shanaka seen me from Day One as a cash cow? So much for 'In love you have to stay a pure heart'.

Then I stop to consider what I would do, in his shoes. If I were born in a country that is beautiful but offers very limited opportunities (ehm... now that I think about it, I was indeed born in such a country!), how would I behave? I would probably try to leave (which is exactly what I did). And how do you manage that, considering the bureaucratic difficulties involved? By landing a foreigner. Or, if you know that this is not so easy to do, you would seek the economic relief that comes from dealing with tourists. A sort of soft prostitution, in a way. 'I feel good with you. We spend so many dreamy moments in this earthly paradise. For you, I am a holiday adventure, while I already love you, though you don't believe me. Anyway, if you go away, can you please leave me some money, which I think is only fair?'

This might be the line of thinking, more or less.

Finally, the kind-hearted and trusting part of me whispers that anyway, given the language barrier, maybe Shanaka has not expressed himself properly. Maybe I have filled the gaps in his faltering English with prejudices I absorbed from others but then took on as my own, to some degree.

#self-persuasion.

Anyway, Shanaka has gone away with a final hug and a kiss, leaving me indeed with the doubt if he was ever only interested in money. One thing's for sure: for someone who claims not to be interested in it, he's been talking about it a lot these last few days. Yet, his WhatsApp tagline is 'I don't care what other people think or say about me. I know who I am (I thought I had understood you, but you got me confused). I respect who has humanity in heart.'

The Pollyanna in me screams happily, 'You see? He respects who has humanity in heart. He's a good guy!'

My cynical side, which I call Samantha Jones, retorts, 'Sure, 'respect' in the sense that he only fucks those with humanity in their heart'.

Ah, ecco.

Better this way, maybe. I am left with a question mark about what his real intentions were, but at least saying goodbye has been easier than I thought.

I am perfectly aware that I'm deceiving myself when I say that I want to have no-strings fun because I am on holiday. In the end, I am the first one to cry when separating from a man I have only just met and with whom I've shared a few special moments. Or this has been my pattern so far at least. Here, instead, I started the whole thing knowing that I wanted to be light hearted. Because the problem is never the fling per se, but how we interpret it. In general, this is the issue with so many things. The problem is the story we tell ourselves, not the one we actually experience. Besides, in this case the detachment has been gradual, so the final goodbye was neither difficult nor sad. I don't hold any grudge against him. No way. This was the first fling of an already marvellous trip.

Thanks anyway, Shanaka. I will remember the nice memories especially. And I wish you every happiness.

The Sri Lanka chapter is really coming to a close. I almost feel as if I have a colourful, sparkling question mark in front of me. What a sense of freedom and lightness. What bliss.

Tomorrow Negombo, for my last two days in Sri Lanka, given that it's only 10km from the airport and is therefore the most logical choice. As Rocky says, 'It's not over 'til it's over'. So let's see if Negombo sends me off with a bang.

Year of the partition of India and creation of Pakistan: 1947
Percentage of the population in Pakistan living in poverty: 30%
Pakistan's position on the UN list by Human Development Index: 150 out of 189 countries
Percentage of the government's expenditure dedicated to the army: 20%
How much this budget has increased in the last two years: 20%
Conclusion I'd be tempted to draw: How about, rather, maybe, the government possibly finds a better way to spend all that funding? Oh, right, sorry, I don't have a well-developed sense of homeland, so I cannot understand.
Curry varieties I've eaten so far: 13
Sri Lankans who have so far asked if they could take a photo with me: 7
Average number of times my thoughts fly to London in a day: 0.7
Rats sighted so far: 0!

DAY 27

'If Bangladesh wins, you dance with me!'
-Negombo, Saturday 10th March 2018-

Wow. I think it's the first time in my life that I've voluntarily left a dance floor because I was feeling uncomfortable. Men here are really relentless sometimes. And, to be honest, today they have been a pain in the arse. But, as usual, let me start at the beginning.

The journey from Mount Lavinia to Negombo was quick, only two hours by bus, and included a nice conversation with a middle-aged gentleman, a lawyer and big American baseball fan (go figure and #notallsrilankansareintocricket), who insisted on connecting with me on LinkedIn. I always feel a fondness towards people like this. A few times now I've met people while travelling in Asia who seem to have a higher-than-average education and social status and apparently want to get something from the interaction, even if it's just a vast array of Western contacts on social media.

I was sitting at the back of the bus, where there were five seats together, like on buses in the UK and Italy. To my right was a local guy, and not a bad looking one, with dreadlocks. He was sitting with his arms crossed. I was quite absorbed by my conversation with the lawyer, so it took me a few seconds to realise that the slight touch I was feeling on my hip was actually the guy stroking me with his finger.

Sure, we are not dealing with the same levels as that pervert who once shoved his full-blown erection against my leg on a night bus in London. That was around eight or nine years ago, the bus was packed, and my only reaction was to move away disgusted, without saying anything. I didn't want to draw attention to myself, creating a scene. I didn't want to be seen as a victim.

Thank God, among the many ways of thinking and attitudes I have changed over the years, I have also changed my response to similar situations. No fucking way would I react that way now. I mean, a pervert takes the liberty of embarrassing me, touching me without permission, and I'm the one who feels guilty? The lawyer was standing in front of me and had no idea of what was happening under the guy's crossed arm. While carrying on my conversation with the lawyer, my only response was to cross my arms so that, hidden by my elbow, I grasped the guy's finger and bent it, even scratching the back of his hand. He didn't utter a sound, but at least he stood up and moved towards the front of the bus, as if he had to get off at the following stop.

I would need to stop and think back over all the trips I've done so far, but I believe I can say with a 97% degree of certainty that this is the first time I've been sexually harassed while travelling. Nothing particularly heavy, but this is because in my culture a finger brushing my hip is not a shocking event. In his culture, however, where men and women live in separate worlds, this gesture becomes way more serious.

I thank God I am able to handle situations like this one and not be scared by them. Some women might fixate on them and say, 'You see? They are dangerous countries. Do you see what can happen when you go travelling alone?' To them, I would answer that in London and Italy I have been harassed several times, so I wouldn't use that as another reason not to go travelling. In fact, if I want to look at the silver lining here, this event has shown me how much I have changed since the last time something similar happened. It's shown me how much stronger and more self-confident I am today, facing behaviour like this without fear. Which is another way of saying, once more, that travelling leads to self-discovery and growth.

I had some trouble finding the hostel, given that I had the wrong address, but once arrived I settled into the dorm and then headed out for lunch in the little restaurant next door, where I treated myself to an omelette. Western food, yes! I'm kind of fed up with curries.

Being a chef, Andre was enthusiastic about how many curry varieties there are, while I instead focused on the fact that they are all basically rice dishes. A perfect and clear example of how some people, faced with two things, tend to notice the differences, while others focus on the things in common.

There was a lady in her mid-60s who was having lunch on her own, and I have to say that I haven't met many women her age travelling alone.

'Ah, you ordered the omelette? Well chosen. It's delicious', she broke the ice first.

'Yes, I've been here for a month, and I just wanted a small break from curries, especially given that I have two more months of this kind of food ahead of me.'

'Oh, you are travelling for a long time. Lucky you.'

After exchanging some more pleasantries, she invited me to join her at her table.

I so love these casual encounters, and how easy it is to make them while on the road!

'My name's Margot', she introduced herself, with a distinct French accent. 'Are you travelling alone?'

'Yes, and you?'

'Yes, me too. I've been doing it for years. I adore it, and until now I never had any problems. Here in Sri Lanka, though, on day one, on the very first day, they stole all the cash I had brought with me from my hotel room – 1,500 euros. Definitely not a good beginning to my holiday.'

Poor her! Me too, I've been carrying around 1,200 pounds in cash, given that every single time I've been abroad I either leave my debit card somewhere, or my bank blocks it fearing that my transactions in Asia are the result of fraud. To avoid all the problems I had in the past, this time I took some extra precautions. I'm travelling with a second prepaid debit card, called Revolut, and also with a lot of cash, which I alternatively lock in the hostels' safe, hide under the mattress, as thousands and thousands of people before me all over the world have done (and still do, I'm sure), or carry with me in my inseparable rucksack, which is now practically an appendage.

I admire women like Margot who, aged around 65, are still ready to go travelling and discover the world by themselves. I sometimes hope to find an adventure-loving and good-hearted man with whom to see new places and enjoy new experiences, but I hope even more that I'll never lose my thirst for discovery and this independence which I see as such a huge gift (or triumph?).

Finding a partner who can understand this need of mine to be on my own sometimes, to rediscover myself, to test myself, to listen to my deepest voice: this is my real dream. Someone who will understand that if I choose me, it doesn't mean that I'm *not* choosing him. If he also happens to be tall, dark haired and athletic, with biceps to sigh for, a simple heart and a complex mind; love children and nature, believe that the world needs more kindness and tenderness; be romantic, generous, deep, sensitive, curious, open minded, strong in body and soul, funny, able to challenge and gently mock me as well as really make me laugh... Well, then, all the better!

I don't know if in my case I made a virtue out of necessity. I don't know if this independence is a gift I was born with or something I have achieved. It's probably more a gift, given that travelling solo comes to me quite naturally nowadays. But then again, it took me a few years of different kinds of travel experiences to get here. At the same time, though, I can see the big gap between my way of thinking and that of the many people who have told me, 'How brave of you! Aren't you afraid (of what, for example?)? Afraid of all the things that could happen. There are so many dangers everywhere... (Oh, okay, so let's stop living and stand still because the world is like Dante's famous 'forest dark'.) Or even just afraid of being bored, or getting lost...'

The behaviours people see as 'courage', my father has always labelled those of 'una testa calda', a hothead. I had never realised that for so many people, especially for so many women, this independence to travel on my own is something inconceivable. And what saddens me the most is that these people miss out on amazing adventures and experiences just because they are blocked by their fears. But in life we have to act out of love, not out of fear. It's one of my mantras. They are afraid to find themselves isolated and lost, but the truth is that the tribe of women travelling on their own is bigger than they think. The fact is, you will never discover this tucked away in your little Italian village or on your package holiday in a tourist resort. And there is so much sisterhood between us female travellers, because we understand all the small difficulties that can arise.

There are many ways to get to know yourself better, sure. Psychoanalysis. Keeping a journal and recording your thoughts. Becoming a mother and having to manage a whole new world, both inside and outside of yourself. Being in a relationship, where you constantly have to deal with someone different from you. Travelling alone is one of my absolute favourite ways of discovering new sides to my personality, learning new things, dismantling or at least reviewing my prejudices and meeting new people, so different from me, and noticing what we have in common and what differentiates us. Above all, facing my days alone in new countries ignites a sense of excitement, adventure, curiosity, which makes me feel tremendously alive. And it shows me, day after day, how many resources I really have. In London I had been feeling emotionally drained for months, like I was running on empty. Here I feel lively, bubbly, so much more at peace with myself and so in love with this gorgeous world.

I have never travelled with a boyfriend, even when I had one. Sure, we went on holiday, up to three weeks, but by 'travelling' I mean backpacking with a lot of time ahead. You really have to be on the same wavelength to feel good in so many out-of-the-ordinary situations. I can think of very few people with whom I'd like to travel, and even with them, after a while, I would like us to go our separate ways. Maybe with a view to reuniting later on. But I know that there generally comes a point when I want to concentrate entirely on myself. Which means doing exactly what I want to do, knowing that my mood depends entirely on me, and seeing what I am capable of, or what I might have up my sleeve to overcome an obstacle... And, for the man who comes into my life and chooses to stay there, I know it might be hard to understand this need.

The conversation with Margot was very pleasant. She has seen so many places. Despite having lost 1,500 euros, she insisted on buying me an ice cream after lunch, and happily licking our cones we went to the beach for a stroll and to continue exchanging travel stories. That was basically my first interaction with Negombo as a place. The sea is not to die for. It doesn't have the colours I've seen in the south, like in Mirissa. A series of big hotels lines the long, sandy beach, and they look almost intimidating with their hundreds of rooms with a sea view. Margot told me that she has hired a driver to take her around Sri Lanka for the next two weeks. I have never travelled in this way. To be honest, I really enjoy taking public transport, mixing with the local population and getting a quick glimpse of their everyday lives.

Shanaka texted me this afternoon. 'Roby, I miss you. Yesterday I am very sad for things. Today I remember you (my congratulations, your short-term memory seems to be working fabulously). I am very sad for you go away. I miss you Roby (and he added not one, but six, s-i-x emojis with a single tear, and four others – four! – desperately crying). I want to see you last minute. I try to come and see you.'

I answered very abruptly, 'Don't be sad. Tonight there's a cricket match!'

I really don't understand his need to play the heartbroken man, overcome by the sorrow of separation. At the same time, right to the end I really cannot decide whether Shanaka has been genuine or not. Oh my God, can *he* be the biggest Secret of Fátima?

Anyway, I knew that tonight there was going to be a cricket match between Bangladesh and Sri Lanka. My Lonely Planet guide recommended the Rodeo pub as a good spot for a fun evening and to watch sports.

When I went in, I was immediately met with a pretty full room. The clientele was made up of tourists and travellers, as well as many local men. When I told the waiter that I wanted to eat, he answered, 'Yes, you can sit there, next to other lonely lady'.

Fantastic. And thanks;-)

I smile over the (hopefully) involuntary mistake. I know there is an abyss between being lonely and being alone. How many times have I felt extremely lonely in a group or, even worse, in a relationship? And how good can I feel in my complete and unadulterated aloneness?

So, I sit next to this other lady on her own.

'Sometimes you can't help but love the locals for the mistakes they make. The waiter told me to sit here because 'there is another lonely lady'. How are you doing? How are you managing all this crushing loneliness?'

'Ah, well, I just arrived today, so I'd say so far, so good. On Monday I'm gonna start an organised tour with 14 other people, so I don't think I'll have this problem', she explained, quite happy to be giving up the pretence of watching the cricket, which probably, like me, leaves her completely stumped (Oh, my God, if this isn't the pun of the day, on the whole planet, I want to know what is!)

Over a burger and fries, I got to know Zoe, a window dresser from Bedford. She has travelled quite a lot and is single, too, probably a bit older than me, and very friendly.

'I'm sorry. I'm so jet-lagged and am falling asleep. Do you fancy exchanging numbers? We could look around Negombo together tomorrow, if you want', she suggested.

'Sure, with pleasure.'

'Perfect. See you tomorrow, then. You can also tell me how the match went. Enjoy your evening and keep the men at bay. There are so many of them tonight.'

'Ah, don't worry, I have my techniques.'

'I have no doubt about it. See you tomorrow, then!'

Indeed, there are plenty of men. Sport matches always attract oceans of testosterone, it seems, and Negombo is no exception. I look around and I see several local guys, and maybe some visitors from other parts of Asia, plus a good few white tourists. A nice mixture.

I moved to the bar to see the TV screen better, pretending to understand something, and this guy Bijay, an Indian from Kerala, starts talking to me. He tells me he exports dry fruits, and within two minutes he is making it abundantly clear that HE WANTS A PIECE OF ME. Like, a huge piece of me. My whole body. All of it.

'If Bangladesh wins, you dance with me', he tells me.

Just like that. He comes up with this bullshit condition after seeing that Bangladesh was winning, and without remotely asking me if I fancied dancing with him. I mean, what do I have to do with Bangladesh's cricket performance? Who'd have thought that an event in my life, even a tiny one, would one day depend on the sporting prowess of eleven Bangladeshi cricketers?

But since I am a cross between Pollyanna at her First Communion and Candy Candy faced with a brood of adorable chicks, I tell myself, 'Okay, basically this guy is just happy to dance a bit with me, so let's make him happy'. However, I had not taken the following into consideration:

1. How uncomfortable and embarrassed I felt dancing with someone whose sense of rhythm was so bad that he could only have been having a seizure while listening to his own music through hidden earbuds.
2. How uncomfortable I felt on the outside and how much I was laughing to myself internally over the sensual and passionate way he was looking at me. Maybe this Bijay attended the same school of seduction as Sanjaya. Or, more likely, he's seen the same movies.
3. How uncomfortable I felt to realise that I was completely surrounded by at least seven or eight local men, all of whom were literally chewing me up with their eyes, without a hint of shame at doing it so openly.

At some point an unspoken contest must have started, which we could call 'Win over the tall white lady (with the strange hair)'. Out of the blue (whale, of course), while I'm super focused on my dance moves, I feel someone put a bottle of beer in my hand. On we go with these beers, which I don't even like. Anyway okay, I smile at the guy and I even clink his bottle with mine, with a half-hearted 'Cheers'. I go to the counter to return the empty bottle, and the moment I turn around to go back to the dance floor another local man turns up, barely reaching my chin, and proffers another beer. Uff... On I go, drinking this beer, too. And congratulations for the perfect timing. Nicely executed.

I went on dancing because the music really was divine and I hadn't gone wild on a dance floor for some time, but I did feel like a bloody seal surrounded by sharks. Not a pleasant sensation, and one I've rarely felt to this extent. When a new guy took my hand and pressed a little piece of paper into it, I decided that it was really too much. I opened that little strip of paper out of curiosity to see that he had written a phone number and the peremptory order, 'Call me'.

I'm sorry, but even if you are the winner of the 'Audacity in Negombo 2018' contest, I won't call you. And, to be honest, you are all stressing me out a bit.

Basically I was now looking at the floor, rather than around me or at the DJ, because I didn't want to meet their eyes and encourage them to take who knows what other initiatives. So for the first time in my life, I have voluntarily deprived myself of the pleasure of dancing. And the music was bloody spectacular, for Horndogs' sake!

Rather than walking back to the hostel I took a tuk-tuk, both because it was my first night in Negombo and I don't know the town at all, and because all this male attention had made me a bit anxious. And I smile as I write this because there will probably come a time in my life when no man will show any interest in me and I will mourn the loss of this kind of attention, perhaps regretting that I didn't deal with it as I could have. *C'est la vie.*

When I arrived at the hostel, surprise! The gate was closed.

But for Curfew and fuck's sake, didn't you think it appropriate to mention that I wouldn't be able to get in after 11pm?

I asked myself one of my favourite questions of all time, and one which has already helped me so much in life: 'What would MacGyver do?'

MacGyver is a mega hottie from an '80s TV series who could make a bomb out of a lock of hair and two toothpicks. In this case, he would have gone looking for something to stand on to help him climb over the wall, which is what I did, taking a chair from the little restaurant next to my hostel where I had lunch with Margot. To be honest, I'd have really liked to see MacGyver jumping a wall while wearing a skirt, but what matters is that nobody saw me, cloaked as I was in darkness.

Today has been another day full of encounters and conversations. And in two days I'm flying to India. I feel so excited, as if I was going home. And, to some extent, that's exactly the case. I'm already smiling at the thought of the usual noisy, colourful mayhem that will assault me from all sides. I can already picture the cows in the street, the monkeys running and jumping all over the place, the bright smiles of street children and the betel-nut stained ones of the men; the colourful saris, the stalls laden with exotic fruits, the bare feet around the city, the tailors working at their sewing machine in the open air by the roadside. And then the bloody rats as big as piglets, people's right hands skilfully mixing rice and curry together and bringing the mixture to their mouths, tuk-tuks adorned with stickers of Hindu deities, the shiny bangles on women's wrists... Plus, India also means seeing Andre and Jacob again. How cool! It's a new sensation for me, this idea of going to a country already knowing that I'll meet certain other travellers there. And let's see if I do some volunteering there as well, and for whom. More importantly, let's see which people will enter my life and what they'll show me. Above all, let's hope I don't get eaten alive by some alien insect or catch the 21st century's worst case of diarrhoea.

But, for now, goodnight Negombo.

From 1 to 10, how much I believed Shanaka's text when he said he would try to come: 0

Men surrounding me at one point on the dance floor: 9

Phone number of the guy who put the strip of paper in my hand: 0094 71 466 7331

Books I've read this month: 4

Years MacGyver aired on Italian TV: 1985–1992

Times in my life I've wondered 'What would MacGyver do now?': 543

Excitement level at the idea of starting the second chapter of my trip: 17!

State of my hair: devastated

Centimetres of regrowth: 1.5

Chances that something will happen with Andre in India: place your bets, guys

Current weight: 71.3kg

Money spent this month: £324

DAY 28
'Have I managed to let it go?'
-Negombo, Sunday 11th March 2018-

Here I am. I woke up one more day (thank you, God) with the intention of exploring until the end! Last night I arranged with Zoe to visit the Sunday market and then maybe go for a bike ride along the Hamilton Canal, as my Bible suggests. So I'm leaving you now, my dear Diary, to go and rent a hopefully not too beaten-up bike to see what mini adventures this last day in Sri Lanka has in store for me. Let's see if serendipity will strike again!

Still 11th March, 10.13pm
It's been a relaxing and pleasant day. Zoe and I, riding our two flashy racing bikes (yeah, right) went first of all to see the Sunday Market which sprawls over quite a large area, along several narrow streets and small squares. In terms of goods, it was nothing special, even if I was really drawn to one of the stalls. It was selling stretch jeans in every possible colour, all so cute. If my backpack wasn't already full, and above all if I didn't have to carry my purchases around for the next two months, I would have definitely bought a few pairs. In terms of a photo shoot, however, Negombo's Sunday Market lends itself very well to photos overflowing with colour. And dried fish, in this specific case. As a matter of fact, if we had started our exploration early, we could have gone to see one of the best attractions in Negombo, which is the fish market, the second largest in Sri Lanka. Here hordes of fishermen lay out their catch on long coconut-fibre sacks, flipping the fish regularly so they dry evenly. And if we had arrived at the fish market much earlier, like around 4

or 5am, we would have seen the real action. That's when the boats start bringing in their catches and the auction begins. The best fish is obviously sold to the best hotels and restaurants, and a lot more is then sold locally in the market itself or, indeed, dried.

While walking from one stall to another two questions arose spontaneously for me:

1. Who has the courage to drink those probably toxic bright pink or blue substances that the locals seem to like so much? What drinks are they?
2. What will they do with all this dry fish? Do they only use it in curries?

To answer this second question, I should have found some fish seller to explain the abundance of dried fish to me. I am talking about dozens and dozens of stalls overflowing with dried fish of every kind and size, and in my ignorance, I could recognise maybe just two or three species. To answer the first question, however, I bought one of those slushy, glowing, cartoon drinks. Just looking at it, I felt like a flashing neon sign lit up in my mind: 'Artificial'.

My verdict? Forget about it. It was disgusting. In fact, drinking this Pink Panther distillate gave rise to certain questions, such as 'What is in this stuff? Why do people find such bright colours appealing? And will I get diarrhoea from drinking something that wasn't sealed?'

More than ten hours later, I can answer to the third question, and it's a no, thank God, the Buddha and Krishna, too.

Afterwards, Zoe and I went cycling along the Hamilton Canal, through which the Dutch have expressed their love for canals more than in any other Sri Lankan city. The Dutch indeed conquered Negombo in 1640, which had been in the hands of the Portuguese until then, before losing it immediately only to win it back in 1644. Around 150 years later, in 1796, the English came to take the city with no major battles. As a lasting sign of Negombo's Dutch past, a series of canals still run through the city, stretching southwards as far as Colombo, and northwards to Puttalam, covering a distance of 120km. Great potential as a bike tour if you had the time for it, but above all if you were sure it was actually possible to cycle freely along the canal. The small stretch Zoe and I cycled this morning was continually interrupted by narrow streets, fishermen's nets or dozing dogs who wouldn't move even if you were to offload a truckload of bones next to them, so in the end we gave up. We went back to the beach and enjoyed a drink there, soaking up the atmosphere and the several activities going on at the Negombo Beach Park, the part of the beach where the locals hang out. There were several stalls and huts selling different snacks, not always clearly identified. Since I have very few Sri Lankan rupees left, and I don't want to change more money, Zoe bought me a Coke. Acts of kindness till the very end! For the same reason, one of the food sellers ended up giving me some free croquettes, though I couldn't say what was inside. Isn't it lovely though? It's these small things, which happen continually, by the way, that convince me that we live in a wonderful world, always and no matter what. The good people do is far greater than the evil, but it speaks more softly, so you have to pay more attention and focus in order to hear it.

The beach is clearly a hot spot for the locals on Sundays. In fact I think that most of the people there were not from Negombo, because so many of them were equipped as if they were on a proper day trip. Everywhere you looked were beach towels and blankets on the sand, with a nice display of dishes, small pots and pans, accompanied by bottles and drinks of all sorts. The beach was literally flooded with people, all of them fully dressed, sitting in circles sharing food, chatting the afternoon away or watching the children jumping waves, fully dressed of course.

And that's where the Fourth Big Epiphany hit me. I feel I can state with a certain degree of confidence that people all over the world love jumping waves. Oh, yes, and myself above all. Even if, after almost drowning in Gallipoli in the south of Italy, exactly by jumping waves, I now approach this universal pastime with more caution.

Overcrowded Negombo Beach is the last image by day that beautiful Sri Lanka has gifted me. It's almost 11pm. My backpack is ready, leaning against my bed. In a few hours I'll be on my flight to Chennai, and from there I will start my tour of the south of India, which will finish in Goa in another month. Between Chennai and Goa I don't have any plans, apart from meeting Jacob and Andre somewhere.

I think back to the blue whale's tail I saw disappearing into the sea in Mirissa. I can still see the vulnerable and slightly disoriented baby turtles scuttling towards the sea in Hikkaduwa, forced to work hard from the moment they hatched. I recall all those candlelit Buddha statues in the Royal Cave Temple and the strange sensations I felt there. I think back to cycling around Polonnaruwa and the elephant's foot I cleaned. I smile remembering Shanaka asking me if I want to swim with him in Mount Lavinia, and the mixture of tenderness and amusement I felt every time he posed as a man of the world. I think back to Andre appearing at my guesthouse and asking if everything was okay, and to the heartbeat I skipped when I switched on my mobile in the morning and was bombarded by messages from Chamath. I am still baffled by the tuk-tuk drivers in Mirissa who recognised me on the street. I think back to Sandula's son and our dictations, and how carefree I felt sitting behind Andre on the scooter. I close my eyes and can feel the foot massage that Sanjaya gave me, and I smile at how he was looking at me. I can still see the butterflies flying about me while I was swimming in the river, and I so clearly remember the fatigue of my night trek up Adam's Peak. I go back in my mind to Mirissa's sunsets, ablaze with red, orange and pink, and to the emotion I felt admiring the elephant family on the safari in the Udawalawe park, with that baby elephant who would trip over his trunk every two minutes. I still find it hard to believe that the guy sitting next to me on the train was the same Jacob that Andre had told me so much about. I think back to the coincidence, which wasn't a coincidence at all, that I was speaking about the Vipassana meditation back at the hostel just before finding a guy in my dorm who had just finished such a retreat. And, to top it off, that there was still a place available in Nepal to go and do that experience at the end of my trip. I recall my chats with Andre under the starry sky, by the sea, not knowing whether he was interested in me or not, telling myself ultimately to let it go, that a man and a woman can enjoy each other's company without things necessarily getting sexual. And, talking of my mantra, 'let it go', I think back on the yellow balloon flying in the sky on the cover of the journal they gave me at the Millennium Elephant Foundation.

Have I managed to 'let it go' this month?

I would say so. I didn't have any plans when I arrived here, apart from having to be at the airport on March 12th to fly to India. I let go of my need to plan, which seems to dominate my life in London, and an amazing month came out of it.

I let go of the need to make something happen, or of the expectation that something had to happen, just because I was getting along well with a man, and in return I enjoyed days of laughter, beers on the beach and nice conversations with Andre.

I also let go of the patterns whereby my moods depended on men. Shanaka sent me a few messages today, too, but for me he's already a closed chapter (and a tiny part of me is wondering in a soft voice if maybe letting it go so soon wasn't a bit much in this case).

I let go of London's bustle, and of the people I've left there. Thanks to the distance I've placed between the United Kingdom and me, I can see some of their behaviours and the things they've said under a new light. It's very likely that, once back, I will have to do a "social clear out" of my life. Or maybe that will have taken care of itself, without any intervention from me, just by letting things run their course.

Have I managed to let go of the pain that I feel is stuck to my skin over not being a mother yet? Not exactly, but I would say I'm definitely working on it, and in any case, I've already made great strides in this direction.

What about the pain of still being single, without knowing if I'll ever meet the right man for me? Have I managed to let that go? Right now, to be honest, I don't feel it, while until a few months ago it manifested as stabbing pains in my heart. At present, I don't feel it at all.

Of course I will find the right man for me, and he will be mega hhhhhhot, Mediterranean and taller than me, with a kind face, complex mind and simple heart, ready with his backpack to discover other wonderful places with me. He will laugh with me about the absurd situations we will end up in, and he will understand that, despite the joy I take in travelling together, at some point I will need to travel on my own as well.

Or on the other hand, considering my infamously tremendous good luck, he won't be remotely like that at all. He will have a limp, a glass eye and a stutter, without a hint of bicep definition, but he will understand me. And I will understand him. I mean, I'd prefer the first version obviously, but anyway.

When travelling I discover and rediscover myself. I reinvent myself and I evolve. I do a lot of soul searching. I feel connected to nature and to others. I ask myself many questions, and I can even answer a few of them. I see parts of me dying and new ones coming up to the surface and blossoming. Above all, I realise how infinitely strong I am and how many hidden resources I have. How, really, 13 kilos of stuff is all we need, and how easy it is to get rid of the mental dead weight oppressing us when we finally decide to do it. Because while it may be true that we don't create our problems, we are certainly the ones who decide to continue having them. Happiness is a choice.

When I was a student at the Advanced School of Modern Languages for Interpreters and Translators in Forlì (ah, those were the days!), on the Italian Literature course in the first year we studied coming-of-age stories. These were amazing texts, which I would devour in one sitting, seeing the link between journeys and personal growth as clear as day; discovering new places outside as a parallel to discovering new ones inside. I still remember a passage by Pier Vittorio Tondelli which instantly sent shivers down my spine when I read it, and which I wrote in the first page of so many of my journals:

> 'But I also know the immense completeness of this solitude of MINE, the attentive ears, the ever-present eyes, the concentration, the epiphanies when you have no one else but you to share a discovery with, and so then, sitting on a rock on any Greek island, wondering why that sun has to be so strong and that sea so blue and that soil so black, you look inside yourself, and there you can see again the suns, the storm surges, the gales and the safe harbours of your life. As long as I have breath in my lungs and strength in my legs, and my arms can drag a bag, I will defend this right of mine to be alone – one like many others – in my completeness.'

Boom!

'THIS RIGHT OF MINE TO BE ALONE': What revolutionary words. They shook me violently when I was 19 years old and still do today. Twenty years later, for Time Flies' sake, they strike a chord deep down.

My sacrosanct right to be alone.

And there's nothing fuller than this solitude.

The right to stop, to think only about ourselves, to realign. The right to do entirely what we want, to cease pleasing others. The right to take the time we need to recharge our batteries, to understand ourselves, to wonder what life we want to lead and what people we want to become.

And now that I think about it... Oh, my God, the Fifth Great Epiphany. Boom! On an unconscious level, perhaps my great desire for freedom and independence could be one of the reasons I attract (or do they attract me?) people who are not available, either because they are commitment phobic or because they've just been sentenced to prison (just a random example, of course!)

Wow, I had never thought about it before... But this line of thought makes perfect sense. Unconsciously looking for those who will allow me to stay free.

These were the sort of realisations I was hoping I'd make during my journey. Looking inside myself and *really* seeing what is there.

'ONE LIKE MANY OTHERS': Yes, I'm special. But not that special. There are millions of other women out there like me who just have to say, 'Enough' to start changing things. Sometimes I would like to hug them all, these women as distressed and stuck as I often felt myself. Insecure, maybe naïve, confused, tired, lonely, trapped in a victim's role they are unable or reluctant to see, in need of validation, with so much love to give, but filled with fear from head to toe (by the way, speaking of heads, I must have 2cm of regrowth by now). I feel like hugging them all and then shaking them like they do in the movies. Do we realise the OPPORTUNITY we have been given, which is refreshed at the beginning of every new day we have the privilege of waking up to? Faced with this incredible generosity, how dare we waste time in apathy, fear, anger, sadness, frustration, anguish or depression? Do we understand that we are in this world to fulfil ourselves, whatever that means for us? Our soul wants to evolve. How can we be so cruel to ourselves as to keep it caged? There's a glorious world all around us just waiting for us to move our butts and share our gifts, which we have kept all to ourselves or repressed for too long.

'IN MY COMPLETENESS': The cherry on the cake. Yes, because I am so damned perfect and complete *on my own*. And we all are, but we haven't looked inside yet to understand this because it's so much easier to look outside and focus on what we feel we lack. Instead I don't need to be in a relationship to feel good. I don't even need a best friend, whom I've relied on so often in the past and who has supported me, yes, but also disappointed me. I am not missing pieces that The Other will provide me with, as if I were a walking jigsaw. All the love we look for in others is already present

328

in ourselves, and it's limitless. However, thanks to a strange sort of irony (or, better, the comicality of the human condition), we end up dispensing our love to everybody except ourselves. We think that love is something given to us from the outside, and so we start expecting huge things from everyone who enters our lives. And I shiver thinking back on all the years when I shared this view. But thank God I have opened my eyes now. I feel like I am awakening. If we managed first to give ourselves this love, which is our natural way of being, taking care of our feelings and our wellbeing, we would feel so aligned and in harmony that other peoples' apparent lacks wouldn't even graze us, let alone wound us. Their opinions wouldn't matter because we would be so sure of our path. We wouldn't accept certain behaviours in friendships and relationships any longer because we would know our worth and what we really need.

Oh, man, if only could I scream to my sisters all around the world how marvellous we are, that it is high time to open up our eyes and shoulder our responsibilities, look at the beauty inside and around us, start with gratitude and work hard to improve the things we don't like, and if I knew they could hear me, I would run back to the top of Adam's Peak to fill the valley with my cries.

Okay, maybe I wouldn't exactly run. I'd walk slowly, stopping to rest every 80 steps.

Instead for now I only have this book, and so I ask you, fantastic woman who's stayed with me until the end of this trip, what do you get out of staying in the situation you're in? What can you do today to move closer to your ideal scenario? What step will you take today for which Your Future Self will thank you? And you too, incredible man who's got this far, what do you want to change in your life today to honour yourself more?

While you're thinking about that, I'm taking a tuk-tuk in the dead of night towards the airport, where a hopefully not too turbulent flight to Chennai awaits me.

One month in India. Here's the step I'm taking now for which My Future Self will thank me.

Ciao, Sri Lanka, and thanks from the bottom of my heart for everything. I am ready for the frenzy of India.

May patience and the bacterial flora be with me.

Universe, I trust You. *E speriamo bene*, and let's hope for the best!

BIBLIOGRAPHY

Brené Brown, *Daring Greatly: How the Courage to be Vulnerable Transforms the Way We Live, Love, Parent and Lead*, Ultra, 2012.

Eckhart Tolle, *The Power of Now*, Hodder & Stoughton, 2005.

John Purkiss, *All in the Mind: How to Succeed by Letting Go*, John Purkiss, 2004.

Gregory David Roberts, *Shantaram*, Scribe Publications, Australia, 2003.

Robert Schwartz, *Your Soul's Plan: Discovering the Real Meaning of the Life You Planned Before You Were Born*, North Atlantic Books, 2009.

Pier Vittorio Tondelli, *Questa specie di patto*, Bompiani, 1993.

NOTES ON THE AUTHOR

Roberta Mussato was born in Padernello, Treviso, Italy in 1978. At the age of eight she started writing her first journal, a habit she would never give up, and by the age of nine she had written her first book, about her dog Briciola ('Breadcrumb') – possibly the least-read book in the world, the only reader being her mother.

After a degree in English and Russian conference interpreting, in 2006 she moved to crazy London, where she is still living today. Before the journey described here, she manoeuvred between working as an interpreter, subtitler and voice-over artist, whilst also finding the time to dance bachata, take care of her beloved plants and notice how many people go around wearing odd socks.

The journey she is sharing here made her understand that all the things which have happened to her are in fact a huge asset in her favour, if framed in the right way, changing the question from, 'Why do they all happen to me?' to 'What for?' And, following a vision she had in Nepal, she now works as a Life and Relationship coach and NLP Practitioner, helping people become unstuck, more aligned and ultimately better versions of themselves.

She trusts the Universe more and more each day and continues to hug trees when the mood takes her. We are also happy to report that, at the time of publication, her hair looks decent (on most days).

NOTES FROM THE AUTHOR

I hope my book has made you smile, maybe even laugh, and gifted you with some pleasurable hours. If you would like to see some of my photos from this marvellous trip, you can do so by scanning the QR code below.

Also, this book presents itself as a travelling diary, but hopefully you have noticed how there are many more themes touched here and there. For those of you who would like to explore more some of them, I have created a freeseries of three short videos to this end. I have also created a longer video series, "Universe, let's explore You", that you can purchase through my website http://www. robertamussato.com, where I go more in depth into six different topics connected to my book.

Happy exploring!

Made in the USA
Middletown, DE
16 June 2023

32321991R00197